MW00465041

# Jefferson's Poplar Forest

UNIVERSITY PRESS OF FLORIDA

Florida A&M University, Tallahassee

Florida Atlantic University, Boca Raton

Florida Gulf Coast University, Ft. Myers

Florida International University, Miami

Florida State University, Tallahassee

New College of Florida, Sarasota

University of Central Florida, Orlando

University of Florida, Gainesville

University of North Florida, Jacksonville

University of South Florida, Tampa

University of West Florida, Pensacola

# Jefferson's
# *Poplar Forest*

## Unearthing a Virginia Plantation

EDITED BY BARBARA J. HEATH AND JACK GARY

University Press of Florida
Gainesville
Tallahassee
Tampa
Boca Raton
Pensacola
Orlando
Miami
Jacksonville
Ft. Myers
Sarasota

Funding for publication generously provided by
the Corporation for Jefferson's Poplar Forest.

Copyright 2012 by Barbara J. Heath and Jack Gary
All rights reserved
Printed in the United States of America on acid-free paper

21  20  19  18  17  16    6  5  4  3  2  1

First cloth printing, 2012
First paperback printing, 2016

Library of Congress Cataloging-in-Publication Data
Jefferson's Poplar Forest : unearthing a Virginia plantation / edited by Barbara J. Heath and Jack Gary.
p. cm.
Includes bibliographical references and index.
ISBN 978-0-8130-3988-6 (cloth)
ISBN 978-0-8130-6299-0 (pbk.)
1. Poplar Forest (Va.)—Antiquities. 2. Poplar Forest (Va.)—History. 3. Jefferson, Thomas,
1743–1826—Homes and haunts—Virginia—Bedford County. 4. Plantation life—Virginia—Bedford
County—History. 5. Poplar Forest (Va.)—Social life and customs. 6. Excavations (Archaeology)—
Virginia—Bedford County. 7. Material culture—Virginia—Bedford County—History. 8. Archaeology
and history—Virginia—Bedford County. 9. Bedford County (Va.)—Antiquities.
I. Heath, Barbara J., 1960– II. Gary, Jack.
F234.P7J44 2012
975.5'675—dc23    2012001072

The University Press of Florida is the scholarly publishing agency for the State University
System of Florida, comprising Florida A&M University, Florida Atlantic University, Florida Gulf Coast
University, Florida International University, Florida State University, New College of Florida, University
of Central Florida, University of Florida, University of North Florida, University of South Florida,
and University of West Florida.

University Press of Florida
15 Northwest 15th Street
Gainesville, FL 32611-2079
http://www.upf.com

# Contents

# Figures

# Tables

# Maps

# Preface

Historical archaeology and the study of plantations have developed together over the past century. Early research designed to facilitate the restoration of great houses and gardens has given way to more explicitly anthropological considerations of the forms and meanings of plantation landscapes and communities. Today archaeologists continue to study mansions and pleasure grounds but increasingly probe the associated vernacular landscapes of quarters, fields, and woodlots, seeking evidence of the individuals and communities of people who populated, developed, and exploited them. Authors of this volume engage with a single plantation, Poplar Forest, over a century of environmental, economic, demographic, and social change that began on the eve of the American Revolution and ended with the Civil War. The historical circumstances of this place, like every historical place, were unique. However, the significant changes observed at Poplar Forest, including environmental degradation, the implementation of increasingly scientific agricultural practices, shifting strategies of provisioning and resource exploitation, the development of multigenerational communities of enslaved people, and plantation owners' and slaves' growing engagement in the consumer economy, have much to contribute to broader dialogues about plantation life across the American South during this period.

We thank the contributors to this volume for their participation, patience, and, most of all, their passion for their work. Each of us has drawn on twenty-five years of archaeology at Poplar Forest. We owe a debt of gratitude to the staff, field school participants, interns, volunteers, and consultants whose work has provided the framework from which we have constructed our research and built our interpretations. We are particularly grateful for the work of Keith Adams, Susan Trevarthen Andrews, Alasdair Brooks, William Kelso, Randy Lichtenberger, Heather Olson, Drake Patten, Elizabeth Paull, and Michael Strutt, whose efforts shaped the course of research over many years. Gail Pond tirelessly collected and shared a wealth of historical research, while Hannah Canel, Steven Deyerle, Ron Giese, Ruth Glass, Donald and Dorothy Cushman, Kathy

Janky, Dot O'Connor, and Chad Valentine contributed their talents and time over many years to forward the program's research, interpretation, and educational missions. Their efforts are greatly appreciated.

In addition to the work of our colleagues and friends, we are grateful for the generosity of foundations and granting agencies for financial support of our work. The Henry Luce Foundation provided funding for all phases of excavation and analysis of the Quarter Site. The Public Welfare Foundation, the Institute of Museum and Library Services, and the SRI Foundation funded several seasons of field and laboratory work at the antebellum slave quarter (Site A) and the ornamental plant nursery (Site B). We also extend our thanks to the numerous corporate, government, and individual sponsors of the Corporation for Jefferson's Poplar Forest who have provided long-term support for the corporation's archaeological research, the Poplar Forest Board of Directors, and Executive Director Lynn Beebe. Mr. and Mrs. Richard Hiner's support for publication costs helped bring this project to completion and is sincerely appreciated.

Laura and Gene Goley have graciously hosted work at the Wingos quarter farm over the course of a decade, while colleagues and students in the Department of Anthropology at the University of Tennessee have contributed to recent research efforts. Funding provided by the university has supported crucial historical and archaeological research.

John and Anja Falcone, Ben Ford, Susan Kern, Chris Mundy, Lynn Rainville, Beth Clites Sawyer, Karen Smith, Steve Thompson, and Derek Wheeler provided access to the various collections in central Virginia containing stone tobacco pipes. They also furnished context information and detailed site histories that revealed connections to African Americans, enslaved and free, who worked for Thomas Jefferson.

Eleanor Breen, Garrett Fesler, Fraser Neiman, and Esther White read earlier drafts of portions of this work and offered valuable comments and suggestions for improvement. Crystal Ptacek prepared maps 1.1, 6.1, 6.2, and 7.1. Edgar Endress created the composite pipe images for chapter 7. Anna Berkes promptly answered a thorny citation question. Kevin Fredette and Reginald Washington assisted with the location of historic records and documents. We are grateful for their assistance.

Lu Ann DeCunzo and Douglas Sanford provided helpful and positive critiques as reviewers. University Press of Florida editors Kara Schwartz and Michele Fiyak-Burkley shepherded this project through review and production. Their advice and encouragement is much appreciated. We would like to particularly thank Kate Babbitt for applying her editorial skills to this volume.

The chapters that follow provide a sample of the range and complexity of data that have been amassed about Poplar Forest by the many dedicated people who have contributed to its study. It is our hope that the breadth of topics and the diversity of approaches presented in the following pages demonstrate how historical archaeology can contribute to richly textured understandings of the past and inspire others to engage with this important place.

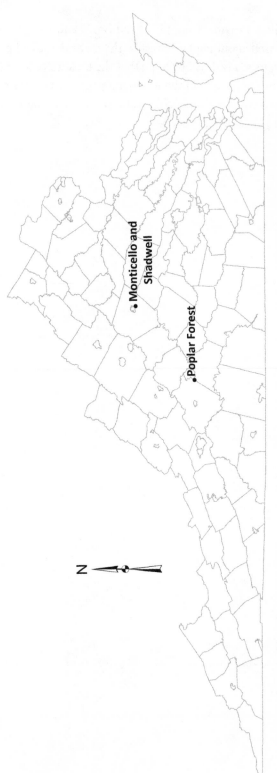

Map 1.1. Thomas Jefferson's two Virginia homes. Poplar Forest is located in Bedford County, and Monticello is in Albemarle County.

# I

## "Two Tracts of Land at the Poplar Forest"

### A Historical and Archaeological Overview of Thomas Jefferson's Plantation Retreat

BARBARA J. HEATH AND JACK GARY

Introducing Poplar Forest, or any site that has been inhabited for generations, is a challenging task. How do we define a place whose physical size, population, landscape, and use have changed dramatically over time? The authors in this book offer varied responses, focusing on written and archaeological evidence of former residents' relationships to the environment, using analysis of buildings and landscape modifications, and to each other, using analysis of acts of consumption and the display and use of consumer goods. Together, these studies provide insights into the specific culture of one plantation and the broader culture of which it was a part during the century that stretched from the eve of the American Revolution to the Civil War.

Today Poplar Forest is a National Historic Landmark, owned and administered since 1984 by the Corporation for Jefferson's Poplar Forest, a nonprofit private preservation organization. Dedicated to preserving, restoring, researching, and interpreting the period from 1806 to 1823, when Thomas Jefferson owned the property and used it as a private retreat and profitable plantation, the administrators of this site attribute its significance to its association with this important figure in American history. However, Jefferson's postretirement use of Poplar Forest is just one part of a multifaceted story that spans thousands of years. While we focus on the property's historic plantation past in this volume, archaeology has demonstrated that native people used this landscape as early as the Paleo-Indian period and as recently as the Late Woodland (Adams 2008). In the twentieth century, families lived and worked at Poplar Forest into the early 1980s.

Historic Poplar Forest

Legally defined by patent in 1745, when colonial minister and planter William Stith joined 4,000 acres of land in what was then Albemarle County, Poplar Forest had become part of newly formed Bedford County by 1754 (figure 1.1). The land apparently remained unoccupied during Stith's ownership and its subsequent possession by his daughter Elizabeth Pasteur and her cousin Peter Randolph (Chambers 1993, 3–4; Marmon 1991, part 1, 5–7).

In 1764, Randolph sold the property to attorney, planter, and businessman John Wayles. An absentee landowner living in Charles City County, Wayles acquired 819 acres of additional land abutting the original tract during the 1760s (Chambers 1993, 4) and developed the property through the use of enslaved labor. Following his death in 1773, the property passed to his daughter and son-in-law, Martha and Thomas Jefferson, along with land in Amherst, Cumberland, Charles City, Goochland, and Powhatan counties and 135 enslaved men, women, and children (Bear and Stanton 1997, 329–332; Jefferson in Betts 1987, 7–9; Chambers 1993, 4).

The Jeffersons were also absentee owners and infrequent visitors to the property. They were engaged in developing their home estate ninety miles to the northeast at Monticello in Albemarle County, raising a family, and pursuing Thomas Jefferson's political and legal career. After Martha's death in 1782, public service called Jefferson away from Virginia. From the mid-1780s through the early nineteenth century, overseers under the overall direction of a steward managed Poplar Forest's labor force, which produced annual crops of tobacco and wheat after 1790. These products were a significant source of income for their employer.

As he planned for his retirement from the presidency in 1809, Jefferson envisioned the property as a retreat from his personal and public responsibilities at Monticello. While still in office, he oversaw the construction of a unique retreat house and the creation of pleasure grounds near the center of the plantation (Brown 1990; Chambers 1993; Heath 2007; McDonald 1994; Trussell this volume).

Jefferson combined elements of ancient Roman architecture with contemporary design from England, France, and the United States in his house at Poplar Forest (McDonald 2000, 190–192). Two stories tall, the structure boasted an upper floor of living space and a lower level of service and storage rooms. Porticos dominated the north and south façades, and stair pavilions to the east and west provided interior access between floors (figures 1.2 and 1.3). Jefferson designed his home in the shape of an octagon, with four elongated octagonal rooms surrounding a central cubical room used for dining. Bedchambers were located east and west of the dining room, the south room served as a parlor,

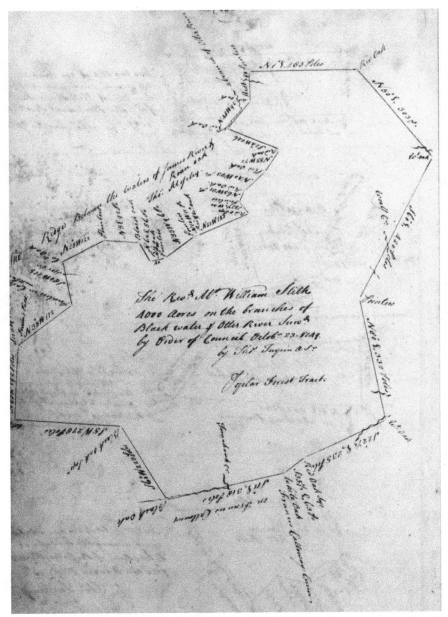

Figure 1.1. *Poplar Forest Tract*, 1749, plat map. Courtesy of Albemarle County Circuit Court, Charlottesville, Virginia.

and the northern octagonal space was cut by a passageway into two small multipurpose rooms.

Less is known about the use of the lower-level rooms, although evidence suggests that an overseer occupied them for a short period and that they were sometimes used as sleeping quarters by enslaved workmen and perhaps do-

Figure 1.2. Aerial view of Poplar Forest house and east dependency wing, looking north. Used by permission of Thomas Jefferson's Poplar Forest, Bedford County, Virginia. Photograph by Les Schofer.

mestic servants.[1] Jefferson used the square room beneath the dining room for storing wine and other goods.[2]

From 1813 to 1816, a dependency wing off the east side of the house was constructed that Jefferson called a "Wing of Offices." It contained an unheated storeroom; a kitchen; a room occupied by Hannah, Jefferson's cook and housekeeper; and a smokehouse. The structure was covered by a 100-foot-long flat roof that served as an outdoor room when the weather was mild. It connected to the east side of the house and was accessible from the east bedroom (figures 1.2 and 1.3) (Chambers 1993, 81; Kelso, Patten, and Strutt 1991; McDonald 2000, 179).

Jefferson carefully designed the five-acre grounds immediately surrounding his house, drawing on published accounts of and visits to contemporary landscapes in England, France, and the United States. This information was filtered through his personal aesthetic sensibilities and the realities of plantation life in rural Bedford County (Brown 1990; Heath 2007; Trussell this volume). During the period of house construction, he ordered workmen and enslaved laborers to excavate a sunken lawn south of the house and to build earthen mounds to the east and west. Enslaved gardeners planted trees and flowering shrubs along the length of the lawn, on the mounds, between the mounds and the house, and

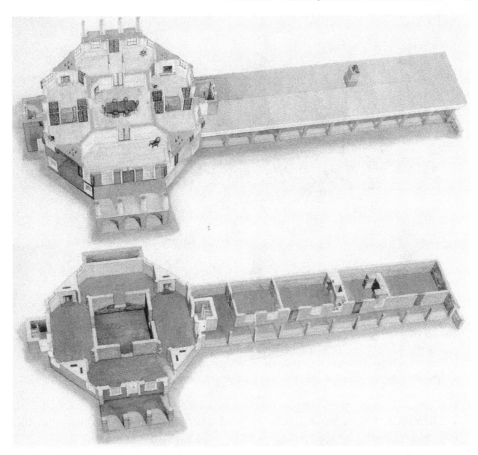

Figure 1.3. Watercolor painting showing sections through the upper and lower levels of the mansion house and the layout of the Wing of Offices. Jefferson's dining room is the cubical room surrounded by four elongated octagonal rooms in the center of the upper level. Used by permission of Thomas Jefferson's Poplar Forest, Bedford County, Virginia. Gail McIntosh, artist.

in the grounds. To the north of the house, a circular carriage turnaround stood within a lawn shaded by young tulip poplars. It was bounded near the north face of the house by oval beds of flowering shrubs. The entire composition was encircled by a road that served as a hub for plantation routes entering from the north and south (figure 1.4). A 61-acre curtilage surrounded the house, containing ornamental plantings, fruit and vegetable gardens, a nursery, orchards, and workspaces related to the household (Brown 1990; Gary 2008; Heath 2007; Trussell 2000; Trussell this volume).

Accompanied by a small retinue of enslaved men and women based at Monticello and occasionally by family members, Jefferson visited the property annually from 1810 to 1823, staying for days or weeks at a time. When the house was near completion in 1816, he began to bring his granddaughters, particularly

Figure 1.4. Watercolor painting showing conjectural view of the development of the Poplar Forest landscape between 1810 and 1820, looking north. Used by permission of Thomas Jefferson's Poplar Forest, Bedford County, Virginia. Diane Johnson, artist.

Ellen and Cornelia Randolph, to Bedford, where they provided companionship and served as hostesses for local callers during his visits (Chambers 1993, 104–5, 128; Gary this volume).

In 1790, Jefferson gave 1,000 acres of Poplar Forest land to his daughter Martha and her husband Thomas Mann Randolph as part of a marriage settlement, along with six enslaved families living on the property (Boyd 1961, 189–191). His hope that future grandchildren from their union would take up residence on that portion of the property were never realized, although he had more success settling the only surviving child of his younger daughter, Maria Eppes, at his retreat. Shortly after they were married in 1823, grandson Francis Eppes and his wife Mary Elizabeth moved to Poplar Forest. When Jefferson died three years later, the Eppeses inherited the house, nearly 1,075 acres of land, and several enslaved men and women. In the 1820s and 1830s, Martha Randolph's son Thomas Jefferson Randolph divided and sold the remainder of his grandfather's landholdings, and in 1827 and 1828 he sold many of Jefferson's slaves to settle debts (Chambers 1993, 167; Marmon 1991, part 2:40-42).

Relatively little is known about Eppes's ownership of the property, as Francis and Mary Elizabeth lived there for only five years (Chambers 1993, 174–175; Proebsting this volume). They sold Poplar Forest in November 1828 to local planter William Cobbs, whose family included his wife, Marian, and daughter, Emma. Following Emma's 1840 marriage to Edward Hutter—a naval officer from Pennsylvania whose brother owned an adjacent plantation—Cobbs turned the property management over to his son-in-law (Chambers 1993, 177; Lee 2008 this volume) (figure 1.5).

A catastrophic fire in 1845 caused substantial damage to the octagonal dwelling. The flames worked slowly, and the Cobbs and Hutter families, who shared the house, escaped with their lives and many of their furnishings. They decided to rebuild, refashioning the dwelling in the popular Greek revival style. They also added an attic story for sleeping and reconfigured the interior plan of the house (Chambers 1993, 181–190).

Just before the fire, William Cobbs had ordered that Jefferson's east dependencies be torn down and had overseen the rebuilding of a smaller detached kitchen and smokehouse on the site of the earlier kitchen and smokehouse (Kelso, Patten, and Strutt 1991).

In addition to rebuilding the house and dependencies, the Cobbs and Hutters made extensive changes to the Poplar Forest landscape during their lives. Among other alterations, they abandoned the southern third of the circular

Figure 1.5. Mid-nineteenth-century photograph of Emma and Edward Hutter. Used by permission of Thomas Jefferson's Poplar Forest, Bedford County, Virginia.

road and planted a large kitchen garden due south of the house with an accompanying subterranean hothouse, built slave quarters southeast of the mansion, constructed a carriage house and barn, changed the location of one major plantation road and stopped using another, and substantially reworked Jefferson's planting scheme. Archaeology has provided important evidence for these significant changes (Chambers 1993, 192–93; Heath et al. 2004, 2005; Heath and Lee 2010; Kelso, Patten, and Strutt 1991).

Edward and Emma Hutter's son Christian purchased Poplar Forest from relatives in the late nineteenth century and used it as a farm and a summer home for his family into the 1940s. Hutter modernized the house by adding running water and electricity and oversaw the construction of a complex of barns and storage buildings southwest of the mansion. The property continued to operate as a farm, with a series of managers overseeing hired black and white farmhands and tenant farmers (Chambers 1993, 195–196).

Members of the Hutter family were keenly aware of their role as stewards of Jefferson's property and cared for a collection of documents and furnishings that had belonged to the former president and his family. During the late nineteenth and early twentieth centuries, they made the property available for patriotic assemblies and private tours, during which Christian Hutter shared family lore with visiting tourists, authors, and reporters (Chambers 1993, 197–200). Nevertheless, the Hutters did not hesitate to make Poplar Forest their own through campaigns that involved building, razing, planting, and modernizing. It was not until the mid-twentieth century, when new owners took possession, that significant efforts were made to restore the physical fabric of the house to a form that would have been recognizable to Thomas Jefferson.

In 1946, Hutter sold the property to the James Watts family. They occupied the house year round and operated Poplar Forest as a dairy farm. Working with Phelps Barnum, a New York architect in partnership with W. Stuart Thompson, they refurbished the main house with the goal of returning it (without major exterior renovations) to a Jeffersonian appearance (Chambers 1993, 200–205). The installation of a swimming pool, bathhouse, and serpentine-walled rose garden south of the house (which was evocative of Jefferson-designed gardens at the University of Virginia) had a considerable visual impact on the landscape and combined modern conveniences with an imagined past. The grading of Jefferson's sunken lawn, part of a larger effort to divert water from the lower level of the house, prioritized practical maintenance needs over the preservation of historic fabric and significantly altered the contours of an important element of the early nineteenth-century grounds. Most unfortunate from the perspective of present-day preservationists, the Wattses sold the majority of the remaining landholdings to a developer, who during the 1970s and early 1980s built a nine-hole golf course and a lake for irrigation north and west of the house and tract housing along much of the eastern and southern portions of the property (Chambers 1993, 195, 200, 207–208).

In an effort to protect what was left of the property, Dr. James Johnson of North Carolina purchased the house and the remaining fifty acres of land from the Wattses in 1980. In December 1983, he sold it to the newly formed nonprofit Corporation for Jefferson's Poplar Forest. Since 1984, the corporation has actively reacquired land that was contained within the early nineteenth-century plantation boundaries. It currently owns 617 acres of the original property, including the historic core, the golf course, farm fields, and woodland. Today this land falls within Bedford and Campbell counties and the city of Lynchburg, Virginia.

## Archaeological Research

Archaeology began at Poplar Forest in 1986 with a short testing project in the area immediately surrounding the house. The results of these tests were so promising that two years later the corporation hired William Kelso to begin a long-term research program. Along with Michael Strutt as field supervisor and Drake Patten as lab supervisor, Kelso's team spent two years excavating the Wing of Offices and carrying out intensive testing of key areas of the ornamental grounds adjacent to the main house, excavating a mid-nineteenth-century hothouse, uncovering portions of the cellar of the main house, testing beneath the floor of one of two extant antebellum brick houses, and testing a nineteenth-century icehouse (figure 1.6) (Kelso, Patten, and Strutt 1991).

Concurrent with the archaeological research, Poplar Forest launched a program of architectural investigation that ultimately led to a full-scale restoration of the house and re-creation of the Wing of Offices, the final phases of which are still in progress. Beginning with Kelso and continuing to the present, the corporation has made it a priority to provide public access to the research and restoration processes, and the ongoing process of archaeological and architectural interpretation and education is now more than twenty-five years old (Heath 1997b, Heath 2003; Lee 2010).

Barbara Heath replaced William Kelso as director of archaeology in 1993 and over the following fourteen years balanced restoration-related excavations, projects to manage cultural resources, and research-oriented field and lab work. In 2000, anticipating a future focus on landscape-related research and restoration, the department was reorganized as the Department of Archaeology and Landscapes. Along with Michael Strutt, Susan Trevarthen Andrews, Alasdair Brooks, Tim Trussell, Heather Olson, Randy Lichtenberger, Scott Grammer,

Figure 1.6. Excavations of Jefferson's east dependencies, known as the Wing of Offices. Used by permission of Thomas Jefferson's Poplar Forest, Bedford County, Virginia.

Keith Adams, and Lori Lee, teams of archaeologists, field school students, interns, and volunteers carried out extensive excavations across the property. Highlights of this period include excavations that focused on the Poplar Forest slave communities at the Quarter Site (1993–1996); the North Hill Site, which was occupied by slaves from 1770 to 1810 (1995–1998); Site A, an antebellum slave cabin (2001–2003); and the Wingos quarter farm (2000, 2001). Extensive research was also done on the ornamental grounds, including excavations of the north yard (1993, 2002), the south lawn (1996, 1998–1999), the east and west mounds (1999–2001), the circular road (2000, 2002), and southeast of the main house in an area known as Site B (2003–present) (see map 1.2) (Andrews 1993, 1999; Brooks 2000; Heath 1993a, 1993b, 1994, 1999b; Heath et al. 2004; Heath et al. 2005; Jones 2001, 2002; Kealofer 1997, 1999; Raymer 1996, 2003). During this period, intensive testing was completed in a ten-acre area around the main house and a comprehensive archaeological and documentary survey of the Poplar Forest property was carried out (Adams 1996, 1997). More intensive

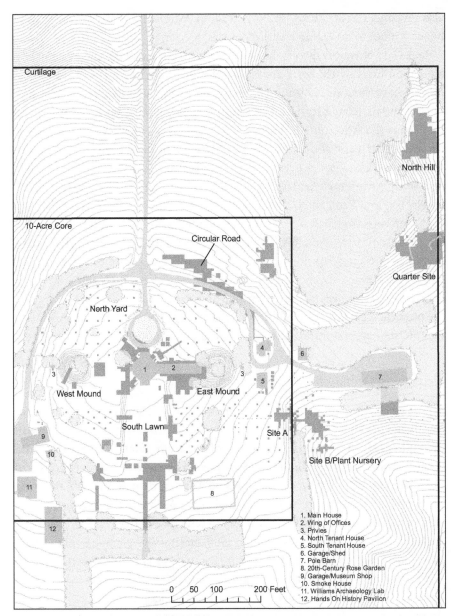

Map 1.2. Areas of archaeological investigation within the 61-acre curtilage at Jefferson's Poplar Forest plantation.

field surveys were performed in the area historically known as the Ridge Field (2000–2002), in the area of Jefferson's prize barn and tobacco barn (1995–1997), and in a field northeast of the main house (1999–2001) (Lichtenberger et al. 2006). The sites of Jefferson's brick kiln and of one of his tobacco barns, neither of which are located on land that was owned by Poplar Forest at the time, were also investigated (Strutt 1998b; Trussell 1999). Heath left Poplar Forest in 2006 but continues to do research at the Wingos quarter.

Jack Gary currently directs the Department of Archaeology and Landscapes, a position he has held since 2006. Together with Lori Lee and Eric Proebsting, he has overseen continuing efforts to understand and locate other support elements related to the retreat and the plantation from the time period that spans the Jefferson era through the twentieth century. A combination of surveys, block excavations, and specialized analysis have been used to search for the sites of stables, vegetable gardens, plant nurseries, and slave quarters that stood within the curtilage during the Jefferson era (2007–present) (Gary 2008; Gary and Paull 2008). Other projects have continued to explore the lives of Poplar Forest's enslaved residents during the Cobbs and Hutter era through an interdisciplinary analysis of a subfloor pit from the Site A antebellum slave quarter (2006–present) (Bowes 2009; Bowes and Trigg 2009 this volume; Lee 2008 this volume). A renewed program of landscape research and restoration began during this period, the results of which are a body of data that will guide the physical reconstruction of the retreat landscape and help steer environmental, interpretive, and infrastructure improvements on the 600-acre property.

## Plantations: Definitions and Approaches

The historical development of one piedmont Virginia plantation forms the central theme of this book. Likely as a result of familiarity with the topic, none of the authors has explored the definition of the term *plantation* explicitly, and yet it is worth noting its multiple meanings. Prior to the English conquest of Ireland in the sixteenth century, *plantation* was a fairly neutral term, referring simply to a place where something was planted. As late as the nineteenth century, gardeners used the word in this way in reference to tree clumps, bushes, or vegetables (see for example McMahon 1806, 46 [nursery plants]; Squibb [1787] 1980, 38–39 [asparagus]; and Whately [1770] 1982, 34 [small thicket]).

Concurrent with colonial expansion, the term *plantation* began to be used to describe New World settlements or the groups of people who occupied them. By the seventeenth century, the modern meaning of the term had emerged; namely a large tract of land where a labor force cultivates crops for regional or international markets (Kolchin 1993, 5; Vlach 1993, 2). Plantations developed within a capitalist system whereby owners were divorced from primary modes of production and created enterprises based on the labor of unfree workers or (at best) men and women whose social, economic, and physical mobility was severely curtailed.

Plantations defined in this way were complex social, economic, and physical entities grounded in specific times and places. The earliest plantations developed in ancient Greece and Rome; those more relevant to historical archaeology and a focus on the Atlantic World began during the Middle Ages with the cultivation of sugar in the eastern Mediterranean, Islamic Spain, the Canaries, and São Tomé and a growing dependence on African laborers (Klein and Vinson 2007, 6–8; Thornton 1998, 34–35). The plantations that developed in the Caribbean and in the Middle Atlantic colonies in the seventeenth century had become the dominant economic system throughout the tidewater and piedmont regions of the American South and in the West Indies by the eighteenth century (Breen [1985] 2001, 40–58; Dunn 1972; Kulikoff 1986; Mintz 1985, 34–46; Morgan 1998, 29–58; Parent 2003).

Plantations were often rural, dispersed, and socially isolated places for owners or managers. In some regions, particularly the Caribbean and the South Carolina lowcountry but also in the Virginia piedmont of the eighteenth century, owners were often entirely absent. At the same time, plantations became population centers and sites where enslaved Africans and other laborers could build community. Social and economic exchanges, mediated within and through the material world of landscapes, buildings, and objects, made plantations important places of cultural continuity and change.

The complex interactions that occurred between diverse Old and New World peoples as a result of colonial and postcolonial processes enacted within plantation contexts have been explained using models of cultural change that include assimilation, acculturation, creolization, hybridization, and ethnogenesis (Cusick 1998a, 1998b; Dawdy 2000, 107; Fennell 2007a, 9; Ferguson 1992; Mintz and Price 1976; Mouer 1993, Singleton 1998). Recent studies have also paid increasing attention to the environmental context (Mrozowski 2006).

Although popular nostalgia equates plantation life with the simplicity of preindustrial societies, planters became increasingly dependent on new technology and industrialization to meet their goal of profitably producing and distributing a single or narrow range of products for a regional or global system of exchange. While most Virginia plantations remained primarily focused on agriculture, plantation-based industries became increasingly common in the late eighteenth and nineteenth centuries. Changing economic and demographic circumstances also pulled many enslaved people off plantations to work in local and regional industrial settings, in a system known as "hiring out." Plantation owners kept the wages of these enslaved industrial workers (Heath this volume; Lee this volume).

After the Civil War, many plantations in the U.S. South experimented with new labor sources, management practices, and crops. By the late nineteenth century, tenant farming, which often was undertaken by former slaves, became the norm. The share-cropping system perpetuated the social and economic inequalities that the war had briefly promised to eradicate.

## About This Volume

The complexity of plantation systems is mirrored in the different approaches archaeologists have used to study them. The many theoretical and methodological changes that have taken place in the field of archaeology have ensured that there is no single approach that archaeologists apply to these large and diverse properties. The authors in this volume use multiple perspectives to address historical ecology, social landscapes, consumerism, identity creation, and community formation at the Poplar Forest plantation site.

Barbara Heath's introductory summary of the history of plantation archaeology in Virginia sets the stage for the chapters that follow, tracing the historical, theoretical, and methodological changes that have transformed plantation studies from particularistic restoration projects to more theoretically informed anthropological investigations of plantation systems. In chapters 3–9, Eric Proebsting, Timothy Trussell, Jack Gary, Barbara Heath, Lori Lee, Jessica Bowes, and Heather Trigg present diverse case studies that examine the landscapes and lives of both free and enslaved residents of Poplar Forest. In the final chapter, Stephen Mrozowski offers a fresh perspective on this body of research and situates it within the larger subdiscipline of historical archaeology.

The volume is organized around several broad themes grounded in readings of material culture, from the individual remains of stone pipes and ceramic plates to the large-scale evidence of designed pleasure grounds and plantation woodlots. Authors explore the interplay between agriculture and the local environment; the multiple roles of plantation landscapes—as economic settings, places for the expression of individual identity and community formation, and spaces of social interaction; and the impact of mass-produced and handmade goods on social life during a critical period of the rise of consumerism among both white and black Virginians.

The significant environmental impact of plantation agriculture is unmistakable in the archaeological and written record of colonial and antebellum Virginia. This theme guides Eric Proebsting's work and is important to the analysis of Jessica Bowes and Heather Trigg as well. Proebsting uses both documentary and archaeological data—derived from excavations and environmental analysis—to explore the processes of human-initiated landscape changes at Poplar Forest and in the surrounding region. These changes still resonate in the area today; the local vegetation, place names, fauna, and topography continue to bear the marks of colonial expansion, agricultural practices, and the economic aspirations of planters. Proebsting uses Poplar Forest to exemplify the powerful cultural and economic forces behind historic landscape changes, particularly those associated with large-scale tobacco production. Poplar Forest provides an example of just how strongly tobacco was ingrained in Virginia culture, despite the drastic impact it had on the local environment and the well-being of the enslaved workforce. The grip of tobacco on the region becomes clear when looking at Poplar Forest's owners. Somewhat anomalously, they all attempted to move away from production of the crop in the nineteenth century, with varying degrees of success. The agricultural histories associated with Jefferson, Eppes, Cobbs, and Hutter demonstrate that significant resources, often outside the financial reach of planters, were needed to reverse the effects of deforestation, erosion, and loss of soil fertility brought about by decades of tobacco production.

The environmental impact of tobacco culture also affected the daily lives of the enslaved residents who lived and worked within these landscapes. Proebsting and Bowes and Trigg have studied plant remains and fuel wood found at Poplar Forest slave quarters; their chapters illustrate that the process of clearing original hardwood forests for the expansion of plantation crops changed the environments from which enslaved laborers gathered food, medicines, and fuel. Abandoned fields that were no longer fertile enough to support tobacco regenerated with a variety of new plant species that had benefits and drawbacks for the people who exploited them. The research contained in these chapters highlights the dynamic relationship between humans and the environments they transform and live within.

The creation of pleasure gardens, set within the raw landscapes of newly opened plantation fields, was one important outcome of the financial success these environmental transformations promised. As tobacco cultivation swept across Virginia in the eighteenth and nineteenth centuries, the art of gardening took root among Virginia's elite. This movement, which drew on neoclassical gardens in France and naturalistic landscapes in England, held great appeal for Jefferson, who used the Poplar Forest grounds to express aesthetic and intellectual preferences. Tim Trussell examines this designed landscape, which was not intended for a large audience, as a point of entry into understanding Jefferson's identity. Trussell connects the documentary and in-ground evidence of the Poplar Forest garden to aspects of Jefferson's personal life, showing how both modern and "ancient" elements were carried out in specific landscape features. His chapter treats ornamental landscapes as expressions of personal identity writ large. At Poplar Forest, this is a reflexive identity; Jefferson's private retreat and grounds reinforced his notion of himself that he had developed through study, observation, and action. Trussell's chapter provides a nuanced approach to formal landscapes that moves away from the traditional issues of status and power to explore their intensely autobiographical nature.

Plantations were also important places that facilitated and structured interactions between diverse people and between people and goods. In this volume several authors discuss the material world of Poplar Forest's residents with regard to the complex interplay between landscapes, buildings, objects, families, and communities.

Author Jack Gary examines consumer choices to better understand how people shaped their everyday lives with mass-produced objects that were important to them. Gary argues that Jefferson encoded messages in the landscape and architecture of Poplar Forest. These messages provided the framework for choosing and acquiring certain ceramic styles for his household, which were intended to reinforce those messages. The social aspects of dining, even at a private retreat, gave Jefferson a stage to create or strengthen relationships among family members, neighbors, and individuals close to him. The imagery contained in transfer-printed wares found at Poplar Forest conveyed an aesthetic value directly tied to the owner, one that visitors and diners would have immediately recognized.

Barbara Heath's chapter introduces Jefferson's enslaved community and explores the debate over the extent to which agricultural systems determine social organization within plantation settings. Specifically, she compares the timing and scope of the transition from tobacco to grain production at Poplar Forest and Monticello and the concomitant changes in plantation management to the spatial organization of enslaved plantation families. Taking issue with a recent model that equates changing sizes and interior features of slave cabins with new styles of management brought about by work regimens associated with wheat production, Heath argues that material changes in living conditions resulted from the historical trajectory of household development that was set in motion by the formation of multigenerational families that began in central Virginia in the 1750s and 1760s.

Lori Lee's work explores the experiences of enslaved men and women at Poplar Forest through the lens of portable material culture. In her chapter on locally produced stone pipes, Lee introduces an important assemblage of handcrafted objects found within early to mid-nineteenth-century contexts associated with enslaved households at Poplar Forest and elsewhere in central Virginia. Rare survivals from a material world that doubtless was populated by a mixture of handcrafted textiles, clay pottery, metalwork, and myriad objects made of wood and leather, these enigmatic pipes suggest that while slaves "bought into" the importance of mass-produced consumables, they also valued qualities inherent in items that they made for themselves. The production of pipes led to the creation of local networks of exchange and use whose scope and meaning we are only beginning to explore.

In a subsequent chapter, Lee explores consumer goods as objects of empowerment within the mid-nineteenth-century enslaved community. The rapid technological, economic, and social changes occurring at that time had a significant impact on the system of plantation-based slavery in Virginia. Lee shows that the result of some of these changes was increased access to the market economy for the enslaved, which in turn affected the social and economic relationships between slaves and planters and among the enslaved themselves. Lee examines the material remains of the possessions of the inhabitants of a cabin excavated at Poplar Forest to elucidate these social changes and demonstrate the power of objects to help enslaved individuals negotiate their daily lives and status within the rapidly changing and unstable system of slavery in the period leading up to emancipation.

Jessica Bowes and Heather Trigg remind the reader that food, like material goods, is charged with meaning. Food in plantation contexts represents the decision-making processes of two parties—the planter who provisioned it and the enslaved people who consumed it and supplemented it with their own food-acquisition strategies. Using the macrobotanical remains recovered from three slave quarters excavated at Poplar Forest, Bowes and Trigg show that the amount of provisioning, gardening, and wild resource procurement changed over time at Poplar Forest. These changes can be connected to plantation management strategies, environmental changes, and the direct actions and decisions of the enslaved.

Future Directions

The chapters in this volume represent only a sample of the rich archaeological research that has been under way at Poplar Forest since the 1980s. Many important projects have yet to be completed and new studies have yet to be conceived that draw on the wealth of the archival and artifact collections currently curated by the corporation. As we write, Gary and his colleagues are uncovering myriad features associated with Hutter-era slave quarters and Jeffersonian landscape elements within the historic grounds surrounding the main house. Additional sites relating to the broader plantation are recorded within the modern property boundaries but have not yet been explored.

Missing from the discussions of the interactions between humans and landscapes that this volume explores is an in-depth consideration of the role animals played in the history of the property (but see Proebsting this volume for an overview). Due to the acidic nature of the Bedford County soils and the plow-disturbed deposits that characterize many of the sites addressed by the authors, bone preservation has been disappointing at most sites and generally faunal analysis has yielded limited results (but see Andrews 1993, 1994, 1999). Happily, that story is changing. Recently analyzed deposits associated with a sub-floor pit in an antebellum slave cabin (Site A discussed by Lee in this volume) have yielded rich and abundant remains that range from domesticated and wild mammals to birds, fish, reptiles, and amphibians. Analysis of this assemblage is nearing completion, and a study of taphonomic processes on fish bones is finished (Klippel, Synstelien, and Heath 2011). Further reporting is anticipated. Additional analysis that is under way includes bone recovered from other Site A contexts and from a late-eighteenth century slave quarter at Wingos.

*Jefferson's Poplar Forest: Unearthing a Virginia Plantation* presents new insights into Jefferson's aesthetic, intellectual, and economic motivations for shaping the setting for his retirement. As Gary's chapter demonstrates, there is tremendous potential for coming to a deeper understanding of Jefferson and his family in the continued analysis and interpretation of the quotidian items he purchased and used in his retirement years.

Beyond the specifics of Poplar Forest's historical context, research has contributed to a broader regional approach to the plantation systems of which it was a part. Collaboration with the Digital Archaeological Archive of Comparative Slavery (www.daacs.org) currently makes it possible for scholars to use Poplar Forest artifacts and context data relating to two plantation quarters within the context of larger comparative regional analysis. Recently, Heath initiated an archaeological research project that seeks to trace the Poplar Forest slave community's roots to properties owned by Jefferson's father-in-law, John Wayles, in piedmont counties to the east. Poplar Forest quartering sites will form an important end to the story of the material and social development of slavery in Virginia as experienced by members of a single community. The resulting data from this project, which is slated to be included in the Digital Archive, will expand the archive and enable researchers to craft a variety of questions about the material conditions of life as experienced by enslaved individuals across the Virginia piedmont.

As Stephen Mrozowski argues in the closing chapter of this volume, historical archaeology has the unique ability to shed new light on lives such as Jefferson's, which is already considered to be well illuminated, and to chase back the shadows and reveal glimpses of the experiences of enslaved people whose legacies have been lost or ignored. To accomplish this, we knit together seemingly incompatible fragments of evidence—soil stains, carbonized seeds, broken pipes, sherds of window glass, mass-produced images of popular scenery, handwritten names in a ledger, notes about a long-ago trip to England—to see the outlines of a bigger picture. This picture, like all interpretations of the past, is incomplete. At plantations such as Poplar Forest, it is also often painful. The material strategies property owners used to manifest and maintain social and economic inequality each day through substandard housing, inadequate provisions, grueling labor, and the physical separation of families succeeded despite the efforts of enslaved men and women to counteract them. Nevertheless, learning from and writing about these past people and the landscapes in which they lived is important to preserving their memories and helping us understand the world in which we live our own lives today.

## Notes

1. Thomas Jefferson to Hugh Chisholm, September 8, 1808, and John Hemings to Thomas Jefferson, November 18, 1819, both in the Coolidge Collection of Thomas Jefferson Manuscripts, Massachusetts Historical Society, Boston, Massachusetts.

2. Joel Yancey to Thomas Jefferson, January 9, 1819, Coolidge Collection of Thomas Jefferson Manuscripts.

# 2

# A Brief History
# of Plantation Archaeology in Virginia

BARBARA J. HEATH

Plantations are complex economic enterprises that interweave commercial and noncommercial agricultural and industrial production with the creation and maintenance of internal transportation, storage, and processing systems and the management of human and natural resources. Historically in Virginia, they have also served as centers of labor for diverse groups of enslaved African and Native Americans and European American indentured servants and as places of work and leisure for owners. Racial boundaries were invented, defined, codified, maintained, and broken in the day-to-day interactions among plantation residents. Paradoxically, plantations were also the birthplaces of multigenerational family lineages, of communities, and of new ethnic identities. For the descendants of both masters and slaves, plantations today constitute powerful reservoirs of cultural memory, serving as home places and cornerstones of regional identity while acting as mnemonics for both gentility and backwardness, power and oppression, and wealth and poverty.

For much of its history, plantation archaeology has worked in the service of restoration and commemoration. Educational missions were guided by a heroic and romanticized vision of the past that preservationists thought was best delivered through restored or reconstructed buildings and landscapes that belonged to colonial and federal elites. Such programs focused on "founding fathers" and the revolutionary generation. Through their labors, practitioners have directly contributed to the physical recreation of historic plantation houses and grounds and thus to the continuation and popular dissemination of this heroic view of the past. However, plantation archaeologists have always encountered the other, more gritty past—the one where mansions overlooked quarters, terraced gardens gave way to workshops and smithies, and erosion, deforestation, and reforestation were the legacies of generations of intensive land use. Over the last three decades, plantation archaeologists have increasingly engaged with *this* past through the study of slavery and the landscape beyond the garden gate, industrial processes and technological changes, and the ways that memories are created and maintained. In this chapter, I provide a brief history of plantation archaeology in Virginia, focusing on the theoretical and social contexts in which projects were undertaken and the research methods and questions that guided the work of generations of architects, landscape architects, and professional archaeologists. I conclude with some thoughts on future research directions.

## Antiquarians to Restoration Architects

In a diary entry for October 1858, Dr. Richard Eppes noted that a flagstone or marble floor to a "large dining room or hall" had been found within the buried remains of a foundation on his property at Bermuda Hundred near Richmond, Virginia. The excavation of such a large, well-finished building prompted the doctor to speculate about the identity of the builders and the use of the structure. His discovery and the detailed diary entry he created about it, is perhaps the earliest reference yet known to historical archaeology carried out on a Virginia plantation (Heite 1967, 94). Throughout the late nineteenth and into the early twentieth centuries, other individuals sporadically dug around Virginia mansions and across abandoned plantation fields, looking for evidence of colonial buildings and collecting artifacts for display (Caywood 1955, 1957; Cotter 1958 as cited in Barka 1996, 5; Dimmick 1929; Hudgins 1985, 27).

Research- and restoration-oriented archaeology traces its roots in Virginia to early twentieth-century architects, draftsmen, and archaeologists tasked with reviving—through exploration, restoration, and reconstruction—the glories of Virginia's past during the colonial and early national periods. The first problem-oriented excavations at a Virginia plantation were carried out as early as 1893 at Mount Vernon. George Washington's Potomac River plantation had been saved for posterity by early historic preservationists, headed by Ann Pamela Cunningham, as part of a larger movement venerating Washington's memory that took shape during the first half of the nineteenth century (Hosmer 1965, 41–63). There, Col. Harrison H. Dodge, director of the Mount Vernon Ladies' Association from 1885 to 1937, excavated the foundations of the plantation's coach house prior to rebuilding it (White 2006, 197). In 1896, he investigated the ducts that heated Bushrod Washington's greenhouse (Pogue 2006, 168–169; E. White, personal communication 2010). That same year, army engineers uncovered portions of brick foundations in an attempt to locate the remains of Wakefield

Plantation, Washington's birthplace in Westmoreland County (Hosmer 1981, 478–79).

Across the state, broader architectural- and landscape-oriented research that incorporated archaeological findings began to take shape in the second and third decades of the twentieth century. In their scope, methodology, and supervision, these projects owe a debt to three organizations: the Colonial Williamsburg Foundation, the National Park Service, and the Garden Club of Virginia. Each organization had a very different mandate and background. Colonial Williamsburg grew out of a private partnership between philanthropist John D. Rockefeller Jr. and local visionary Rev. William Archer Rutherfoord Goodwin. The goal of these two men was to purchase, restore, and interpret the colonial capital of Williamsburg (Hosmer 1981, 11–73). Founded in 1916 as a federal agency, the National Park Service was tasked with preserving and maintaining important natural and archaeological resources. By 1930, with the acquisition of Wakefield Plantation in Westmoreland County and the establishment of Colonial National Monument in James City and York counties,[1] the park service entered the field of historic preservation (Hosmer 1981, 483–488, 494–499). The Garden Club of Virginia was formed in 1920 as a privately administered statewide alliance of local garden clubs. Through its Restoration Committee, the club promoted restoration and public access to historic landscapes throughout the commonwealth by providing funding and oversight for projects that club members believed to have significant historical merit (Williams 1975, xi–xii). Together, these three organizations were instrumental in launching research and restoration projects at plantation sites across the state beginning in the 1930s.

With the commencement of the restoration of Williamsburg in 1928 and the birth of the archaeological program at Jamestown six years later, the ground rules were set for how, by whom, and for what purpose archaeology at historic sites in the area should be carried out. Important differences in the approaches of both organizations had emerged by the mid-1930s, exemplified by the hiring in 1936 of professional archaeologist J. C. Harrington to direct the Jamestown project. Initially, however, the two organizations took a similar approach that had been pioneered at Williamsburg. There, a team of consulting architects, landscape architects, and architectural draftsmen devised a process that included large-scale excavations of trenches to locate and study major foundations and landscape features such as walls, pavements, pathways, drains, and steps (for example, see Ragland 1930); the removal of fill within foundations; the recording of important features through measured drawings, photography, and brief descriptive reports; and the selective collection of associated artifacts.[2]

The project team followed a similar course in the early years at Jamestown. Harrington noted that before he arrived, as a result of disagreements between staff members, "the architects were assigned sole responsibility for the excavation of structural remains and the archaeologists for everything else, up to an arbitrary three-foot line from any foundation" (Harrington 1994, 4). This procedure changed when he took over the project and hired a staff of experienced field archaeologists who understood the importance of following stratigraphy, recording artifact provenience within a master grid, and keeping meticulous records (Cotter 1994, 29).

The primary goal of Colonial Williamsburg's restoration team was the physical re-creation of the eighteenth-century town that had served as Virginia's capital. Architectural reconstruction was the main focus of this work. Although accuracy was of prime concern for building projects, the concerns of cost, maintenance, and visitor comfort and pleasure took priority in the grounds (Hosmer 1985, 69). Landscapes were intended to provide a beautiful setting where visitors could experience a romanticized past instead of demonstrating the realities of southern urban life during the colonial period. While project founder W. A. R. Goodwin envisioned Williamsburg as a place to educate and inspire visitors about life in the pre–Revolutionary War era, a focus on architecture and (to a lesser extent) landscapes pushed his broader agenda aside in the early years (Hosmer 1981, 43–44, 61).

These values and attitudes—prioritizing architectural restoration, seeing landscapes as backdrops rather than as artifacts as deserving of careful research as buildings, and focusing on the built environment as an end in itself rather than as an aspect of material culture useful in conveying broader interpretations of the past—influenced landscape research and restoration decisions at plantation sites for years to come and continue to influence decision-making today. Indeed, one legacy of the early work of preservationists is the continued perception of archaeologists as technicians at worst or junior partners at best, who supplement rather than challenge historical "truths" (Deagan 1996, 23–25; Little 1996, 43–44).

In 1930, Arthur Shurcliff, a professor of landscape architecture at Harvard University and the primary consultant on landscape restoration for Colonial Williamsburg, was invited to undertake research at Stratford Hall, the ancestral home of the Lee family. His project was sponsored by the Garden Club of Virginia (Williams 1975, 18). In a report to that organization, he argued for "patient study of the actual facts of the old design before we attempt the restoration of the grounds." This patient study included, at least in part, archaeological evidence collected during excavations undertaken that summer (Hosmer 1985, 63–64). Two years later, his colleague Morley Williams completed work at the plantation's East Garden, and in 1934, Williams undertook additional work on the property (Beaman 2000, 5; Williams 1975, 14, 19).

Williams went to Virginia in the late spring of 1931, funded in part by a grant from Harvard University entitled "American Landscape Design as Exemplified by the Plantation Estates of Maryland and Virginia 1750–1860." The impetus for the research was Shurcliff's work at Stratford and the need for better documentation of historic southern gardens that this work demanded (Williams 1975, 19). The grant also funded Williams's research at Mount Vernon, where he and his team undertook topographic surveys, looking for evidence of colonial and early federal landscape design (Beaman 2000, 4–5; Pogue 2006, 167; Williams 1932, 165, 1938). During the summer of 1931, he mapped the grounds surrounding the mansion and began a multiyear archaeological project that resulted in the discovery of the foundations of a pre-1775 complex of outbuildings that included a kitchen, a dairy, a washhouse, and a storehouse. Williams was hired as Mount Vernon's director of research and restoration in 1936. Williams spent the next three years overseeing the excavation of a blacksmith shop along the North Lane and a dung repository (stercorary) on the South Lane; locating features associated with two nineteenth-century structures; and exploring enclosed gardens and the broader landscape design. He left the project in 1939, having contributed significantly to understanding the landscape of Mount Vernon during George Washington's ownership (Pogue 2006, 167–168).

Because of their training in landscape architecture, Shurcliff and Williams prioritized buildings and hardscape evidence in their efforts to understand landscapes. Neither man placed much emphasis on artifact recovery or analysis. This lack of interest in non-architectural material culture was common in the 1920s and 1930s (Cotter 1994, 27; Harrington 1994, 10; Sanford 1999a, 5). However, excavators in these early projects did pay attention to basic stratigraphic sequences in the test trenches they dug. At Mount Vernon, Williams left behind a wealth of documentation that is still valued by archaeologists and restoration architects (Pogue 1996, 167).

During the 1940s and 1950s, plantation archaeology remained largely focused on illuminating the homes and landscapes of the colonial elite, but practitioners increasingly began to consider sites with little or no standing architecture.[3] Historical archaeology continued to be carried out by people trained in a variety of disciplines, including architecture, landscape architecture, and anthropology, and by some with no formal training at all. Architect Fiske Kimball's work at Monticello exemplifies the continuities and changes of this period. Harvard-trained like Shurcliff and Williams, Kimball had held a variety of academic positions prior to becoming director of the Philadelphia Museum of Art in 1925.

Early in his career he became known as a Jefferson scholar, largely because of his landmark study *Thomas Jefferson, Architect* (1916). Although he was based in Pennsylvania until his retirement, Kimball served as director of the Monticello Restoration Committee from 1925 until 1955, the year of his death (Stephenson et al. 2010). There he worked closely with the foundation's restoration architect, Milton L. Grigg. During the 1930s, under the direction of Kimball and Grigg, excavators investigated Jefferson's north and south dependencies and the west lawn of the mansion (Grigg 1939).

In 1941, the two men embarked on a research project at Shadwell, Jefferson's birthplace and the site of his father's eighteenth-century plantation (Kimball 1943). They attempted the relatively new technique of aerial survey, but it unfortunately proved unsuccessful for locating features.[4] The project used a then-standard combination of trenching and almost completely excavating foundation interiors. Test pits were also placed strategically, but they failed to reveal additional information.

Excavators made some attempt to save artifacts from the trenches and fill from within the foundations. While the focus of the project remained firmly on architectural remains associated with an important family in Virginia's history, Kimball placed some value on identifying and using non-architectural historic artifacts (mostly as dating tools), a practice that became increasingly common as attention to historic artifacts intensified (Harrington 1994, 10–11; Barka 1996, 7).[5] This growing interest in developing artifact typologies and constructing chronologies fit within a broader cultural-historical framework that dominated U.S. archaeology at the time.

Excavators involved in the Shadwell project unearthed the remains of a large brick and a smaller stone foundation at the east end of a ridge above the Rivanna River and two smaller brick features associated with what Kimball believed to be "smoke or bake house[s]" about 100 feet to the west (Kimball 1943, 321). He concluded that the smaller stone foundation likely represented the remains of the house where Jefferson was born, but a lack of eighteenth-century artifacts associated with either foundation left troubling questions (Hosmer 1981, 753; Kimball 1943, 324).

Members of the Thomas Jefferson Memorial Foundation, a private organization that had purchased the Shadwell property in 1945, were unsatisfied with Kimball's conclusions. They hired National Park Service archaeologist Paul Schumacher to resume excavations in 1954 in an area where a nineteenth-century farmhouse had recently been torn down. His testing covered limited ground and proved unsuccessful in locating the Jefferson home. Later that year, Roland Robbins began work at the site, continuing into the spring of 1955 (Linebaugh 1996, 191–196).

Robbins used small test units, placed at ten-foot intervals along a master grid, to study artifact distributions and look for features. Dug by hand and mechanical posthole digger, the 540 test units provided systematic coverage of the ridge top but failed to unearth evidence of additional foundations (Linebaugh 1996, 199–200). After this phase of investigation, Robbins removed topsoil and plow zone within each grid square, recovering artifacts by hand and piling the back dirt by grid unit to be screened at a later date.[6] Robbins's goal for this part of the project was to use artifact concentrations, particularly of architectural materials such as brick, mortar, and window glass, to predict the location of the original dwelling.

In addition to the testing, Robbins re-excavated one of the two small brick features that Kimball and Grigg believed were related to a bake house or smokehouse, found and excavated an unlined pit 100 feet further east, and re-excavated the stone and brick foundations, seeking evidence of chimney bases (Linebaugh 1996, 196–197, 206). Based on an evaluation of artifact distributions, evidence of extensive erosion at the site, and the absence of a chimney adjacent to either large foundation, Robbins erroneously concluded that the main house stood in the center of the ridge above Kimball and Grigg's smokehouse or bake house features (Linebaugh 1996, 207).

Unlike his predecessors, who had academic training in architecture (Kimball and Grigg) or anthropology and archaeology (Schumacher), Robbins was self-taught. He had learned his craft through experience and by combining "business success, historical knowledge, and popular appreciation of the past" in his approach to the emerging profession of historical archaeology (Linebaugh 1996, xiii). In his evaluation of Robbins's work, biographer Donald Linebaugh notes that he used new field techniques and research methods, including careful stratigraphic excavation, often by hand; precise horizontal and vertical controls carried out through gridded excavation units; systematic testing; and accessing the expertise of local soil scientists to meticulously collect, record, and interpret site data (Linebaugh 1996, 208–211). Like Kimball, Robbins used artifacts to date and interpret features, familiarizing himself with the emerging literature on colonial material culture and working with specialists. C. Malcolm Watkins[7] and his mother Lura Watkins, both well-known experts in historic ceramics, helped with the identification of Shadwell ceramics, while H. Geiger Omwake analyzed and reported on the white clay pipes (Linebaugh 1996, 212). Yet while Robbins used more modern excavation methods, his questions were antiquarian in nature, geared more toward establishing another commemorative shrine than to understanding the broader historical and cultural context of Jefferson's mid-eighteenth-century origins.

## Archaeology and the Post–World War II Park Service

In 1954, after a hiatus of more than a decade, archaeologists resumed research at Jamestown under the direction of John L. Cotter. In addition to the valuable work undertaken at that site, the project played an important role in bringing academically trained and field-tested archaeologists to plantation studies, including Paul Schumacher.[8] Although plantation-based research was not the primary focus of the work at Jamestown, it benefited from the skills, methods, and professionalism that Cotter and his colleagues brought to such sites.

The celebration of the 350th anniversary of permanent English settlement in America in 1957 provided the impetus for resuming work at Jamestown. Broad in scope, the celebration also highlighted the role of Williamsburg and Yorktown in early American history. Federal and state commissions working together on the planning and oversight for the anniversary year recommended that the ruins of Green Spring, the plantation home of seventeenth-century governor Sir William Berkeley—as well as of the later Ludwells and Lees—be restored as one of the initial projects. Under the supervision of archaeologist Louis R. Caywood, excavations began in November 1954 and were completed in May 1955 (Caywood 1957, 67).

An early twentieth-century owner of the property had previously carried out extensive excavations at Green Spring, uncovering foundation walls for the house and excavating five rooms down to the floors of their cellars. He located several outbuildings and portions of substantial brick garden walls as well (Caywood 1957; Dimmick 1929). Caywood's team dealt with these earlier excavations by creating a close-interval topographic map of the site, mapping standing ruins and previously exposed foundations, and carefully examining and recording exposed brickwork and flooring. They uncovered and excavated portions of a trash-filled drainage depression east of the house ruins and an earlier trash-filled pit adjacent to the east garden wall; a stone foundation with cellar that was associated with the oldest part of the house; portions of an adjoining basement room; and two cellars in a later part of the structure (Caywood 1957, 64, 76–77, 81–82). They also tested an earthen mount northeast of the structure, excavated a circa 1660–1680 pottery kiln located near the mount, explored a kitchen/blacksmith building, and uncovered the foundation of an unidentified structure (Caywood 1957, 73–74, 79–81).[9]

Although Caywood's focus was largely architectural, his writings on Green Spring placed the mansion within the context of broader plantation activities, described aspects of a sophisticated garden design, acknowledged the presence and contributions of enslaved labor (he referred to them as "servants"), and investigated a few of the industrial activities at the site such as pottery making and blacksmithing (Caywood 1955, 114–15, 1957, 70).

As early as the 1930s, plantation-based research had begun to broaden to include a consideration of industrial activities and work spaces. Caywood's work is but one example. Interest in the technology, organization, and products of plantation industry and agriculture grew in the 1950s and 1960s, although this attention was only minimally extended to the enslaved work force that drove such operations (Markotic 1958; Pi-Sunyer 1963; Pi-Sunyer and Bear 1957; Pogue 1996, 168–169). Caywood's work and the anniversary celebration of which it was a part also increased interest in the archaeology of seventeenth-century plantations and resulted in the completion of numerous small- to medium-scale projects over the next decade (see, for example, Buchanan and Heite 1971; Caywood 1955; Painter 1958; Painter 1959; Weaver 1979).

New Directions?

During the fifteen years that spanned the early 1960s to the mid-1970s, the field of archaeology underwent fundamental changes in theory, methodology, policy, and practice. Led by Lewis Binford (1962, 1965), processual archaeologists challenged older cultural-historical models, offering a neo-evolutionary view of the past that focused on defining and exploring cultural regularities and generalized processes of culture change (Trigger 2006, 295). Historical particularism gave way to generalizing models that crosscut cultures and time periods. Proponents of the New Archaeology were materialists rather than mentalists. They saw archaeology's major strength as its ability to examine evidence of technology and subsistence practices to explain the large-scale adaptive strategies used by past cultures to respond to the natural world (Trigger 2006, 298–299).

To accomplish these goals, methodological changes included large-scale survey to aid in the discovery and analysis of settlement patterns, which gave rise to the subfield of landscape archaeology. Small-scale efforts were also undertaken at this time to develop a system for recovering environmental and subsistence-related evidence through water separation (water screening and flotation) and standardizing quantitative methods for analyzing macro- and microbotanical samples and faunal remains (Grayson 1973; Gremillion 1993, 140–141). While the new goals and methods of faunal analysis were adopted relatively quickly by archaeologists working with assemblages from Virginia plantations (Barber 1976; Crader 1984, 1990; McKee 1987, 1989), studies of macro- and microbotanical remains did not begin to appear until the 1990s (these will be discussed below). Also within the context of the New Archaeology, quantitative artifact analysis replaced earlier descriptive studies to the extent that individual objects were subsumed by broad functional typologies. Recognizing patterns associated with specific site types became an important goal within the broader field of historical archaeology (South 1977).

Independent of theory and methods, the passage of several key pieces of legislation fundamentally altered the practice of archaeology in the United States during this period. The National Historic Preservation Act (1966) mandated that federal agencies consider the effects of their undertakings on historic properties included on the National Register of Historic Places, Executive Order 11593 (1972) extended federal protection to sites deemed eligible for listing on the register and established criteria for eligibility; and the Archaeological Resources Protection Act (1979) provided guidance for managing the disturbance of archaeological resources on federal and tribal lands (Barka 1996, 9; King 1998, 15–20). This legislation resulted in an explosion of archaeological projects throughout the country and was instrumental in the growth of the cultural resource management industry. Over time, the context of most archaeology shifted from universities and government agencies to private companies. Preservation laws and resulting projects brought archaeologists to sites they had previously overlooked or deemed uninteresting or unimportant. Among these were plantation slave quarters (Ferguson 1992, xxxviii–xxxix).

The development of plantation archaeology was furthered by the nation's heightened awareness of African American history brought about by the Civil Rights Movement of the 1960s (Ferguson 1992, xxxv–xxxviii). Beyond undertaking legally mandated excavations, archaeologists engaged with African American organizations and historical associations whose members were eager to explore and promote their history (Singleton 1995, 120–121). While many of the sites they were interested in were far removed from slavery, archaeologists began to recognize the research potential of plantation quarters. Charles Fairbanks's work in Florida and along the Georgia coast represents a disciplinary shift away from the study of wealthy owners and the goals of restoration to an anthropological focus on understanding cultural continuities and changes and African and African American lifeways in plantation contexts across the U.S. South (Singleton 1990, 71–72, 1995, 119–120).

Finally, historical archaeologists became increasingly aligned with anthropology and the new social history during this period. Anthropology departments began training a new generation of scholars interested in studying the recent past. At the same time, the approach to the past advocated by the Annales School of French historians, who sought to investigate the "total history" of societies, including groups of people previously deemed historically unimportant, had a strong influence on anthropologically trained archaeologists and gave rise to the new field of social history in history departments at U.S. colleges and universities (Schlereth 1982, 36–37).

The establishment and growth of professional societies in the 1960s and 1970s provided archaeologists with new communities for the regular exchange of ideas through conferences and publications. The Society for Historical Archaeology was formed in 1967 as a national (and now international) organization; while the Middle Atlantic Archaeological Conference (1970) and the Council of Virginia Archaeologists (1975) served regional communities and encouraged the growth and professionalization of historical archaeology.[10]

Plantation archaeology in Virginia during the 1960s and 1970s must be viewed within these broader contexts. Some practitioners resisted the New Archaeology and continued to refine earlier descriptive approaches rather than depart from them. This conservatism is perhaps best exemplified by the Colonial Williamsburg Foundation's hiring in 1957 of British archaeologist Ivor Noël Hume (Barka 1996, 7).[11]

A historian in training and approach, Noël Hume had little patience for the goals of New Archaeology, arguing that archaeology belonged in the ranks of the arts rather than the sciences (Noël Hume 1969, 15). In his assessment of the relationship between the historian and the archaeologist, he stated that although the latter "cannot hope to equal the historian who holds a document" that provides the essential outlines of past events, archaeology's strength lay in its ability to "fill in details from the written record" and "even correct previous interpretations" of that record (Noël Hume 1969, 18–19).

Noël Hume was (and remains) an outspoken advocate of historical archaeology for its own sake. In *Historical Archaeology* in 1969, he lamented the fact that most sites had been excavated as a means to an end as a restoration, an exhibit, or a tourist venue (Noël Hume 1969, 11). He argued that "the time has come to think of American historical sites as being worthy of excavation simply to obtain information." He criticized many of his anthropologically trained contemporaries for failing to understand that historical artifacts were well documented and could therefore be dated with a high degree of accuracy. He believed that as a result of this misunderstanding of the nature of historical material culture, his colleagues had failed to develop rigorous field methods in stratigraphic excavation that would enable them to capture and record small-scale temporal changes (Noël Hume 1969, 13). His own work and the work of the people he trained emphasized careful field techniques, including tight horizontal and vertical control of strata and artifact proveniences, detailed artifact identification and analysis, and lively historical interpretations of his results for both professionals and members of the public. Theoretically, his work continues to be largely particularistic, descriptive, and typological, while methodologically he has been disinclined to incorporate advances such as systematic screening for artifacts and comprehensive sampling for environmental remains into his research.

Both Noël Hume and his wife Audrey, also a professional archaeologist at Colonial Williamsburg, believed that the small-scale material culture of the colonial period had a profoundly important role to play in historical archaeology, and their collaboration at Colonial Williamsburg resulted in a number of important artifact studies, the best known of which is *Artifacts of Colonial America*, first published in 1970. While much of the work of the Department of Archaeology was carried out in Colonial Williamsburg's historic core during the late 1950s and 1960s, Noël Hume also undertook projects at the plantation sites of Rosewell, Clay Bank, and Tutter's Neck (Noël Hume 1962a, 1966a, 1966b). At Rosewell, a large, rich trash pit—and not the impressive brick ruins of the eighteenth-century mansion—provided the impetus for excavations, for Noël Hume saw in its stratigraphy and the variety of artifacts it contained an important resource for constructing a tight chronology of eighteenth-century domestic objects. Another important outcome of this plantation work was his study of low-fired, hand-built earthenware found there and at sites within Williamsburg. He believed that this "colono-Indian ware" was produced by Pamunkey potters and sold to slave owners for use in the quarters (Noël Hume 1962b, 133). More important, he tied it to a much broader regional tradition that stretched from Delaware to South Carolina and drew native peoples into the economic spheres of plantation slavery (143). A third important outcome of research outside of the Williamsburg core was Noël Hume's excavation of a Virginia slave quarter containing multiple subfloor pits. His Tutter's Neck excavations are likely the first to carefully record, excavate, and report on a complex of such features, although he did not recognize their significance at the time (Noël Hume 1966b).

In 1965, the Department of Anthropology at the College of William and Mary hired Norman F. Barka to teach archaeology. A recent graduate of Harvard University, he was an early author of a dissertation in historical archaeology. For thirty-nine years, Barka trained students, many of whom went on to work on plantation sites throughout the state.[12] While his fieldwork in Virginia covered a variety of prehistoric and historic sites, from 1971 to 1978 he directed some of his best-known excavations at Flowerdew Hundred in Prince George County, where he explored the development of one of Virginia's earliest plantations. Together with his colleagues and students, he uncovered the remains of houses and outbuildings on the property dating from the 1620s through the late eighteenth century (Altshuler et al. 1979; Barka and Altshuler 1976; Deetz 1995, xi–xii; Hodges 2009; Veit 2009, 3). Subsequent work by James Deetz and his students and colleagues from the University of California, Berkeley during the 1980s and early 1990s expanded on Barka's work and explored additional plantation sites dating from the eighteenth century to the period of the Civil War (Deetz 1988, 1995).

## Plantation Archaeology Expands Its Scope

Archaeologists crisscrossed the state during the 1970s and 1980s, excavating at Bacon's Castle, Carter's Grove, College Landing, Governor's Land, Jordan's Point, Jordan's Journey, Kingsmill, Shirley, and Wilton in the Virginia Tidewater; at Ash Lawn, Germanna, Montpelier, Monticello, and Poplar Forest in the Piedmont; at The Clifts, Corotoman, Newman's Neck, and Wakefield on the Northern Neck; at Belle Grove in the Shenandoah Valley; at Belvoir, Gunston Hall, Mount Vernon, Pohoke and Portici, and Sully in northern Virginia; and at Arlington on the Eastern Shore, among other sites (Barka 1978; Barka and Sanford 1976; Hodges 1990; Hudgins 1977, 1985; Kelso 1971, 1982, 1984a; Kelso et al. 1984, 1985, 1991; Lembo 2001; Luccketti 1989, 1990; McLearen and Mouer 1994; Mouer et al. 1992; Neiman 1978, 1980a, 1980b; Noël Hume 1982; Outlaw 1974, 1990; Parker and Hernigle 1990; Parker et al. 1996; Pogue 1988a; Pogue and White 1991; Polk 1991; Reinhart 1984; Rockwell 1974; Rust 1985; Sanford 1990; Schott 1978; Williams 1975).

In the 1980s, several public sites, including Mount Vernon, Montpelier, Monticello, and Poplar Forest, established permanent departments of archaeology to engage in long-term research, often tied, as it had been in the past, to planned restorations.[13] While they have been criticized for their focus on the plantations of the elite and on restoration-driven questions, archaeological programs established at these sites have made major contributions to our understanding of eighteenth- and early nineteenth-century plantation life. Because of the excellent preservation of archaeological sites on these properties; long-term commitment to preservation on the part of the organizations that own them; continuity of staff and methodology; archival, curatorial, and financial resources; and the variety of sites that have been explored, these properties continue to provide unique settings for in-depth research on plantation communities, the landscape, industry, and associated material culture.

Despite the geographic and temporal diversity of sites explored in the 1970s and 1980s, shared methodologies and research questions resulted in the fairly rapid accumulation of important sets of data largely relating to colonial architecture, landscapes, and artifacts. This movement has been referred to as New Plantation Archaeology (Hudgins 1996, 47–48). As Kimball, Caywood, and other archaeologists had discovered on earlier projects, many abandoned domestic sites on plantations were incorporated into agricultural fields over time. Because plowing caused extensive vertical disturbance, archaeologists considered the soils that overlay these sites to have little research value and regularly removed them with scant attention to the artifacts they contained. What set the archaeology of the 1970s and 1980s apart was the routine exposure of large areas through the mechanical stripping of plow zones and the broader scale of research questions this approach facilitated (Hudgins 1996, 47–48; Noël Hume 1982, 9–10). Large-area stripping exposed landscape elements such as fence lines, terraces, paths, ponds, cemeteries, and myriad smaller-scale features, as well as multiple accompanying structures—planters' houses, slave quarters, tenants' and overseers' houses, and agricultural outbuildings.

For the first time, plantation archaeologists were able to routinely expose, excavate, and analyze complex landscapes, moving beyond recording above-ground features or trenching for brick paving and walls to considering entire gardens, home lots, and fortified settlements. Through this work, plantation-based research made significant contributions to the emerging subfield of landscape archaeology. Landscape archaeology and plantation archaeology share a focus on the interrelationships between people and their environments that created the "connective tissue" between houses and communities (Deetz 1990, 1).

From 1970 to 1990, several projects illuminated our understanding of colonial and antebellum plantation landscapes. Fraser Neiman's work at The Clifts in Westmoreland County revealed several generations of late seventeenth- and early eighteenth-century landscape enclosures bounded by ditches and fence lines that at the time of their discovery appeared to have been more functional than designed (Neiman 1980a, 1980b; but see Heath 2010a). Nicolas Luccketti's work at Bacon's Castle in Surry County exposed a remarkably early example of an academic formal garden dating to the late seventeenth century (Luccketti 1990). William Kelso documented a series of early to mid-eighteenth-century gardens at Kingsmill; a mid-eighteenth-century garden at Carter's Grove; the early nineteenth-century kitchen garden, the orchards, the ha ha, and other aspects of the ornamental grounds at Monticello; and portions of Jefferson's designed landscape at Poplar Forest in Bedford County (Kelso 1982, 1984a, 1984b, 1990; Kelso, Patten, and Strutt 1991). At Mount Vernon, Dennis Pogue and Esther White unearthed Washington's vineyard enclosure and explored the south grove, an area between the mansion and plantation kitchen that contained a significant historic midden (Breen 2004; Pogue 1992; White 2006).

These projects and other excavations throughout the Chesapeake laid the groundwork for tracing the development of plantation landscapes. By the mid-eighteenth century, vernacular, utilitarian, and "organic" home lots composed of simple enclosures adjacent to dwellings had given way to elite terraced geometric gardens designed in harmony with the great houses they supported. Archaeologist James Deetz attributed this trend to a cognitive shift during the colonial period from communal to individual, while Mark Leone read emerging capitalist ideologies in the geometric gardens that appeared in contemporary urban settings (Deetz 1977, 1996; Leone 1984). In the post–Revolutionary War period, picturesque landscapes that blended utility and beauty replaced the rigidly geometric gardens that had preceded them (Heath 2007; Trussell this volume).

Large-area excavations also revealed defensive aspects of historic plantation landscapes. In the late 1960s, excavators at the Hallowes Site in Westmoreland County recorded a series of ditches surrounding an earthfast dwelling but failed to recognize that they formed corner bastions for a fortified house and extended away from the house to form additional palisade lines (Buchanan and Heite 1971; Hodges 1993, 205–208). Subsequent excavations at the nearby Clifts plantation clearly revealed the outlines of a fortified house there, which led to a reassessment of the features associated with Hallowes (Neiman 1980a, 1980b). Additional excavations during the 1970s and 1980s demonstrated that these houses marked the end of a historical trajectory that had begun with larger privately funded fortified settlements at several early seventeenth-century Virginia plantations. Palisaded enclosures along the James River at Flowerdew Hundred, Martin's Hundred, Jordan's Journey, and Nansemond Fort, all of which were constructed before 1650, revealed both the vulnerability of early settlers to attack and the strategies they adopted from colonial experiences in Ireland to cope with conflict on the new frontier (Hodges 1993, 2009; Mouer et al. 1992; Luccketti 2010; Noël Hume 1982; Pecoraro 2010).

One of the most important outcomes of plantation archaeology during this period was the amassing of conclusive evidence that demonstrated the importance of "impermanent" construction on rural sites throughout the Chesapeake. Earthfast buildings characterized most plantation architecture before 1720 and continued to be constructed even later in the form of agricultural outbuildings and slave quarters. In a seminal article published in 1981, Cary Carson and his archaeological and historical colleagues outlined the development of a tradition of impermanent architecture in Maryland and Virginia and offered an interpretation for its longevity (Carson et al. 1981). Based on excavations at Governor's Land, Martin's Hundred, Flowerdew Hundred, Kingsmill, The Clifts, and other sites, they observed that an early diversity of house plans and construction styles had given way to a standardized form by the mid-seventeenth century. The "Virginia house" consisted of hole-set structural posts that formed simple timber framing that was roofed and sided by riven clapboards (Carson et al. 1981, 148–155, 158–159, 160–162). Carson and his colleagues argued that the persistence of impermanent architecture in the Chesapeake was attributable to two factors: planters in an unstable tobacco economy investing their limited resources in land and labor rather than in housing and furnishings, and demographic instability that extended frontier social conditions for decades and encouraged spending on small-scale comforts rather than long-lasting houses (168–169).

Other important studies of architecture used the floor plans of plantation houses and the placement of their associated dependencies to explore changing ideas about the use of space that accompanied increasing social stratification from the late seventeenth century into the eighteenth century. After examining standing structures and archaeological footprints, Fraser Neiman and Dell Upton argued that seventeenth-century communal hall-parlor structures, which combined living and work areas, gave way to increasingly segmented and formalized spaces over time. Work areas were pushed out of the house into separate outbuildings, while the rooms within dwellings were divided by function and arrayed around a central passage that served to keep social inferiors at bay (Neiman 1978, 3121–3128; Upton 1982; see also Epperson 1990 and Wells 1993). Donald Linebaugh (1994) later countered these authors, arguing that the movement of domestic functions from the dwelling to outbuildings was motivated as much by environmental factors as by changing social relations, while Anne Yentsch (1996) attributes the architectural segmentation of work spaces to changes in gender relationships.

Concurrently, researchers expanded the scope of their work to include the living spaces of enslaved laborers, engaging with the growing subfield of African American archaeology. Enslaved workers lived in a variety of house types, including single-room, multiresident barracks; two-room duplexes; single-room cabins; and lofts, sheds, kitchens and other "make-do" spaces scattered among plantation outbuildings and within the main house (Kelso 1984a; Sanford 1996; Sobel 1987; Vlach 1991).

Starting with Kelso's work at Kingsmill, archaeologists began to interpret rectangular pit features as root cellars, spaces the enslaved had created and used for storage and for hiding stolen tools or foodstuffs within plantation quarters (Kelso 1984a, 200–202; Kelso 1986). Previously, Noël Hume had interpreted such features at Tutter's Neck as refuse pits and Kelso had interpreted them as tanning pits at Carter's Grove. These features, now commonly called subfloor pits (Neiman 1997), appeared in large numbers on late seventeenth- through mid-eighteenth-century quartering sites in the vicinity of Williamsburg and in lesser numbers at eighteenth- to mid-nineteenth-century quarters elsewhere in the tidewater, in northern Virginia, and in the Virginia piedmont. The function and meaning of these pits, the explanations for their fluctuating numbers over time, and the nature and extent of their relationship to house size have all been major questions for plantation researchers since the 1970s (Fesler 2004b, 280–341, 434–436; Hatch 2009; Heath this volume; Heath and Breen 2012; McKee 1992; Neiman 1997, 2008; Samford 1996, 93–94, 2007).

Artifacts recovered from subfloor pits and other quarter-site contexts provided an important avenue for investigating plantation life among enslaved African Americans. As with assemblages recovered from quarters elsewhere in the Middle Atlantic and Southeast in the 1970s and 1980s, interpretations of artifacts associated with slave dwellings focused on three interrelated areas: the material culture of daily life (Gruber 1991; Kelso 1984a; Kelso et. al 1985; Kelso 1997, 51–74, 88–101; Parker and Hernigle 1990; Pogue and White 1991); intra-plantation relationships between masters, overseers, domestic slaves and field slaves, including social and economic distinctions, internal power struggles, and paternalistic behavior such as the distribution of gifts or hand-me-downs (Crader 1984, 1990; Gruber 1990; Kelso 1984a, 200–202, 1986, 1997; Parker and Hernigle 1990, 101, 188; Pogue and White 1991, 42–43, 49–50); and the study of material expressions of ethnicity (Gruber 1991, 7; Heath 1996; McKee 1987; Mouer et al. 1999; Pogue and White 1991, 44–46, Pogue and White 1994, 42–43; Renaud 1996; Klingelhofer 1987).

While investigations of slave quarters intensified, archaeologists continued to explore industrial aspects of plantation economies. Work at the Monticello nailery and nailers' addition, the Mount Vernon smith's shop, and the Montpelier ironworks considered not only physical remains of the shops, ancillary spaces, and artifacts associated with ironworking but also explored the extent of production and trade through surviving documentation (Bessey and Pogue 2006; Parker et al. 1996; Sanford 1984, 26–61). While James Madison's Montpelier operation supplied neighbors and relatives throughout Orange County and as far afield as Kentucky and Pennsylvania with products from their shop, the Mount Vernon shop filled purely local demand (Bessey and Pogue 2006, 179–181, 183; Parker et al. 2006, 192). Washington's industrial endeavors at Mount Vernon went beyond blacksmithing, however, to include a commercial weaving operation, a fishery, a mill for grinding grain, a distillery, and a cooperage (to package fish, flour, and whiskey for shipment), while at Monticello, Jefferson operated a sawmill, a mill for grinding grain, a weaving and spinning shop, and a cooperage (Betts 1987, 421–495; Breen and White 2006, 209–211; Parker et al. 2006, 197; Heath 1999b; Stanton 1993, 153–162).

The study of plantation industry proved to be possible at domestic sites as well as shops. At Monticello, I investigated a house occupied by William Stewart, a smith, and Elisha Watkins, a carpenter, who worked for Jefferson in the early nineteenth century. Both men supervised construction projects on the plantation and taught enslaved laborers their specialized crafts. Their household belongings contained a mix of domestic and industrial artifacts (tools and blacksmithing waste material), demonstrating that the line between domestic and work life was faintly drawn. Work at this site laid the groundwork for understanding the material conditions of life for free white plantation laborers (Heath 1991a, 1991b, 1999b).

Plantation Archaeology Today, 1990s–2010

Since 1990, intensive excavations have been undertaken at numerous plantation sites across Virginia, including Fairfield, the Governor's Land quarter, the Palace Lands Quarter, Richneck, Southall's Quarter, the Utopia quarters (at Kingsmill), and Wilton in the Tidewater (Agbe-Davies 2003; Brown 2006, Brown and Harpole 2007, 2007a, 2007b; Fesler 2003, 2004a and 2004b; Franklin 1997, 2004, 2007; Higgins et al. 2000; Mahoney 2007; Maloy 2007; Muraca, Levy, and McFaden 2003; Pullins et al. 2003; Samford 1991); Stratford Hall on the Northern Neck (Bell et al. 1998; Sanford 1999a, 1999b, 2000, 2003; Wilkins 2009); Ferry Farm, Gunston Hall, Mount Vernon, and the Barnes Site in northern Virginia (Bessey and Pogue 2006; Breen 2004; Breen and White 2006; Pogue 1996, 2001a, 2002; Veech 1998); and Montpelier, Monticello, Poplar Forest, and Shadwell in the piedmont (Bowes 2009; Bowes and Trigg this volume; Fischer 2001; Gary this volume; Gary and Paull 2008; Heath 1999a, 1999b, 1999c, 2004a, 2004b, 2004c, 2008a, 2008b, 2010b, Heath this volume; Heath and Bennett 2000; Heath et al. 2004; Heath et al. 2005; Lee 2008, Lee this volume; Kelso 1992; Kern 1999, 2005a and 2005b, 2010; Neiman 2008; Proebsting this volume, Trussell this volume). In addition, new archaeology programs were established at Gunston Hall and Fairfield (2000–present).

A variety of theoretical perspectives has informed recent work at plantations. Structuralism, grounded in the idea that culture imposes and is structured by subconscious ordering of the world based on oppositions, is most clearly seen in the discussions of "Georgianization" that characterized much historical archaeology discourse during the 1980s and has been the subject of subsequent critique (Deetz 1977, 1996; Mrozowski 1996; Pogue 2001b). Interpretive archaeology, a postprocessual approach, stresses agency, context, and multivocality while supporting systematic scientific data collection and analysis and is widely practiced (Beaudry 1996; De Cunzo 1996; Hicks and Beaudry 2006). Evolutionary archaeology, drawing on principles of Darwinian evolution to explain cultural phenomena (Galle 2010; Graham et al. 2007; Neiman 2008), and cultural ecological approaches that explore the intersection of culture and the environment (Bowen 1996, 1999, 2010; Carson et al. 2008; Mrozowski, Franklin, and Hunt 2008; Proebsting this volume) are also applied today.

The analysis of intraplantation social relations has continued with consider-ations of the roles of race, ethnicity, gender, and class in establishing and main-taining social boundaries (Edwards-Ingram 2001; Epperson 2000, 2001; Fesler 2004a, 2004b; Franklin 2001; Kern 2010; Samford 1999, 2004). Researchers have increasingly moved away from seeing artifacts as static reflections of past activi-ties or ways of thinking in favor of studying their active role in shaping cultural interactions through day-to-day exchanges, especially in the contexts of con-sumerism and slave spirituality. A variety of quotidian artifacts have gained im-portance as evidence of the decisions that individuals and groups made about how best to express their place within families, plantation communities, and the broader societies in which they lived, while other artifacts attest to strategies of household-based production that people used to meet their consumer needs (Galle 2006, 2010; Hatch 2009; Heath 2004a; Lee 2008 this volume; Martin 2008; Pogue 2001a).

Artifacts, features, and environmental evidence have also been examined for their ability to convey clues about African and emerging African American spiritual beliefs that honored ancestors, mediated conflict between the living and the dead, strengthened communities, and contributed to individual well-being (Edwards-Ingram 1998; Franklin 1997, 238–254; Lee 2008; Mrozowski, Franklin, and Hunt 2008; Patten 1992; Samford 1996, 107–10, 1999, 2000). Through the transformative research of Atlantic World historians, archaeolo-gists now have a much clearer understanding of the clusters of ethnic groups of Africans imported into colonial Virginia in the late seventeenth and eighteenth centuries (Chambers 1996, 1997, 1999; Walsh 2001). As a result, efforts to study the retention or recreation of ethnic identities have become more nuanced, although there is still much work to be done on in this area (Franklin 1997; Samford 1999, 2000, 2004, 2007, 149–173).

Throughout the recent past, a focus on landscapes has defined much of plan-tation archaeology. Intensive research on planters' yards, gardens, and pleasure grounds continues to flourish alongside more limited investigations of quarter yards and gardens and broader studies of plantation management and the plan-tation environment (Bon-Harper 2010; Bowen 1996; Breckenridge 2009; Brown and Harpole 2007; Fesler 2004a, 2004b, 2010; Gary 2008 this volume; Gary and Proebsting 2010; Heath 2001, 2007, 2008b, 2010a, 2010b; Heath and Bennett 2000; Mahoney 2007; Muraca, Levy, and McFaden 2003; Neiman 2008; Proeb-sting this volume; Ptacek 2009; Reeves 2010; Strutt 1999; Trickett 2010; Trussell this volume; White and Breckenridge 2010). While defining the plans of gar-dens has always been a mainstay of plantation archaeology, current researchers are increasingly interested in considering change over time and are attempting to look at the microstructure of gardens through specialized analysis.

Plantation archaeology at historic house museums continues to be driven by site-specific questions as well, and restoration and educational goals continue to influence site selection and research questions (Bessey and Pogue 2006; Reeves 2010; White 2008). While public interpretation has been a component of plantation archaeology since its inception, during the last two decades, a fundamental shift in thinking has taken place about how professionals should engage with the public. The inclusion of descendant communities and other stakeholders in formulating, conducting, and disseminating research and the emphasis on reaching out to and including the public through volunteer opportunities, internships, field schools, public tours, lectures, and popular publications has expanded the reach of our research and helped demonstrate the relevance of plantation archaeology to a wider constituency.

Methodologically, the pendulum has swung away from plow-zone stripping and large-area excavations toward a greater focus on sampling, geophysical surveys, smaller-area excavations, and understanding sites at the micro-scale. Historical archaeologists have come to realize, in large part due to work conducted at St. Mary's City and other colonial Maryland sites, that even though plow zones are disturbed, they retain important spatial information (Gibb and King 1991; King 1990; King and Miller 1987; Pogue 1988b; Riordan 1988; see also O'Brien and Lewarch 1981). They are now routinely sampled for artifacts and environmental data.

Over the last twenty years there has been an exponential growth in the use of environmental sampling—from geomorphology to soil chemistry to macro- and microbotanical remains recovered from planters' gardens, outbuildings, and slave quarters—and the integration of such evidence into broader interpretations of plantation landscapes (Anderson and Brunner-Jass 2000; Archer 2004; Bowes 2009, Bowes and Trigg 2009, this volume; Cummings 1995, 2008; Fesler 2010; Fischer 1993, 2001; Heath 2001; Jacobucci 2009a, 2009b; Jones 2001, 2002; Kealofer 1997, 1999; McKnight 1999, 2000, 2003, 2004a, 2004b, 2006; Mrozowski, Franklin and Hunt 2008; Neiman, McFaden and Wheeler 2000; Neiman et al. 2003; Raymer 1996, 2003; Shick 2005; Wilkins 2009, 2010; Windingstad 2008).

Research focused on industrial landscapes has also continued, primarily represented by White and Breen's work at George Washington's distillery at Mount Vernon. White and Breen have pieced together the layout and inner workings of a late eighteenth-century whiskey distillery, explored the living areas associated with distillery workers, and excavated an associated well (A. Anderson 2002; Breen and White 2006).

The growth of computer technology and the Internet has transformed the ways archaeologists preserve and access data and distribute their work. Archaeologists are now able to catalogue artifacts, context records, historical data, images, and other evidence in searchable databases; quickly process and analyze aggregate data using a variety of statistical packages; manipulate and display a variety of spatial data in GIS; and create and store quantities of high-quality digital still and video images. Many archaeological projects routinely maintain a web presence that disseminates research summaries and reports, and social networking has enabled researchers to communicate findings and follow the work of their colleagues in real time. The accessibility of information to myriad visitors, volunteers, and archaeologists working at a site and the ease of dissemination of that information is beginning to challenge field and laboratory researchers' authority over interpretive messages and to raise questions of who controls rights to images and other site-based information. Social media will doubtlessly continue to transform methods of communicating findings in the future and result in new (and sometimes controversial) interpretations.

Comparative research between plantations has been facilitated by the creation of web-based archaeological datasets and databases hosted at sites such as the Comparative Archaeological Study of Colonial Chesapeake Culture (Maryland Archaeological Conservation Lab 2005–2007) and the Digital Archaeological Archive of Comparative Slavery (DAACS 2004). Material culture research has been facilitated by sites devoted to artifact identification and dating and databases of museum collections (see Maryland Archaeological Conservation Lab 2002; Bureau of Land Management 2010; and Museum of London 2010 for a few examples). The existence of online databases is making gaps in the data evident and is thus beginning to affect how research is conceived and conducted.

While comparative studies, aided by data compilations, are vital for the future of archaeology, archaeologists must continue to wrestle with the problems of data rendered incompatible by idiosyncratic methods of record keeping, divergent field recovery methods, and different cataloguing standards. Although important regional-scale and limited temporal-scale studies are already emerging (Graham et al. 2007; Carson et al. 2008; Galle 2006, 2010), significant gaps in geographic representation and time periods within datasets make comparisons between regions and across time problematic, a situation that will continue until these gaps are addressed.

Added to these archaeology- and material culture–based websites are numerous digital resources compiled by historians, architectural historians, geographers, and other scholars that make important documentary and spatial sources easily available. Archaeologists are also increasingly drawing on an array of digital tools to interpret their sites and publish these interpretations to a varied audience (Freeman and Heath 2008; Freeman 2010; Proebsting, Gary, and Lee 2010). While it is unlikely that the Internet will replace physical archives, the accessibility of primary sources, articles, books, and diverse databases online is revolutionizing how archaeologists conduct research and distribute their results and how the public learns about the past.

Finally, archaeologists and historians have become increasingly attuned to the richness of the documentary record relating to plantations and have become more sophisticated and imaginative about ferreting out relevant sources and applying them to archaeological sites and problems. New attention to and applications of documentary evidence are particularly strong in studies of the consumer behavior of both planters and enslaved men and women (Heath 1997a, 2004a; Martin 2008); in reconstructing slave biographies (Chambers 2005; Fesler 2004b; Franklin 1997; Walsh 1997), and in understanding how the political and economic patterns of the slave trade affected regional demographics and material culture (Chambers 1996; Samford 2007; Walsh 2001).


Future Directions

Future research questions and methods will respond to broad social, economic, and technological transformations and to specific changes in anthropological and historical theory and practice. However, some future directions are apparent today from a consideration of gaps or trends in current work. First, although research on all time periods and regions of Virginia will continue to be productive, plantation settings in the piedmont, the Northern Neck, northern Virginia, and the Shenandoah Valley remain understudied and are much less clearly understood than plantations in the tidewater. This disparity is quite evident in compilations of data regarding slave housing, but is true for most other aspects of plantation life as well (Heath and Breen 2012). Surprisingly, the late antebellum period has garnered relatively little archaeological attention in plantation contexts. Many questions remain to be explored concerning changes brought about by improvements in farming technology and methods in the face of land divisions and degrading environmental conditions; improvements in transportation systems; increased consumerism across all classes of society; a divisive political climate; and radicalizing ideologies and their impact on individuals divided by class and race  Overall, while a much clearer picture of life on plantations for owners and enslaved men and women has emerged in the last thirty years, the experiences of planter's wives and children, and hired free laborers of both sexes and all ages call for much more attention. Planters' wives brought important resources of land and labor to their marriages. Understanding property transfers that resulted from marriage settlements and dowries can elucidate relationships between planter families and can clarify relationships between enslaved individuals and families that may have passed through elite female lines for generations. More specifically, women were responsible for the management of the household, and it is the material outcomes of their practices and preferences, and the practices and preferences of the enslaved and hired women whom they supervised, that comprise the bulk of assemblages relating to foodways and domestic crafts (textile and clothing production), health and well-being, and, to a lesser extent, adornment and other items of personal consumption.

The role of children and their influence on household economies and consumer behavior is also of interest. Although methods of discerning their presence are poorly developed, this area is well worth further exploration. Enslaved plantation children—and likely children of free laborers and tenants—performed important roles in plantation operations and worked outside their homes from an early age. They also contributed to household economies through gardening, foraging, raising poultry, and assisting with housework and crafts. Limited evidence from Monticello suggests that the presence and age of children within an enslaved household was an important factor in determining that household's participation in the consumer marketplace (Heath 2004a). Expanding the scope of this study to include the impact of children on consumer behavior within all aspects of plantation society and over time and space is an important avenue for future research.

Archaeologists have long recognized the need to add tenant farmers and free laborers to discussions of plantation communities but have made limited progress in this direction. Overseer and artisanal jobs were filled by a diversity of men of varying social, economic, and skill levels, and evidence suggests that on larger plantations such as Monticello they lived in a competitive and contentious atmosphere. These men occupied a shifting middle ground between owners and enslaved laborers. They were required to reflect their employer's prosperity and not challenge his superiority, to meet his quotas and follow his managerial orders, and ensure an adequate level of cooperation, either voluntary or coerced, from the enslaved men and women among whom they lived and often raised their families. How these men were perceived by owners can be seen in the siting, size, and materials of their houses and work spaces; how they lived (and aspired to live) can be seen in the remains of their household furnishings, food, and tools; in the landscapes surrounding their dwellings; and in the detritus of their workshops.

A stronger understanding of the lives of free laborers, both black and white, might also highlight differences in housing, the use of space, preferences and practices regarding foodways, consumer behavior, or other aspects of daily life that help make differences in race and class more visible archaeologically. Currently, poorly documented sites with ephemeral architectural evidence, one or two subfloor pits, and sparse artifact assemblages tend to be attributed to enslaved inhabitants, but without a better understanding of the material culture of other laborers, those assumptions cannot be tested.

Archaeologists studying the African diaspora are increasingly focusing on postbellum life, and in the coming years, plantation sites will provide important evidence for understanding how political, social, and economic transformations played out materially among freedpeople, planters, and white farm laborers. Within a decade of emancipation, the promise of freedom gave way to new forms of oppression. The study of the material culture of the Jim Crow era has much to contribute to our understanding of how inequalities were manifested, reinforced, and resisted in daily practice on plantations across the state and how regional demographic, economic and social conditions affected the experiences of freedpeople.

Future work can look backward as well as forward. Postbellum nostalgia on the part of white Southerners gave rise to many of the early twentieth-century preservation efforts carried out on plantations whose histories began this chapter. Conducting archaeology at the sites where early preservation efforts were undertaken will bring us full circle to our roots as a scholarly field and enable us to critically examine the evidence upon which many popular understandings of colonial and antebellum plantation life were developed.

More recent research merits revisiting as well. The boom in plantation archaeology in the 1970s and 1980s added to an already substantial inventory of sites that were not thoroughly analyzed following excavation or that are ripe for reanalysis given current methodological and theoretical advances. In the coming years, work with existing collections will no doubt lend considerable insights into plantation relations through reexamination of the material culture that maintained and supported them (see for example Heath et al. 2009).

Although in this chapter I've encouraged researchers to pay greater attention to certain groups within the plantation community, I'd like conclude with a call for increased attention to the entire plantation as an analytical unit. Plantations were complexly interwoven social and economic systems that cannot be understood piecemeal. Sites such as Poplar Forest, which has been studied by archaeologists for decades, has abundant documentary evidence, has preserved or restored architecture, and has significant land holdings are ideal places to attempt such synthesis. The following chapters provide an important starting point in capturing the rich and complex story of one plantation through time.

## Notes

1. Colonial National Monument consists of most of Jamestown Island and the site of the Yorktown battlefield.

2. Among the cadre of professionals involved in the Williamsburg restoration, consultants Fiske Kimball and Arthur Shurcliff, resident architect Walter Macomber, and architectural draftsmen Milton Grigg, A. Edwin Kendrew, and Singleton Morehead (and likely others) went on to oversee excavations at a number of Virginia plantations in the ensuing years (Hosmer 1981, 19–71; McDonald 2006–2007, 50; Williams 1975, 45, 49, 50). Fiske Kimball and Milton Grigg worked together during the 1930s on excavations at Monticello and in the 1940s at Jefferson's Shadwell birthplace (Kimball 1943). Shurcliff worked at Stratford Hall (Sanford 1999a, 5) and introduced his colleague Morley Williams to that project (Beaman 2000, 4). Macomber became "architect for restoration" at Mount Vernon from 1941 to 1974 (Pogue 2006, 168). Edward Kendrew and Singleton P. Morehead oversaw excavation at Warren House (Smith's Fort Plantation) (Johns 1935, 205).

3. Excavations at Wakefield, undertaken briefly in 1896 and again in 1926 and 1930, are among the earliest done in association with a plantation that no longer had a standing mansion. The goal was to confirm the mansion location, which had been confused in the nineteenth century by the movement of a commemorative marker, itself originally misplaced, before reconstruction. The reconstructed house was dedicated in 1932 in the wrong location (Hosmer 1981, 478–493). Jesse Dimmick also conducted extensive excavations on his Green Spring plantation property before 1929 (Dimmick 1929).

4. This was not the first use of this technology. As early as 1929, aerial photography was used to study the ruins of Green Spring plantation in James City County (Anonymous 1929, 290 and plate between 294 and 295).

5. Kimball sent the ceramics to the Philadelphia Museum of Art, where they were identified by Joan Prentice, assistant curator of decorative arts and a ceramics specialist, and Jean Lee, assistant curator of Eastern art (Kimball 1943, 318; Philadelphia Museum of Art 1946). These collections were subsequently lost.

6. Unfortunately, this was never done, and while the back dirt piles remained in place into the 1990s, their relationship to the original grid was lost.

7. C. Malcolm Watkins was a 1934 Harvard graduate whose curatorial career included work for the Wells Historical Museum (later Old Sturbridge Village) from 1936 to 1948 and for the Smithsonian from 1949 until his retirement in 1980. He and Frank M. Seltzer excavated Mercer's eighteenth-century plantation at Marlborough, Virginia, from 1953 to 1969 (Watkins 1968). He was a founding member of the Society for Historical Archaeology. Lura Woodside Watkins was an expert on historic ceramics and glass (Hosmer 1981, 111; Mapp and Wojcik 2004).

8. Schumacher's association with Jamestown likely prompted J. C. Harrington to recommend him for work at Shadwell.

9. In 1980, James Smith reexcavated the kiln and studied its construction. Subsequent study of pottery from Jamestown and Governor's Land place construction of the kiln to circa 1646–1650 (Straube 1995, 17–18).

10. The Archeological Society of Virginia, which combines the interests of professional and avocational archaeologists, was formed in 1940 but incorporated in 1963.

11. Originally hired as director of archaeology, Noël Hume became director of a separate Department of Archaeology in 1964. The Department of Archaeology divided in 1982 when Marley R. Brown III was hired as director of the Office of Excavation and Conservation. Ivor Noël Hume headed up the Department of Archaeological Interpretation (Barka 1996, 13). Brown's department became the Department of Archaeological Research in 1991. In 2008, the department was divided; collections and curatorial staff moved to the Department of Collections, Conservation, and Museums and field staff became part of a new Department of Architectural and Archaeological Research.

12. The Department of Anthropology began training M.A. students with a concentration in historical archaeology in 1979. Norman Barka served as graduate chair for 20 years (Veit 2009, 2).

13. Scott Parker, the first permanent archaeologist to work specifically at Montpelier, was hired in 1987 and was funded by the National Trust for Historic Preservation, which owned the property at that time. In 2000, the Montpelier Foundation acquired Montpelier and took over the operation of a long-term archaeology program that was headed by Matthew Reeves. The other programs were established by the nonprofit organizations that own and administer each site.

# 3

## Seasons of Change

Community Life and Landscape at the
Foot of the Blue Ridge Mountains, 1740–1860

ERIC PROEBSTING

The landscape is a dynamic place where people interact with their environment. Some of the most dramatic of these relationships center on how people make a living each day. Over time these economic aspects of life often create powerful changes—both positive and negative—in the world in which we live (Balée 1998, 19, 22–23; Crumley 1994, 5–6).

Perspectives provided by historical ecology frame my discussion of the Poplar Forest plantation, which I situate in its broader environmental and cultural context (Balée 1998, 2006; Balée and Erickson 2006; Crumley 1994, 1998; Egan and Howell 2001; E. Russell 1997). I examine the people who came to this portion of the Virginia piedmont starting in the mid-eighteenth century as well as the plants, animals, soils, and slopes with which these and later settlers interacted over time. The history of these changes at Poplar Forest is found in the historical writings, surveyors' maps, pollen grains, household artifacts, and archaeological features people left behind. By weaving together these different strands of evidence, we are able to broaden the history of Poplar Forest to one that also includes the story of environmental change. And by placing the history of Poplar Forest within the context of the surrounding community, we can also understand Poplar Forest's role in the larger social, economic, and ecological changes that took place in the piedmont of Virginia from the beginning of colonial settlement to the eve of the Civil War.

### The Native Landscape

In the years before colonial settlement, groups of Monacan Indians lived in villages along the James River Basin of central Virginia (Gallivan 2004). Archaeologists estimate that by 1600 AD, between 10,000 and 15,000 Monacans were settled in central Virginia, where they hunted and fished, gathered wild plants, and practiced agriculture (Hantman 1990, 1992, 2001). During the seventeenth century, the Monacan and other Native Americans living in the piedmont were assaulted by European diseases and increased warfare, but remnant groups remained in the region during the years that followed. No longer residing in large villages along the James and Rappahannock Rivers, the small number of Monacans that remained relocated to the more secluded James River uplands (Egloff and Woodward 2000, 48–50; Hantman 2001, 116).[1] Their continued presence in the region is suggested by the fact that in 1750, when he was a child, Thomas Jefferson witnessed a small group of Native Americans pay an emotional visit to a large earthen burial mound located along the Rivanna River, about eighty miles northeast of Poplar Forest, near his boyhood home of Shadwell (Hantman 1990, 683, 2001, 108; Jefferson [1787] 1954, 100)(Map 1.1). Other Native Americans, mostly Cherokee, passed through Shadwell plantation and other parts of central Virginia during the mid-eighteenth century (Kern 2010, 190–199).

In addition to learning from encounters with Indians living in the piedmont, eighteenth-century settlers carried knowledge of the Virginia landscape that they had gained from over a century of previous interactions between colonists and Native Americans. These encounters created a cultural exchange of ideas and objects and a biological exchange of diseases, plants, and animals. These exchanges had already transformed the lives of Native, European, and African people living along the mid-Atlantic coast of America when colonists began making their way into the interior portions of Virginia in the early 1700s (Blanton and King 2004; Bowen 1999, 2010; Crosby 1972, 1986, 1994; Kern 2010, 199–200; Silver 1990).

Over the past twenty-five years, archaeologists have recovered the remains of over 10,000 years of Native American history at Poplar Forest. Although there is no evidence that Native Americans used Poplar Forest during the colonial period, small stone arrowheads found during archaeological surveys and excavations along Tomahawk Creek and elsewhere on the property show native people were actively shaping the local landscape during the Late Woodland Period (900–1600 AD), which preceded colonial settlement (Adams 2008; Egloff and Woodward 2000, 26–37). These Native Americans would have likely impacted the ecology of Poplar Forest during occasional hunting trips and other associated activities such as burning the woodlands to help kill pesky insects, create more open woodland pathways, and make it possible to spot game animals more easily (Delcourt and Delcourt 1997; Druckenbrod and Shugart 2004, 207; Silver 1990, 59–64). It was likely because of these native burning practices that colonists found the forests of central Virginia dominated by large, open tracts of mature deciduous trees at settlement. Species of oak and hickory were most common across the region (Orwig and Abrams 1994). At Poplar Forest, black, white, and red oak were recorded by surveyors as they staked out the property's original colonial land grant, in addition to the tract's namesake groves of tulip poplars.[2]

Numerous animals lived in the forests and river bottoms of the Virginia piedmont. German-born explorer John Lederer described a wealth of animals inhabiting the interior of Virginia in the spring of 1669 during his trip over the south branch of the upper Rappahannock River (Briceland 1987, 5–6; Clayton 1912, 145–149). These animals included "great herds" of deer and elk "feeding on the hillsides" and "bears crashing mast like swine." Beavers and otters were found in "every river that [he] passed," and the woods were filled with bobcats, gray foxes, and wolves. Lederer also saw ample evidence of mountain lions in the skins worn by the Native Americans living in the area (Clayton 1912, 147–148).

Place names recorded by colonial surveyors who came to central Virginia

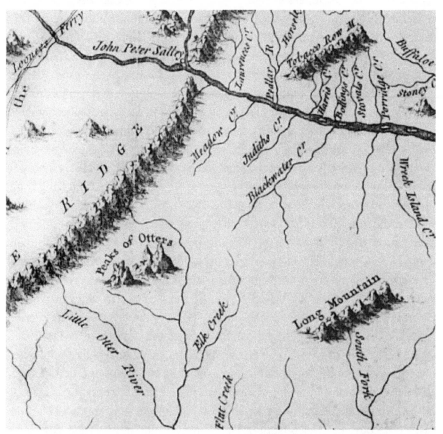

Figure 3.1. Detail from Joshua Frye and Peter Jefferson, *Map of the Inhabited Part of Virginia Containing the Whole Province of Maryland, with Part of Pensilvania, New Jersey, and North Carolina*, 1775. Peter Jefferson, Thomas Jefferson's father, and Joshua Frye prepared the first edition of this map in 1751. Poplar Forest (not shown) is located between the Peaks of Otter and Blackwater Creek. Courtesy of Geography and Map Division, Library of Congress.

to lay out the Poplar Forest tract in the mid-eighteenth century echo many of Lederer's earlier observations. For example, Bear Branch ran through Poplar Forest, while Wolf Branch and Buffalo Creek were located along its boundaries. Elk Creek was also located nearby, and the Peaks of Otter rose on the western horizon as the highest point of the Blue Ridge Mountains. In addition, the presence of local landmarks with family names, such as Judith's Creek, Harris' Creek, and Bolling's Creek, suggests that at least a handful of European settlers had already established themselves as important parts of the local landscape by the 1750s (figure 3.1).[3]

## Tobacco Culture

When colonial settlers arrived in central Virginia in the eighteenth century, they not only described the land as it was, they also portrayed the landscape as they wished it to be.[4] Tobacco Row Mountain, located about fifteen miles north of Poplar Forest on Joshua Frye and Peter Jefferson's 1751 map of Virginia, describes both the physical realities of the rugged piedmont, which rose like a series of tobacco hills on the horizon, and the lofty expectations of Virginia's colonial planters, who were eager to clear ground and sell crops from these new tobacco lands for profit (figure 3.1).[5]

Tobacco equaled wealth in colonial Virginia. Tobacco had become the English drug of choice, and this fact launched the economic success of the Virginia Company at Jamestown and greatly contributed to the growth of the colony. Despite downturns in tobacco prices during the first half of the eighteenth century, tobacco remained Virginia's most valuable export and the focus of everyday life for most enslaved and free persons living in the colony (Breen [1985] 2001; Kulikoff 1986; Morgan and Nicholls 1989; Robert [1938] 1965, 3–8; Walsh 1993).

As colonists moved west from the tidewater to the piedmont, surveyors quickly staked out some of the region's best tobacco lands. Such surveys benefited rich land speculators who lived in the tidewater region. Many of these speculators were interested in expanding their land holdings and believed that acquiring new agricultural lands would provide the fertile soil needed to ensure a wealthy future for themselves and their families. Others were betting on the growing demand of tidewater farmers and planters for land and hoped, in a few short years, to turn a nice profit by leasing or selling their investments in the Virginia frontier to new piedmont settlers (Nelson 2007, 31–35).

William Stith, who lived from 1707 to 1755, was among the wealthy tidewater land speculators during the first half of the eighteenth century. One of his acquisitions was the first patent on the Poplar Forest tract in 1745. Thomas Jefferson's father, Peter, who helped survey much of central Virginia, also speculated on lands in the local community, using his privileged position as the Albemarle County surveyor to obtain several promising tracts of land near Poplar Forest in the mid-eighteenth century (Bedini 1990, 8–11; Chambers 1993, 2–4; Kern 2010, 170–179).

Soon after colonists began settling this portion of the piedmont in the 1740s, Bedford County was created from Albemarle and Lunenburg counties in 1754 (Chambers 1993, 2). Many patented lands, including Poplar Forest, remained vacant for several years. Others lands began to be developed soon after they were surveyed; at which time owners would send their slaves and overseers to begin clearing ground and establishing quarters, barns, and tobacco fields (Heath 2008a, 110, this volume; Nelson 2007, 33–34).

Tobacco touched nearly every aspect of agrarian life for the slaves, planters, and overseers who lived in mid-eighteenth-century Virginia. Along with structuring their daily work routines, it served as a medium of exchange for a wide variety of commercial transactions and as a means to pay taxes collected by counties located across the commonwealth (Breen [1985] 2001, 41). From the outset, nearly all of Bedford County's business was centered on tobacco. Court documents recorded at the county seat of New London, located about four miles south of Poplar Forest, show that taxes and wages were paid in tobacco by the pound (T. L. C. Genealogy 2000).

So were wolf bounties, which had been established throughout the American colonies to protect colonists' livestock from harm (V. Anderson 2002, 380; Coleman 2004; Linzey 1998, 233–234). In Bedford County, bounties consisted of one hundred pounds of tobacco for each grown wolf and fifty pounds for each whelp killed (T. L. C. Genealogy 2000). Designed to reduce the number of predators in the local landscape, wolf bounties were also tied to the larger process of commodification that was taking place across the eastern seaboard. Through these kinds of economic practices, English colonists often attempted to change the plants, animals, land, and people they encountered into items that could be bought and sold (Cronon 1983; Mrozowski 1999; Silver 1990, 2001).

Two of the most valuable of these commodities colonists needed for producing tobacco were fertile land and reliable labor. By the early eighteenth century, enslaved Africans and African Americans had become the backbone of tobacco agriculture in Virginia. Since land on the piedmont frontier was relatively cheap and plentiful, owners and overseers often sought to maximize their profits by instructing slaves to clear new fields instead of improving old ones after soils were depleted by several seasons of growing tobacco (Kulikoff 1986, 76; Nelson 2007, 24).

When John Wayles purchased Poplar Forest in 1764, his slaves and overseers began transforming the property from woods and creek bottoms into a working tobacco plantation. Enslaved laborers cleared the land in late winter, removing brush and stripping bark from the trees to prevent the sap from rising. Without sap, the branches did not bud in the spring; this killed the trees and allowed light to reach the ground. When trees died, tobacco could be cultivated among the rotting tree trunks and decaying roots. In some cases, slaves also felled and burned trees. This practice provided a boost of nutrients to the soil and was often used to help create fertile beds for tobacco seed, which was planted in the early spring (Heath 1999b, 21; Nelson 2007, 44–45; Robert [1938] 1965, 33–34).

Young tobacco plants required constant care from enslaved workers. As the seedlings grew, they were placed in hills on freshly cleared fields. Tobacco fields were enclosed by split-rail fences made of cleared timber. Like most Virginia rail fences, their purpose was to protect crops from free-ranging livestock. Frequent cultivating and pruning was needed to ensure that the plants produced healthy tobacco leaves. In the early fall, tobacco was harvested and hung in log barns, where it was cured for at least a month. Then the leaves could be stripped, packed into large wooden barrels known as hogsheads and shipped to market (Giese 2003, 7–18; Heath 1999b, 21–26; Morgan 1998, 166–168; Nelson 2007, 76; Robert [1938] 1965, 35–50).

Tobacco production was intense and was hard on the health of the people who produced it (Jefferson [1787] 1954, 166–168). Since it took well over a year to bring each crop from the field to the market, there was never a season of rest for enslaved laborers (Breen [1985] 2001, 45–55). The plant also could cause skin irritations and sickness in workers who handled its harsh leaves and breathed in the dust of the dried product as it was processed and sorted (Savitt 1978, 107–108).

Likewise, tobacco was a strain on the land. Soils were depleted after a few years of tobacco production. In addition to robbing the soil of nutrients, tobacco production caused erosion that could devastate cleared fields as water ran down hillsides, washing away topsoil and cutting deep gullies in the landscape (Ambers, Druckenbrod, and Ambers 2006; Craven 1926, 35; Nelson 2007, 46, 238; The Farmers' Register 1837, 651).

At Poplar Forest, the largest of these gullies was discovered at Site B. The excavated portions of this gully—which was part of a much larger landscape feature—measures up to twenty-five feet wide, as much as four feet deep, and more than eighty feet long. The gully seems to have been washed as a result of agricultural activities that took place along this southeastern slope during the second half of the eighteenth century. This gully was then filled with soil and covered by an ornamental plant nursery, which Jefferson established in the early nineteenth century (Gary 2008, 140; Gary, Proebsting, and Lee 2010, 14–21; Windingstad 2008).

An 1801 map of Poplar Forest suggests that well-established field boundaries surrounded Site B (Nichols 1984a, 39 [N266]). Several tobacco houses and a prize barn were also placed across the Tomahawk Quarter Farm (Nichols 1984a, 39 [N255][6]). The Tomahawk Quarter Farm included not only the houses and people who made this portion of Poplar Forest their home but also the surrounding fields and outbuildings that comprised this plantation community during the late eighteenth and early nineteenth centuries. These basic elements of tobacco agriculture structured the daily routines of the enslaved African Americans who lived at Poplar Forest and helped shape the domestic landscapes in which they lived.

The North Hill slave cabin was established on the Tomahawk Quarter Farm about 200 yards northeast of the Site B gully in the 1770s, along the edge of cultivated tobacco land (see map 1.2). Water-eroded gullies were found beneath the North Hill Site (ca. 1770–1785) and the nearby Quarter Site (ca. 1790–1812). These gullies, along with a deeply incised soil-filled spring valley located along the western edge of these archaeological sites, suggests that enslaved workers were purposefully placed on marginal land that had been abandoned after the initial period of field clearing and tobacco cultivation at Poplar Forest (Heath 1999b, 32–33; 2004b).

Since a constant supply of fresh land and slave labor was needed to produce tobacco in eighteenth-century Virginia, many piedmont planters became entangled in an annual cycle of debt to maintain their plantations (Nelson 2007, 51–68). In many cases, these debts were allowed to grow during a long tobacco boom, which lasted from 1750 to the mid-1770s. During this period of high prices, tobacco production seemed to be such a sure investment that it was easy for planters and speculators to obtain credit for land and slaves from British merchants (Kulikoff 1986, 118–119; Sheridan 1960).

Such was the case for John Wayles, who purchased Poplar Forest in 1764 and invested in a number of other tobacco lands located across the Virginia piedmont and tidewater. In addition to his landholdings, Wayles owned many slaves and became heavily involved in the Atlantic slave trade near the end of his life (Chambers 1993, 4; Heath 2008b, 125). In fact, due to an unsuccessful slave-trading venture in 1772, Wayles became deeply indebted to the English tobacco firm Farell and Jones. As a result of these and other debts, some of Wayles's land and slaves had to be sold after his death in 1773 to pay his creditors in Bristol (Boyd 1958, 642–677; Malone 1948, 441–445; Sloan 1995, 14–15, 254). Poplar Forest was kept intact, and it passed to his daughter, Martha, and her husband, Thomas Jefferson (Chambers 1993, 4–5; Heath 1999b, 9–10; Heath this volume).

## Settling the Local Landscape

When Jefferson inherited Poplar Forest, it consisted of nearly 5,000 acres, ranking it, in terms of size, in the top 1 percent of landholdings in Bedford County (Heath 2008a, 110; Martin 1993, 265). As changes in ownership and agriculture occurred at Poplar Forest, they were reflected in the environmental transformations in the plantation landscape. One of Jefferson's first changes was to move additional slaves to Poplar Forest to increase the amount of tobacco being produced (Heath 1999b, 10–11; Heath this volume). Jefferson hoped Poplar Forest would provide a way to stave off his mounting debts and a means to support the wealthy lifestyle he expected for himself and his family (see Boyd 1958, 658; Ellis 1997, 134–144; Sloan 1995, 14–26, 30–32; Stein 1993).

By 1800, several decades of slash-and-burn agriculture would have left a patchwork of active fields and fallow thickets at Poplar Forest. Even though woodlands were likely present between cultivated lands, many trees had been cleared by two generations of enslaved African Americans who had been directed to make fields; build homes, barns, and fences; and collect firewood on the Poplar Forest quarter farms of Tomahawk, Wingos, and Bear Creek (Heath 1999b; Heath this volume).

These changes were especially dramatic on the lands surrounding Tomahawk Creek, which were among the most intensively cultivated portions of Poplar Forest. Charcoal fragments found in the subfloor pit of the North Hill log cabin, which was located on the Tomahawk plantation in the 1770s and 1780s, show that enslaved residents relied on oak (63 percent) and hickory (12 percent) for most of their firewood needs. Since these pieces of charcoal were found along with the charred remains of at least fourteen other native tree species; the assemblage suggests that a mature, ecologically diverse, hardwood forest was within easy reach of these slave quarters during the early years of agriculture at Poplar Forest (Bowes and Trigg this volume; Heath 2008b, 129; Raymer 2003, 68–71).

Charcoal from the remains of the nearby Quarter Site (ca. 1790–1812), however, suggests a very different local environment for this portion of the property just twenty years later. It appears that pine (67 percent), rather than oak (27 percent) and hickory (5 percent), had become the most available source of firewood. As a fast-growing softwood tree, pine would have been a poor source of fuel compared to the hardwoods, which burn much hotter. Slaves in households that relied on pine for firewood would have had to burn more wood to create the same amount of heat as a hardwood fire would create, which meant they would have had to spend more of their time gathering firewood in the early 1800s than in previous decades. However, pine would have been common in the new brush that regenerated over the abandoned tobacco fields of Tomahawk

Creek, where the mature hardwood forest had once stood (Heath 2008b, 132; Raymer 2003, 68–71; see also Orwig and Abrams 1994, 1221).

To revive these and other worn-out fields at Poplar Forest, Jefferson began experimenting with a system of crop rotation that he first used at Monticello in the early 1790s (Betts 1944, 192–202; Neiman 2008, 174). As part of his plans for his Tomahawk Creek quarter farm, tobacco and corn—which extracted large amounts of nutrients from the soil—were to be grown in moderation. Written and archaeological evidence shows that as early as the 1780s, wheat, which was less extractive, served as a new cash crop at Poplar Forest, while rotations of clover, timothy, oats, peas, and periods of rest were used alongside wheat by at least 1809 to help rebuild soil fertility over time (figure 2) (Giese 2003, 78–82, 2007, 179–182; Heath this volume). In addition to changing the color and layout of the fields at Poplar Forest, these shifts in agriculture created new tasks, demands, opportunities, and skill sets within the enslaved community, thereby changing both the cultural and environmental landscapes of the plantation (see Irwin 1988, 302, 316; Lee this volume; Morgan 1998, 170–175; Neiman 2008, 181–182; Walsh 1993, 185–187).

Jefferson's movement toward more scientific methods of agriculture occurred alongside the efforts of other enlightened planters during the early years of the U.S. Republic. To help advance their ideas, Jefferson and his longtime friend, James Madison, founded the Albemarle Agricultural Society in 1817 to promote agricultural education and innovations within the local community and elsewhere (Nelson 2007, 66–77; Turner 1952, 81).

One of Jefferson's favorite innovations was horizontal plowing. This technique used a hillside plow that Jefferson's son-in-law, Thomas Mann Randolph, had designed to decrease soil erosion by following the natural contours of the landscape instead of running the plow against the slope. Jefferson also used his own design, called "the mouldboard of least resistance," to reduce the time and labor needed to plow fields (Bedini 1990, 260–262, 418; Giese 2007, 135–156). Although these innovations were received enthusiastically by enlightened agriculturalists, evidence suggests that they did not eliminate erosion. In fact, recent archaeological excavations at Monticello suggest that erosion increased during this period, when deep plowing and wheat-based agriculture was implemented for the first time across large portions of the plantation (Bon-Harper 2010; Neiman 2008, 183–185; Neiman et al. 2003; see also Earle 1988, 198–199; Earle and Hoffman 2001).

While Jefferson's plans for enlightened agriculture worked well in theory, they proved difficult to put into practice. One of the main obstacles at Poplar Forest was that Jefferson needed the plantation to produce a steady source of revenue to pay interest on his mounting financial debts. The prices paid for

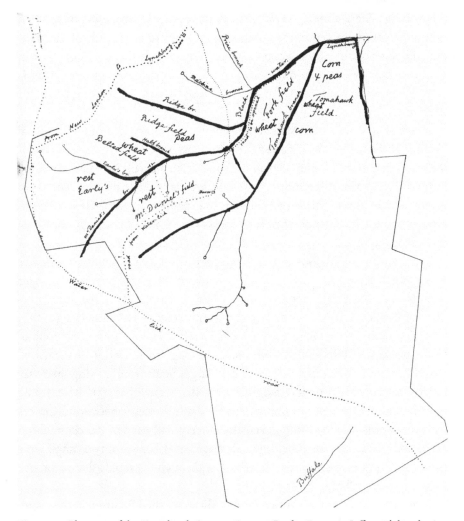

Figure 3.2. Plat map of the Tomahawk Quarter Farm at Poplar Forest in Jefferson's handwriting, watermarked 1809. Names of the fields and other topographic features, including the retreat home, roads, creeks, and springs, are drawn in pen, while the crops are written in pencil, perhaps so Jefferson could make yearly changes (Chambers 1993, 72). Used by permission of the Hutter Family.

wheat fluctuated widely throughout the first decades of the nineteenth century due to periods of war, poor weather, insects, and crop-related disease (Ellis 1997, 138–139; Giese 2007, 85–123, 222–232). Because of this instability in price, wheat could not be relied on as a steady source of income for Poplar Forest.

Tobacco remained an important way to establish the lengthy lines of credit Jefferson needed to maintain his plantations, provide for his work force, and purchase the amenities he required as part of his wealthy lifestyle (see Gary this volume; Giese 2003, 45–122; Sloan 1995, 30–32). Hence, tobacco production remained ingrained in the culture and ecology of Poplar Forest throughout Jefferson's lifetime (Giese 2003, 113–124). This meant that the Poplar Forest slave community was required to focus on the daily demands of tobacco agriculture while also handling the many tasks associated with growing wheat for the market.

Jefferson was not alone. Many other planters who owned ground in central Virginia at the turn of the nineteenth century also relied heavily on tobacco for their wealth and well-being. Lynchburg's rise from a small river-ferry crossing in the 1780s to a bustling tobacco town in the early 1800s reflected the rapid pace at which tobacco farms and plantations expanded, in both acres and earnings, across the local landscape (Chambers 1981, 6–29; Christian 1900, 21–38; Weld 1800, 155–156).

Lynchburg's growth was due in large part to its location along the James River, which served as a major highway between the piedmont and tidewater regions. A commercial shipping industry had developed along the upper portions of the James River by the late eighteenth century (Chambers 1981, 6–7; Christian 1900, 61–62; Giese 2003, 95–98; Terrell 1992, 105–106). Long double-ended bateaux had drafts that were shallow enough to allow downriver travel, past the rapids of the "fall line," which kept larger boats from making their way into the interior of Virginia (Chambers 1981, 510; Terrell 1992, 13).[7] River traffic was also aided by a series of improvements that included a network of sluices and wing dams designed to quicken the current and deepen the channel between Richmond and the Blue Ridge Mountains. Also, a set of two canals were completed in 1800 to carry river boats safely through the rapids that ran above Richmond (Terrell 1992, 20–24).

After tobacco, wheat, and other commodities reached Richmond, they were sold by planters or their representatives to national and international commodity brokers. The resulting credit was used by planters to purchase the wide variety of staple goods they needed and the luxury items they desired, which were then shipped back by the James River (Terrell 1992, 49–96; see also Gary this volume).

The Spring Tobacco Warehouse, which was built by 1793, was among the first businesses tied to the new shipping industry being established in Lynchburg. The warehouse served as an inspection center and holding place for much of the Richmond-bound tobacco being grown in the region (Chambers 1981, 25; Christian 1900, 25).Over 600,000 pounds of tobacco passed through Spring Tobacco Warehouse between December 1793 and November 1794, including nearly 50,000 pounds of tobacco from Poplar Forest.[8]

As the surrounding countryside filled with tobacco farms and plantations,

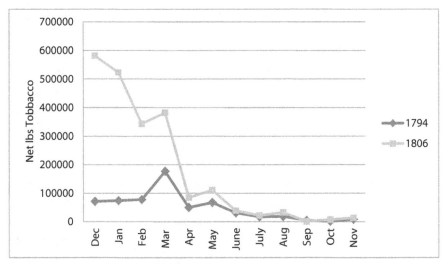

Figure 3.3. Pounds of tobacco received in 1794 and 1806 at the Spring Tobacco Warehouse, Lynchburg, Virginia. From Ledgers of Spring Tobacco Warehouse, December 1793–November 1794 and December 1805–November 1806, Albert and Shirley Small Special Collections Library, University of Virginia, Charlottesville, Virginia.

the amount of tobacco that moved through Lynchburg skyrocketed. By the beginning of 1806, more than two million pounds of the season's tobacco crop were being inspected by the Spring Warehouse alone, making it among the busiest warehouses in Virginia (figure 3.3).[9] To help meet the community's rising demand, six other warehouses were established in Lynchburg by the end of that year (Chambers 1981, 25, 29). The expansion of Lynchburg as a tobacco town not only reflects the rapid growth of the local economy and population at the turn of the nineteenth century (Chambers 1981, 28–39; Christian 1900, 31–42); it also reflects the speed at which ecological changes were taking place within the local agricultural landscape. The dramatic increase in tobacco production in just ten years meant that much of the fertile land in the local landscape had been cleared by slaves and planted as tobacco fields.

## Raising Stock and Using the Commons

Animals were an important part of plantation life from the beginning of colonial settlement. Enslaved workers began raising livestock for food, labor, and transportation in the mid-1700s, when white owners and overseers began establishing quarter farms across the Virginia piedmont. Historical documents and archaeological remains show that at Poplar Forest, pork and beef were provisioned to enslaved African Americans who lived at the North Hill and

Quarter sites from about 1770 to 1812. Food remains and written documents also indicate that slaves living at the Quarter Site raised chickens and turkeys to provide themselves with fresh meat and eggs and a source of income. Jefferson purchased these items for food during his periodic visits to Poplar Forest. Slaves would then use this extra money to purchase everyday items such as rum, buttons, thread, and cloth according to surviving store ledgers and account books from the merchant John Hook's store in the nearby town of New London (Heath 1999b, 50-53, 59–60; see also Martin 2008, 79–186).

Like free whites, slaves would hunt and fish to add fresh meat to their diets. Gun flints and pieces of lead shot were found at the North Hill, Wingos, and Quarter sites (figure 3.4). Archaeological evidence of rabbit, squirrel, raccoon, opossum, venison, turkey, and freshwater fish suggest that enslaved households cleaned and butchered these animals close to their homes and had considerable control over this wild portion of their diets (Andrews 1993, 1999; Heath 1999b, 59–61; Heath this volume). Changes in crops grown at Poplar Forest would have had a significant effect on the type and number of animals that were available to enslaved and free hunters. Grain crops would have provided a new source of

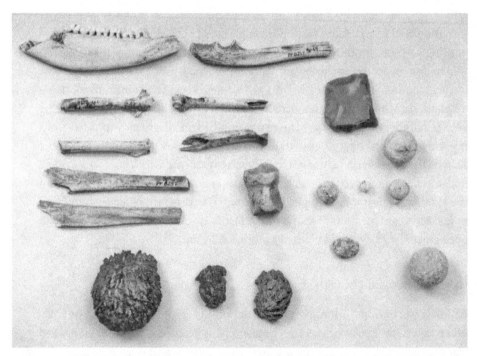

Figure 3.4. A collection of Quarter Site artifacts related to hunting and diet, including (*clockwise, from upper left*) animal bones, a gunflint, lead shot, walnut shells, and a peach pit (Heath 1999b, 60). Used by permission of Thomas Jefferson's Poplar Forest, Bedford County, Virginia. Photograph by Les Shofer.

food for many types of wildlife, while tobacco is toxic and even deadly to most mammals when ingested (Knight and Walter 2001, 247).

Hunting and fishing practices coincided with the tradition of the commons, which British colonists brought with them as they settled the piedmont (Nelson 2007, 39–43; see also Anderson 2002, 387-403). Under this system, unfenced lands and many wild plants and animals were used as common resources by Virginians throughout the colonial period and during the decades that followed.[10] At Poplar Forest, botanical evidence from archaeological features discovered at the North Hill and Quarter sites suggests that slaves often added to their diets by gathering wild fruit, such as blackberries, cherries, huckleberries, grapes, and persimmons. In addition, slaves gathered nuts from oak, hickory, and walnut trees (Heath 1999b, 60, 2008b, 129–132; Raymer 2003).

Livestock grazing practices within the community also followed the tradition of the commons (Nelson 1998, 118–125, 2007, 40–41). Hogs and cattle were often let loose to forage across open forests, meadows, river bottoms, and abandoned fields for much of the year. They were then collected in the fall to be fattened on corn and killed for food. Jefferson continually worked to improve the breeds of his animals, but the reliance on free-range practices at Poplar Forest kept his hogs much leaner than he would have liked (McEwan 1991, 116–122).

The persistence of these practices is well depicted in an 1819 letter from Jefferson's Poplar Forest overseer, Joel Yancey. In the letter, Yancey reported that he had a herd of seventy hogs rounded up from the surrounding forests and creek bottoms that fall and penned for fattening, with five more being "a little shy" and difficult to catch. Nevertheless, Yancey was confident they would get these stragglers in a day or two, so that they could count on fattening a total of seventy-five hogs for slaughter that winter. Twenty-five to thirty other hogs were left to run wild, since corn was in short supply, making it impossible for them to be fattened by the end of the year. However, Yancey explained, a diet of wild "mast" such as acorns and chestnuts over the winter and spring months, "with a little corn to keep them gentle," would have them large enough for butchering by the next fall.[11]

## Signs of Wear

By the first decades of the nineteenth century, sixty years of raising livestock, clearing fields, and cultivating crops in central Virginia had dramatically changed the local landscape. In August 1817, Jefferson took his granddaughters Cornelia and Ellen on a journey from Poplar Forest to Natural Bridge. Cornelia wrote of their experiences as they traveled into the Blue Ridge Mountains, where they encountered extreme heat, dilapidated bridges, "savage-looking" backcountry farmers, filthy guest quarters, and beautiful scenery (Chambers 1993, 108–110).

These encounters reinforced the granddaughters' perception of the Blue Ridge as a "wild and picturesque . . . new world" compared to their home at Monticello.[12] These fantastic experiences only added to their surprise when they learned from locals that many of the wild animals they expected to see, such as "bears, wolves, panthers, and rattle snakes," had been "nearly exterminated."[13] Decreased habitat and increased hunting had led to the disappearance of these and other once-prominent animals, such as buffalo and elk, from the piedmont landscape by the early nineteenth century (Linzey 1998, 288, 297).

As these wild species disappeared from central Virginia in the 1810s and 1820s, worn lands continued to be used and new lands continued to be cleared for tobacco cultivation at Poplar Forest. Despite Jefferson's desire to revolutionize Poplar Forest's agriculture by implementing crop rotation and introducing contour plowing, his efforts to restore the fertility of the plantation's soil failed miserably. In the end, poor weather, price fluctuations, and financial difficulties forced him to abandon his dream for a more sustainable wheat-based system of agriculture in favor of balancing it with the more established system of tobacco production.

Historical documents suggest that when Francis Eppes took over the management of Poplar Forest in 1823, he continued to operate the plantation in much the same way as his grandfather had (Giese 2007, 204). With Jefferson's blessing, Eppes directed enslaved laborers to apply gypsum plaster to the fields for the first time in 1826. Eppes was excited to find that plaster quickly worked wonders on old tobacco fields. Treated soils "produced dark green plants," while soil without the gypsum produced only "pale sickly yellow" plants.[14] However, Poplar Forest was hit with three devastating rain storms that year, which destroyed many of the tobacco hills and washed away most of the fertilized topsoil. In despair, Eppes recorded that "nothing but the clay is left behind."[15]

These storms marked the beginning of the end for Francis Eppes's tenure at Poplar Forest. Eppes soon found that plaster was expensive and that when crops failed because of natural events such as flash floods and drought, even an ample supply of gypsum could not ensure the financial success of his plantation. In 1827, a year after Jefferson's death, Francis's wife Mary Elizabeth wrote, "These gullied and worn out fields. . . . Tobacco is the only thing that can be made here, and after vast labour and expense, in raising and manufacturing the vile weed . . . to find still no profit . . . is disheartening indeed."[16]

A year later, Francis agreed. He wrote to his cousin-in-law Nicholas Trist that "the soil is exhausted." The income from tobacco at Poplar Forest was "reduced almost to the prime cost of the materials," and Eppes could no longer find a reason to remain in Virginia.[17] As a result, like other frustrated farmers and planters in Virginia, Eppes and his family decided to leave for more fertile fields (Fischer and Kelly 2000, 135–201). In the spring of 1829, they moved from the piedmont with a number of their slaves to start their new life in northern Florida, having sold Poplar Forest to a local planter named William Cobbs (Chambers 1993, 174–177).

The New Plantation

Some families responded with plans to make better use of their land, labor, and other resources instead of leaving the community. New agricultural organizations were formed to promote better agricultural practices in much of central Virginia. For example, in 1833, the New London Agricultural Society was formed within a few miles of Poplar Forest (Bruce 1932, 11–12; Daniel 1985, 81–84). Agricultural journals also emerged that promoted improved agricultural practices across the South. These included *The Farmers' Register*, which was founded by Edmund Ruffin in 1833. Another popular journal was *The Southern Planter*, which was published in Richmond beginning in 1841 (Swanson 2009, 108, 123).

Edward Hutter, William Cobbs's son-in-law, was an avid reader of *The Southern Planter*.[18] Hutter began to apply many of the progressive farming practices it advocated soon after he retired from the navy and took over the management of Poplar Forest in 1842 (Marmon 1991, part 2, 67). Hutter's daily farm journal, which he kept from 1844 to 1854, shows that he developed a sophisticated farming system that used wheat as the main cash crop. The records he kept demonstrate an exhausting annual routine of ditching, grubbing, plowing, and working wagonloads of manure and other fertilizers into the soil, all of which was done by enslaved African Americans who were literally rebuilding the fields of the plantation from the bottom up.[19]

Hutter's journal shows that a variety of additives were applied in his efforts to reclaim old fields. Gypsum plaster was used from 1844 to 1850 to help enrich the soil at Poplar Forest. Around 1850, plaster was replaced with Peruvian guano, which was the newest and most exotic soil fertilizer on the market. Guano was hailed across the Old South for its almost-miraculous ability to revive worn-out soils, and it quickly became Hutter's fertilizer of choice. He purchased 320 pounds in the fall of 1850 and three years later, he purchased nearly 12,000 pounds.[20]

Imported fertilizers were supplemented by more traditional means of enriching the soil, especially seasonal burning and the use of animal manure. Using manure meant that livestock had to be supervised much more closely than before. Jefferson had experimented with the use of this type of fertilizer during his time at Poplar Forest. He instructed that his sheep be penned each night within his new vegetable garden in 1811 and that dung be spread over portions of his agricultural fields in the fall of 1813 and over his vegetable garden in the winter of 1814.[21] These farming practices, which were first applied on a limited basis by Jefferson, were expanded during Hutter's tenure at Poplar Forest. Gone were the days when hogs were allowed to roam free through the commons for much of the year. Instead, these and other livestock at Poplar Forest were penned so slaves could pile manure into carts and wagons and spread it on old fields.[22]

Livestock was also rotated across fallow fields so that their manure would be dispersed as they grazed. Hutter recorded several instances in the 1840s and 1850s when he had his hogs placed on old or recently harvested fields to help clear the ground and improve the soil. This increased control of animals required tremendous amounts of new timber for fencing. During the period 1844 to 1852, Hutter's farm journal recorded 83 days of splitting rails and 145 days of hauling rails.[23]

The decreasing size of woodlots could have made finding the timber needed for fences an increasingly difficult task for Hutter and his neighbors during the antebellum period. Some planters, especially those living in the Virginia tidewater, lobbied hard to end free-range practices. Among other things, these planters argued that their plantations no longer had the mature hardwood trees they needed to build the fences necessary to protect their croplands against wandering herds of livestock (Swanson 2009, 110–116).

A shortage of quality timber at Poplar Forest is suggested by several surviving structures built on the property during the 1840s and 1850s. For example, the large poplar wall plates found in the detached kitchen and smokehouse, built to replace Jefferson's Wing of Offices in the early 1840s, had a series of older notches. These notches had been cut during the Jefferson period to fit their original role as roof support beams for the office wing (Chambers 1993, 190–192; Kelso, Patten, and Strutt 1991, 26–29; McDonald , personal communication 2011). In another case, dendrochronology shows that a wooden granary built west of the Main House in 1856 was composed of a mixture of reused hardwood logs from an earlier structure that dates to the Jefferson period and wood from recently felled trees (figure 3.5) (Heikkenen 1997; Strutt 1998a). This could have been part of a larger, plantation-wide effort to conserve the remaining mature hardwood trees on the property, in part by reusing old building materials and investing in building technologies that did not require as much wood. In the following year, bricks rather than logs were used to build a new slave quarter and an overseer's residence.[24]

Figure 3.5. This granary was built in 1856 and is the only surviving wooden outbuilding from the plantation era of Poplar Forest history. It was partially constructed from Jefferson-period timber. Courtesy of the Prints and Photographs Division, Library of Congress. Photograph by Jack E. Boucher for the Historical American Buildings Survey, 1986.

Despite these efforts to conserve timber, new logs were still being cut by slaves to construct buildings across the plantation throughout the antebellum period. In his farm journal, Hutter noted that wood was cut for at least five buildings at Poplar Forest from 1844 to 1854.[25] It is likely that many of these buildings used relatively young timber, since most mature hardwood trees had been cleared from the plantation to create fences, firewood, homes, and out-buildings over the past eighty years. As with the granary, the detached kitchen, and the smokehouse, we can surmise that other buildings built at this time incorporated materials from older structures from the Jefferson period whenever possible.

In 2003, archaeologists uncovered one of these antebellum structures 100 yards southeast of the Main House and named it Site A. The cabin was likely made of log and was occupied by slaves from the mid-1830s until the eve of emancipation. Features included the remains of a stone-and-brick chimney as well as a small subfloor storage pit filled with artifacts (Gary, Proebsting, and Lee 2010, 22–25; Heath et al 2004, 16–30; Heath and Lee 2008; Lee 2008, 166–168). Seeds found within the subfloor pit have revealed that the individuals who were living in this home had access to a wide variety of plants that could have been used for food and medicinal purposes. These plants could have been produced by the occupants in their home garden, traded within the local slave community, gathered from common lands at Poplar Forest, or received as provisions from the larger production of the plantation (Bowes 2009, 26–65; Bowes and Trigg this volume; Gary, Proebsting, and Lee 2010, 26).

Charcoal remains show a diverse collection of twelve different species. High-quality hardwoods such as oak, ash, and hickory constituted 76 percent of the charcoal remains, while low-quality fuel woods such as chestnut, tulip poplar, and pine constituted only 24 percent (Bowes 2009, 61–62, 97–105). In fact, when compared to other slave cabins found at Poplar Forest, the fuel remains found at Site A more closely resemble those recovered from the North Hill site, which was in use around the 1770s and 1780s, than those from the Quarter Site, which was in use in later decades, from about 1790 to 1812.

This diversity speaks to the resilience of native forest species, which seem to have rebounded on portions of the Tomahawk Quarter Farm after being largely replaced by pine following its initial clearing during the Jefferson period. However, unlike the North Hill quarter, where enslaved African Americans gathered firewood from mature hardwood forests, the fuel the residents of Site A collected was likely taken from areas where young hardwoods had reestablished themselves on worn-out lands or along field margins by the mid-nineteenth century. In addition, fragments of a deadly tree fungus, known as hypoxylon, have been found throughout the subfloor pit fill, suggesting that the residents of Site A were relying on severely stressed trees and deadwood for at least a portion of their firewood needs (Bowes 2009, 30–31).

Alongside these changes in farming practices and forest composition, the advent of railroad transportation was another important change for the local community. The postal community of Forest Depot was established for the area around Poplar Forest soon after the Virginia and Tennessee railroad began running through Central Virginia in 1852 (Daniel 1985, 109–112; Goode 1998, 83).

Manuscript U.S. census records for Forest Depot provide a snapshot of the local landscape in 1860. These documents depict a highly stratified society in which the top 25 percent of the community's landowners owned over half of the community's acres (57 percent), tobacco (56 percent), and livestock (63 percent). Hutter and the rest of these relatively wealthy plantation landowners also owned the majority of the community's farm machinery (62 percent), produced a large amount of the wheat (69 percent), and raised nearly all of the community's sheep (92 percent). They also owned 575 (47 percent) of the community's 1,231 enslaved African Americans (table 3.1).[26]

Hutter grew very little tobacco during his tenure at Poplar Forest and produced no tobacco in 1860; however, the plant was still an important cash crop

Table 3.1. Property owned by Edward Hutter, the top quartile of landowners, and all free households in Forest Depot, Virginia, 1860

|  | Edward Hutter | Top 25% of Landowners (N = 16) | All Free Households (N = 93) |
|---|---|---|---|
| Acres (number) | 1,070 | 19,345 | 34,152 |
| Slaves (number) | 37 | 575 | 1,231 |
| Tobacco (lbs.) | 0 | 168,800 | 304,060 |
| Wheat (bu.) | 1,065 | 28,095 | 40,766 |
| Livestock (number) | 230 | 3,136 | 4,945 |
| Value of farm machinery ($) | 1,000 | 10,670 | 17,170 |

Source: Agriculture Schedule, Free Schedule, and Slave Schedule, Forest Depot, Bedford County, Virginia, U.S. Manuscript Census, Eighth Census of the United States, 1860, Microfilm M653, Records of the Bureau of the Census, 1790–2007, Record Group 29, National Archives and Records Administration, Washington, D.C.

within the local community. The agricultural census shows that over 300,000 pounds of tobacco were produced in Forest Depot alone and 4,100,000 pounds were produced in Bedford County.[27] Therefore, in addition to their other work, many slaves living in this portion of the Virginia piedmont still spent a considerable portion of their time each year doing the same grueling tobacco-related tasks that had occupied the center of daily life for the past hundred years.

Why did tobacco remain such an important crop within the local community on the eve of the Civil War amid so much environmental change? Despite the ecological problems with growing this crop on plantations in this portion of Virginia, it was difficult for local farmers to change their long-standing practice of growing tobacco. New fertilizers made it possible for tobacco to remain a bankable commodity for piedmont planters, even at the end of the antebellum period (Nelson 2007, 171–176).

In addition to the century-old agricultural routines of planting, cultivating, harvesting, and packing tobacco that had become ingrained in the daily life of many local plantations, Lynchburg's antebellum economy also remained wedded to marketing "the vile weed." Even though the tobacco market remained notoriously unstable throughout the antebellum period, individuals grew wealthy as Lynchburg became one of America's leading manufacturers of chewing tobacco, making it the second wealthiest city, per capita, in the nation (Tripp 1997, 6–8). The result was that many planters living in central Virginia found themselves either unable or unwilling to follow the drastic measures that Edward Hutter instituted at Poplar Forest to accomplish what Thomas Jefferson could not; abandon tobacco for what promised to be a more sustainable system of mixed-grain agriculture.

## Conclusion

The historical ecology of Poplar Forest and the surrounding landscape is a story of dramatic change. Beginning with colonial settlement in the 1700s, slaves cleared forests for tobacco production, which had spread throughout much of this portion of central Virginia by the turn of the nineteenth century. In addition to raising crops and livestock, enslaved and free people also took advantage of the commons for hunting and fishing, gathering plants for food and firewood, and addressing many other daily wants and needs. Despite attempts to establish other ways to make a living through new farming techniques and mixed-grain agriculture, tobacco agriculture persisted in the following decades.

At Poplar Forest, we see how ecological changes and agricultural practices—from settlement onward—helped shape the daily lives of the people who lived and worked on the plantation over the years. The archaeological and historical records also show a dynamic landscape—one where communities were closely connected with the ecology of the world they lived in. Individuals had a dramatic impact on this world through their daily routines and long-term actions. People's actions were guided not only by personal choices but also by the historical circumstances of the time and place in which they were born.

Future research will continue to explore how cultural and ecological transitions, such as the shift from tobacco to mixed-grained agriculture, played out on the ground and in the quarters of Poplar Forest. The fruit of this research will produce additional insights into how environmental changes were expressed over time in the conditions and quality of life for the enslaved laborers, owners, and overseers who made their home here, at the foot of the Blue Ridge Mountains.

## Notes

1. Descendants of the Monacans ultimately purchased a small tract of land on Bear Mountain, located about fifteen miles northeast of Poplar Forest, where some still live today (Egloff and Woodward 2000, 50; Hantman 2001, 116).

2. Albemarle County Surveyor's Book 1, part 1, 1744–1750, Library of Virginia, Richmond, Virginia. See also Chambers (1993, 2).

3. Chambers (1993, 1–2); Joshua Frye and Peter Jefferson, *Map of the Inhabited Part of Virginia Containing the Whole Province of Maryland*, 1751, Geography and Map Division, Library of Congress.

4. Although central Virginia includes a much larger area, this chapter's main focus is on the western portion of central Virginia that was settled during the eighteenth century, particularly the land now included within Bedford and Campbell counties.

5. Frye and Jefferson, *Map of the Inhabited Part of Virginia Containing the Whole Province of Maryland*. See also Verner (1967).

6. See Wenger (1997, 240) for evidence supporting a 1781 date for this undated Poplar Forest plat.

7. The fall line in Virginia is a geological boundary created where the higher elevations of the piedmont region reach the lower elevations of the tidewater. This change in topography helped shape colonial settlement and had a significant impact on the regional commerce and politics that took place within the state of Virginia throughout the first half of the nineteenth century (Twyman 2003).

8. Poplar Forest's 28,262 pounds of tobacco was from Jefferson's holdings at Tomahawk and Bear Creek, while 21,018 pounds was produced on the Wingos quarter farm, which at that time was owned by Jefferson's son-in-law, Thomas Mann Randolph. Ledgers of Spring Tobacco Warehouse, 1793–1806, Albert and Shirley Small Special Collections Library, University of Virginia, Charlottesville, Virginia; Chambers (1993, 14).

9. Ledgers of Spring Tobacco Warehouse 1793–1806; Chambers (1981, 29).

10. In Virginia, common lands were unfenced grasslands, woodlands, and river bottoms where individuals were often allowed to hunt and fish and livestock were allowed to roam free. This arrangement often suited settlers who enjoyed having access to extra acres for hunting, fishing, and pastureland. But it also caused common lands to be abused. As geographer Garret Hardin explained in his classic article "The Tragedy of the Commons," people are easily tempted to overuse common land over the long term when they see short-term benefits (Hardin 1968). For a poignant, present-day discussion of how this process is currently affecting the commons in our world's oceans, see Carl Safinia's *Song for the Blue Ocean* (New York: Henry Holt, 1997).

11. Joel Yancey to Thomas Jefferson, November 19, 1819, Coolidge Collection of Thomas Jefferson Manuscripts, Massachusetts Historical Society, Boston, Massachusetts (hereafter Coolidge Collection, MHS).

12. Ellen Randolph to Martha Randolph, August 18, 1817, Edgehill-Randolph Family Papers, Albert and Shirley Small Special Collections Library, University of Virginia, Charlottesville, Virginia (hereafter Edgehill-Randolph Family Papers, University of Virginia).

13. Cornelia Randolph to Virginia and Mary Randolph, September 24, 1817, Nicholas Philip Trist Papers, Southern Historical Collection, Louis Round Wilson Special Collections Library, University of North Carolina, Chapel Hill, North Carolina (hereafter Trist Papers, University of North Carolina).

14. Francis Eppes, Memoranda, 1826, 4–5, The Corporation for Thomas Jefferson's Poplar Forest, Forest, Virginia. See also Giese (2003, 123–124).

15. Francis Eppes to Thomas Jefferson, June 23 1826, Coolidge Collection, MHS.

16. Mary Elizabeth Eppes to Jane Randolph, April 1, 1827, Edgehill-Randolph Family Papers, University of Virginia.

17. Francis Eppes to Nicholas Trist, March 2, 1828, Trist Papers, University of North Carolina.

18. Edward S. Hutter, Income and Expense Journal, July 1, 1856–January 1, 1862, The Corporation for Thomas Jefferson's Poplar Forest, Forest, Virginia (hereafter Hutter Income and Expense Journal).

19. Edward S. Hutter, Farm Journal, January 1, 1844–December 31, 1854, The Corporation for Thomas Jefferson's Poplar Forest, Forest, Virginia (hereafter Hutter Farm Journal).

20. Ibid. See also Jordan (1950); Skaggs (1994); Stoll (2002, 187–194).

21. Thomas Jefferson to Jeremiah Goodman, November 14, 1814, Gilder Lehrman Institute of American History, New York, New York. See also Betts (1944, 467, 517–518).

22. Hutter Farm Journal.

23. Ibid.

24. Hutter Income and Expense Journal. It is likely that the use of brick for slave housing at Poplar Forest was also influenced by the agricultural reform movement taking place in the antebellum South, which advocated that planters provide clean, durable housing for slaves (Vlach 1993, 163).

25. Hutter Farm Journal. See also Chambers (1993, 183–193).

26. U.S. Manuscript Census, Eighth Census of the United States, 1860, Microfilm M653, Records of the Bureau of the Census, 1790–2007, Record Group 29.

27. Daniel 1985; U.S. Manuscript Census, Eighth Census of the United States, 1860.

# 4

# A Landscape for Mr. Jefferson's Retreat

TIMOTHY TRUSSELL

A landscape, whether utilitarian or ornamental, is an intensely cultural creation. It is both a product of and a reflection on the assumptions and purposes of those who fashioned it. Once created, the very existence of the landscape influences the lives and choices of those who dwell within it, forming a feedback loop whereby people's actions continually shape the landscape and it in turn shapes their actions. The varied and interesting possibilities for historical interpretation of a relic landscape are suggested by the many topics discussed in this book. This chapter will examine one small corner of this field of possibility by discussing the ornamental landscape design of Poplar Forest in relation to Thomas Jefferson and his life.

Thomas Jefferson inherited Poplar Forest in 1773 and designed an ornamental landscape as part of the retreat he created at his Bedford County plantation in the first two decades of the nineteenth century (Heath and Gary this volume). The landscape as it exists today at Poplar Forest contains partially intact portions of this original landscape. In addition to Jefferson's restored home, which now functions as a house museum, the unusual octagonal privies that he designed are present and are almost completely original (figure 4.1). The constructed ornamental mounds to the east and west of the main house as well as the sunken lawn and terraces to the south are also still extant (figure 4.2). A portion of the circular road is intact on the north side of the core area, as is the southwest axial road. Intact portions of an old fence line surrounding the core area of the property may be a much-replaced remnant of the Jefferson-period ten-acre interior curtilage fence that appears on an 1813 map of the property (figure 4.3).[1] The area within this ten-acre enclosure is known as the "core area" and forms the boundary of the Jefferson-era ornamental landscape. To the north of the house, several ancient tulip poplar trees still stand, living remnants of a larger grove that was incorporated into Jefferson's design (figure 4.4) (Heath 2007, 137–144; Trussell 2000, 4–15).

Figure 4.1. Brick octagonal privy located at the base of the west mound. Used by permission of Thomas Jefferson's Poplar Forest, Bedford County, Virginia.

In 1807, Jefferson instructed that a sunken lawn ninety feet wide be excavated south of the house.[2] The house was sited at the top of a gentle hill and was built into the top of the hillside in such a way that from the front, or northern, aspect, the building appeared to have only one story. On the south side, however, it was clear that the building had two levels; the sunken lawn extended away from the basement story at a regular slope until it reached grade.

For nearly twenty years, Jefferson constructed and modified both his retreat home and the ornamental landscape surrounding it. No landscape is ever static, however, and upon his death in 1826 Poplar Forest entered into a long process of change whereby many of the original landscape elements were modified or destroyed.

Landscape research questions have been explored archaeologically at Poplar Forest since 1989, and with well over 1,000 individual units excavated within the core area of the property, a considerable amount of information is now available for interpretation. No relic landscape can ever be perfectly understood, however, and despite two decades of research our knowledge of the ornamental landscape at Poplar Forest remains imperfect. Similarly, Jefferson's design goals and the specific intellectual influences he used to formulate and create his de-

Figure 4.2. The view from the southwest core, showing the sunken lawn and the east mound. The wing of dependencies, which was built in 1813, cuts into the mound, which had been created earlier from the earth excavated for the foundation of the house and the sunken lawn. Used by permission of Thomas Jefferson's Poplar Forest, Bedford County, Virginia. Photograph by Jack Henley.

sign are also only partially understood. This essay will therefore use a recursive approach that draws upon what we know about Jefferson to understand the ornamental landscape design information recovered archaeologically at Poplar Forest and in turn, applies what we have learned about this landscape to shed light on Jefferson and his landscape design influences.

## The Context of Time and Place

Much of Jefferson's life was spent interacting with the economic and political elite of Europe and America. His extensive travels abroad in the 1780s and his political status brought him into contact with a social class that was in the midst of an explosion of interest in gardening and ornamental landscapes. Jefferson was immersed in a culture that saw a revolution in the style and fame of large-scale gardening and landscape design. Across Europe, immense tracts were laid off on the estates of the powerful and wealthy and enormous sums of money were spent to create elaborate visual landscapes. The cultural impact of this movement, which took place in France but was especially intense in England, was very important to the social circles in which Jefferson was traveling

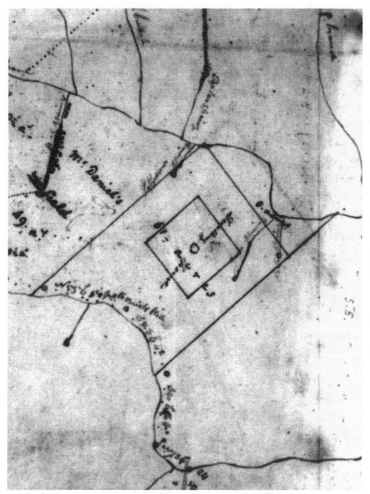

Figure 4.3. Joseph Slaughter, *Map of Tomahawk Creek Lands,* September 13, 1813. This section shows the rectangular 61-acre curtilage surrounding ten acres of Poplar Forest. Jefferson's retreat house, which had been completed the previous year, is in the center. Courtesy of Thomas Jefferson Papers, Special Collections, University of Virginia Library.

(Brown 1990, 121–131; Hunt 1991, 231–242; Hunt and Willis 1990, 17–28; Shackelford 1995, 144–187).

Constructing a large ornamental landscape made a powerful and very explicit statement. The observation that the "size and pretensions of [estate] houses were an accurate index of the ambitions of their owners" (Girouard 1978, 13) applied to ornamental gardens as well. However, simply constructing a big garden or wilderness walk was not enough. The creator of a garden landscape was judged not simply by the fact that he was wealthy enough to build it but, perhaps more important, by the taste he showed through his creation. Receiv-

Figure 4.4. Extant tulip poplar trees in the north core. Based on tree-ring dating of tulip poplars of similar size removed from the north core, these trees are thought to predate the main house by several decades. Used by permission of Thomas Jefferson's Poplar Forest, Bedford County, Virginia.

ing approval or prestige of this kind was so valued as social capital that it gave rise to a professional class of landscape architects whose job it was to create ornamental landscapes that would reflect gloriously on the refinement of their benefactors (ibid.). In order to be considered educated and of good taste, it was necessary for a wealthy person to become fully versed in ornamental plant species, current gardening theories, and even classical literature, which was often used for the themes of individual or sequenced scenes in designed landscapes (Hunt 1991, 233–238).

Understanding how Jefferson viewed this movement and how he was influenced by it is clearly an important element in discerning his intentions and actions in the ornamental landscape at Poplar Forest. Several contexts of gardening and landscape influence may provide a starting point for understanding the mature Jefferson's work at Poplar Forest.

During his long stay in France, Jefferson saw many of the baroque-style geometric garden designs that were still maintained in the last quarter of the eighteenth century. However, French architectural and landscape thought was undergoing a transformation that was heavily influenced by the English naturalistic, or picturesque, style (Rice 1976, 95–98). Thomas Whately's *Observations on Modern Gardening* (1770), which delineated the latest theory of the pictur-esque style, was translated into French almost immediately upon publication and was widely read. *Observations* seems to have sparked a flurry of publishing on beauty and landscape in France. It was followed by the publication of Wate-let's *Essay on Gardens: A Chapter in the French Picturesque* (1774), Duchesne's *Traité de la formation de Jardins* (*Treatise on the Making of Gardens*; 1775), Mo-rel's *Théorie des jardins* (*Theory of Gardens*; 1776), and Girardin's *De la composi-tion des paysages* (1777; translated as *An Essay on Landscape* in 1783) (Middleton 1992, 48–51). These works all deal with interpretations of the picturesque theory, and while there is no evidence that Jefferson owned any of these books, they certainly would have been well known to his aristocratic acquaintances. The La Rochefoucauld family estate of La Roche-Guyon, for example, contained modern irregular gardens as well as a working *ferme ornée* (ornamented farm) based directly on Morel's prescriptions in *Theory of Gardens* (Adams 1997, 121). In fact, Jefferson's friend the Duchess D'Enville implored Jefferson to send her selected American species to plant in the grounds of La Roche-Guyon. The list included *Liriodendron tulipifera,* which Jefferson described as "the Juno of our groves." The seeds arrived in time to be planted in the spring of 1792 (Rice 1976, 113). In sum, it would seem that Jefferson's exposure to aristocratic French landscape taste around 1786 would have informed him that the most stylish "modern" garden designs were grounded in the rococo irregularity of the *jardin anglaise,* but during his travels in France he would also have seen the elegance of the older geometric designs.

One particular detail of Jefferson's time in France may relate directly to the grounds at Poplar Forest. While he spent the bulk of his time in Paris, Jefferson occasionally went "into retreat" in the country at a peaceful mountaintop mon-astery called Mont-Valérien that was run by a religious community of lay broth-ers known as the Hermites. Jefferson's daughter Martha later wrote, "Whenever he had a press of business, he was in the habit of taking his papers and going to the hermitage, where he spent sometimes a week or more till he had finished his work. The hermits visited him regularly in Paris, and the Superior made him a present of an ivory broom that was turned by one of the brothers" (Randolph [1871] 1978, 48).

This community, which was part of the Pilgrimage Church, produced honey, wood, and wine from large terraced vineyards surrounding the mountaintop retreat. Jefferson would stay in a boardinghouse kept by the brothers, where he "enjoyed good air, a magnificent view, and found comfort for body as well as for soul" (Rice 1976, 106–107). Jefferson's pleasure at the prospect of a visit to this idyllic retreat is plain from a note he wrote on October 18, 1787: "The sky is clearing, and I shall away to my hermitage!"[3] There are obvious parallels

Figure 4.5. The view toward the north up the center of the sunken lawn. The right bank is slightly canted, while the left bank runs parallel to the north-south axis of the house. Used by permission of Thomas Jefferson's Poplar Forest, Bedford County, Virginia.

between Jefferson's visits to this hermitage and the experience of being "in retreat" that he wished to create at Poplar Forest. The grounds at Mont-Valérien contained a central house overlooking a parterre flanked by rows of trees canted slightly outward (figure 4.5). Jefferson chose a strikingly similar landscape form for Poplar Forest, where he modified the sunken-lawn parterre to cant outward from the house in the exact manner as at Mont-Valérien.

If the effect of Jefferson's education in landscape gardening while in France is not easy to identify, there is no such ambiguity regarding the influence of English garden design on his tastes. He wrote, "The gardening in that country is the article in which it excels all the earth. I mean their pleasure gardening. This, indeed, went far beyond my ideas."[4] Like many cultural phenomena, the English style changed over time. John Dixon Hunt notes that originally the term "picturesque" denoted any subject worthy of inclusion in a painting and that the term did not come to denote "an experience of landscape" based on the irregular or natural until the end of the eighteenth century (Hunt 1991, 231). It was considered by the English aristocracy, whose members were in the midst of a fervent love affair with grand-scale landscape gardening during Jefferson's time in Europe, to be the most aesthetically advanced landscape style. Jefferson's six-week tour of famous gardens and grounds in England with John

Adams provides an intimate glimpse into Jefferson's tastes in landscape design, as he looked with a highly critical eye on the various ornamental grounds he surveyed. He stated that the purpose of the trip was to ascertain the expense and practicality of creating an ornamental landscape, an indication that that he intended to put his evaluations to future use.

Jefferson used the tour as an opportunity to observe the "state of the art" of the landscape garden at the time. During the trip he distilled his thoughts on the subject and showed a keen appreciation for the beauty of well-executed natural landscapes and landscape features. Martin notes: "What Jefferson liked very much in a few English landscapes, and what he later would try to create at Monticello . . . was the soft and pastoral" (Martin 1991, 146). Jefferson's critical eye noted and discarded the contrived or artificial elements of these landscapes, in the process crystallizing a personal vision of landscape based loosely on the best of what he observed in English landscape designs.

## Jeffersonian Landscapes: The Modern and Ancient

Jefferson was a lifelong enthusiast of landscape gardening. He featured the topic prominently in traveling notes that he prepared for fellow Americans, which were later published as "Objects of Attention for an American," in which he stated that gardens are "particularly worth the attention of an American, because it is the country of all others where noblest gardens may be made without expense. We have only to cut out the superabundant plants" (Boyd 1956, 269). This note clearly indicates the degree to which Jefferson was willing to adapt himself and his creative vision to the natural landscape; a designer prepared to change, and be changed by, that which was already extant. It is a revealing comment. To Jefferson, nature was not an impediment to be cleared away and reconstructed; it was a valued contributor to good landscape design. It also indicates his preference for naturalistic landscape ideas, as one could hardly create a baroque or neoclassical geometric garden by merely cutting out selected abundant plants. Later in his life, Jefferson noted that "to England, we are surely to go for models of this art." [5] Poplar Forest represents Jefferson's personal forays into the world of the late eighteenth- and early nineteenth-century garden landscape design.

The ornamental landscape at Poplar Forest appears to have contained an interesting juxtaposition of rococo or naturalistic landscape elements and geometric, neoclassical symmetry (figure 4.6). Jefferson particularly respected Thomas Whately's *Observations on Modern Gardening*. Whately wrote: "Regularity can never attain to a great share of beauty, and to none of the species called picturesque; a denomination in general expressive of excellence" (Whately [1770] 1982, 146). Jefferson shared this view, discarding the most artificial or contrived elements of ornamental landscape design in favor of tastefully ex-

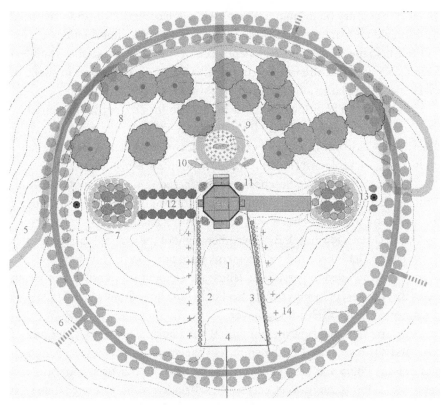

Figure 4.6. Schematic of the core area showing major landscape features: 1) sunken lawn; 2 and 3) shrub plantings on the banks of the sunken lawn; 4) stone drain; 5) circular road lined with paper mulberry trees; 6) southwest axial road (one of three entering the circular road); 7) mound covered in willow trees and ringed with aspens; 8) north yard with grove of tulip poplars; 9) carriage turnaround; 10) oval beds of flowering shrubs; 11) clumps of ornamental trees; 12) double row of paper mulberry trees; 13) octagonal privy; 14) Kentucky coffee trees on top of the sunken lawn. Used by permission of Thomas Jefferson's Poplar Forest, Bedford County, Virginia.

ecuted natural-looking features, a philosophy described as based on the "soft and pastoral" (Martin 1991, 147).

At Poplar Forest, the influence of Jefferson's knowledge of English landscape gardening is expressed through his use of several types of landscape elements. The north core area in particular appears to have been designed almost exclusively around features emblematic of English picturesque garden design of the late eighteenth and early nineteenth centuries. Planting clumps at the diagonal angles of the house contained trees and shrubs that were densely packed to produce a wild thicket of foliage. The form of the planting clump had been developed over the course of the eighteenth century in England, where it evolved from broad wildernesses and thickets into the "shrubbery" of the mid- to late nineteenth century (Laird 1991, 154–165). Although composition and size varied with individual plantings and sites, the style of planting clump Jefferson used had taken shape in the mid-eighteenth century. Whately describes the ideal form as being "a mixture of trees and shrubs, or wood and grove; in short, of every species of plantation" (Whately [1770] 1982, 53–55).

Jefferson began planting clumps at Monticello in 1807, perhaps inspired by the clumps he remembered from his 1786 visit to Esher Place, Surrey, which he described as "a lovely mixture of concave and convex" (Betts 1944, 112). Paper mulberries, prickly locust (*Robinia hispida*), mountain ash, poplars, prickly ash, chokecherries, and purple beeches were purchased in the spring of 1807 from Thomas Main's nursery in Georgetown. These formed the core plantings around the house and were augmented with horse chestnut and redbud from Jefferson's own stock (Heath 1993b, 52). By November, eight of the original thirty-six trees in the clumps had died, and replacements were purchased. How long a clump of trees was intended to persist as a landscape element is unknown, but Heath notes that by 1825, paintings of Monticello do not show clumps matching those documented in 1807 (Heath 1993b, 54).

Jefferson's 1812 planting memorandum for Poplar Forest notes the mix of trees and shrubs he used in the clumps at the angles of the house: "Athenian and Balsam Poplars at each corner of house. Intermix locusts, common and kentucky, redbuds, dogwoods, calycanthus, liriodendron" (Betts 1944, 494). If Jefferson followed Bernard McMahon's *American Gardener's Calendar* instructions for organizing these species within the clump, the tallest specimens would have been placed in either the background or center of the clump, with the whole arranged "according to their gradation in height" (McMahon 1806, 62–63). Laird notes: "One central idea seems to run through the composition of all eighteenth-century shrubberies and flower gardens: plants should be arranged in a graduated array" (Laird 1999, 16).

The oval bed grew out of the same evolution in landscape gardening that produced the shrubbery clump. Comprised primarily of low-lying flowers, oval beds also occasionally contained a flowering shrub in the center and were typically composed with the same gradation in height that governed the construction of clumps. Jefferson began to plant oval beds at Monticello in 1807, occasionally including fraxinella and guelder rose in the centers of some beds. Other oval beds were composed entirely of flowers (Betts 1944, 334). He was evidently pleased enough with the results to continue the practice at Poplar Forest. In a November 1, 1816, planting memorandum for Poplar Forest, Jefferson noted: "Planted large roses of different kinds in the oval bed in the N. front. Dwarf roses in the N. E. oval. Robinia hispida in the N. W. do." (Betts 1944, 563). Archaeological investigations have located the northwest oval bed and indicate that it was not aligned geometrically with the house (Heath 1993b, 68–75). The angled placement of this feature recalls the naturalist style oval beds and serpentine path shown in Jefferson's plan for the west lawn at Monticello.

Another important aspect of the north core design is brought to light by the five tulip poplars still standing along the circular road (figure 4.4). Numerous circular depressions eight to ten feet in diameter from large removed stumps were recorded across the north core during modern surveys of the property, hinting that the five remaining specimens are the last remnants of a larger grove that likely once covered the north core area. Jefferson argued that the execution of the naturalist style of landscape gardening should be, of necessity, different in America than in England. In writing to William Hamilton in 1806, the same year that he began construction of the house at Poplar Forest, Jefferson stated:

> Their sunless climate has permitted them to adopt what is certainly beauty of the first order in landscape. Their canvas is of open ground. . . . But under the beaming, constant and almost vertical sun of Virginia, shade is our Elysium. In the absence of this no beauty of the eye can be enjoyed. . . . The only substitute I have been able to find is this. Let your ground be covered with trees of the loftiest stature. Trim up their bodies as high as the form of the tree will bear, but so that their tops shall still unite and yield dense shade. A wood so open will have nearly the appearance of open grounds.[6]

This quote surely describes the effect Jefferson wished to achieve in the north core area at Poplar Forest and suggests one way that Jefferson adapted to and incorporated existing landscape elements in his design. Dendrochronological analysis of two surviving specimens suggests that these trees were twenty to thirty years old when Jefferson built the house and designed the landscape. That these poplars were intentionally left in place also points to the intended setting Jefferson wished to achieve in the north core area at Poplar Forest. The planting clumps, the angled oval beds, and a cover of native trees to provide English-style open grounds in a Virginia climate all illustrate a coherent landscape composition strongly influenced by Jefferson's knowledge of and exposure to the English naturalistic landscape gardens of his time.

The southern half of the core area landscape at Poplar Forest represented a different aesthetic. Drawing upon the neoclassical Palladian inspiration of the house, Jefferson created a more formal geometric landscape. The central feature was a classical sunken "parterre" measuring 70 by 210 feet, which created a large rectangle in a one-to-three ratio that suggests the deliberate use of dynamic symmetry (Heath 2007, 140). Sloped banks to the east and west rose to meet the natural ground level and were each planted with a row of flowering ornamental shrubs (figure 4.6). The effect was strongly linear and geometric, and the sunken parterre visually dominated the southern landscape.

This linear landscape feature is not immediately congruous with a soft pastoral landscape atmosphere. However, it likely overlooked a utilitarian garden of some type at the end of the sunken lawn, beyond which was a very pastoral view of gently undulating agricultural fields that descended to a wooded creek. In addition, the two allées of paper mulberries and the earthen mounds east and west of the house were symmetrical landscape features that appear to have been built to sculpt Palladian architecture from nature. Jefferson's use of these landscape features as architectural forms is shown by comparing the elevation of Poplar Forest with Palladio's own design for the Villa Barbaro, which was constructed between 1549 and 1558 (figure 4.7). The double rows of paper mulberry trees east and west of the house formed the *barchessas,* or wings. The earthen mounds at each end, which were initially planted with willows, functioned as the dovecotes, forming the familiar tripartite Palladian scheme (Farber and Reed 1980, 22–56). The visual architectural function of these landscape features is demonstrated by the fact that in 1813, Jefferson replaced the paper mulberries on the east side with an actual brick-and-mortar wing of offices, a building that was later destroyed in the 1840s (Kelso, Patten, and Strutt 1991, 46). This construction also indicates Jefferson's willingness to change (and be changed by) the house and landscape at Poplar Forest.

Jefferson's experience living on the property convinced him of the need to build a storage room, a kitchen, a cook's room/laundry and a smokehouse; he added these spaces in 1813 in a wing that was twenty-three feet wide by one hundred feet long. Similarly, it appears that viewing the geometric sunken lawn from his rear portico convinced him that a redesign was in order at this same time. Jefferson had the east bank cut back to form an angled parterre. The changes to the building, mirrored by changes to the landscape, illustrate the intimate blend of nature and architecture Jefferson sought to create at Poplar Forest.

It is significant that several elements of the landscape appear to have been based on dynamic symmetry. Jefferson's use of dynamic symmetry at Poplar Forest was first identified by landscape historian C. Allan Brown (Brown 1990). Although subsequent excavations have revealed that some landscape elements were not as symmetrical as Brown had posited, landscape features using dynamic symmetry included the mounds (seventy-five feet), and the wing of offices and allées of trees east and west of the house (one hundred feet), all based on the base measurement of the house of fifty feet.

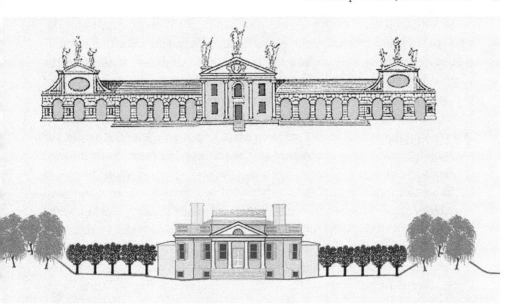

Figure 4.7. A comparison of Palladio's Villa Barbaro and the design for Poplar Forest, ca. 1812. Note how trees create wings and mounds serve as end pavilions. By permission of Thomas Jefferson's Poplar Forest, Bedford County, Virginia.

Thus, while the overall design of the landscape reflects a Palladian physical harmony between the measures of various elements, the form and organization of those elements shows Jefferson's personal affinity for the English "natural"-style landscape. The combination of these two design influences is not necessarily contradictory. Whately noted that a physical harmony between the measures of constituent parts is not only amenable to the picturesque style but should actually be sought as a design element in some instances:

> The style of every part must be accommodated to the nature of the whole.
> . . . On the same principle, the proportion of the parts may often be adjusted; for though their size must be very much governed by the extent of the place; . . . a character of greatness belongs to some scenes, which is not measured by their extent but raised by other properties, sometimes only by the proportional largeness of its parts. (Whately [1770] 1982, 13–14)

The organization of landscape features within the core area sheds light on Jefferson's vision of his own interaction with (and presumed activity within) the Poplar Forest house and grounds. In addition to functioning as corollaries to Palladian architectural elements, the paper mulberries and earthen mounds would have visually split the core into two halves. Stretching for 350 feet from east to west, these features would have confined one's view to whichever half of the core landscape the viewer was standing in. This was an intentional design goal to avoid presenting the viewer with a discordant scene of natural irregularity on the north side and linear geometric landscape features on the south side. The seemingly contradictory division between the natural style of the north core area and the geometric linear south core area may become more harmonious when one envisions entering the house through the first landscape and viewing the second landscape from a fixed position within the house. The natural-style north core would have set the scene as Jefferson passed through the landscape and entered his villa through the north portico. When he retired to the south room, the sunken lawn bounded by shrubs would have provided an exterior frame to Jefferson's view of the garden and distant rural landscape from his study, through the triple-sash windows or the sash doors on the south wall of the house.

Clearly, Jefferson the gardener would never have been content simply to view the landscape from his study. He would have enjoyed being "in" these landscapes he created too much to merely observe them from the platform of the house. Nonetheless, a strong case can be made that the *primary* view informing the design of the south core area was the view from the south portico and study.

The interpretation of a divided landscape north and south in the core area at Poplar Forest may also be strengthened by the fact that Jefferson had previously used this concept architecturally. At Monticello, the east elevation (the building front and main entrance) was designed in the fashion of the French hotels or town houses Jefferson admired so much (Beiswanger 2000, 595–596). An important innovation of this "modern" architecture—and a departure from traditional classical models—was the use of a single-story front with a low, horizontal look containing hidden volumes of space. Jefferson designed the second-story windows on the east elevation at Monticello to be just four feet square and placed them at floor level. The base of these second-story windows met the top of the first-story windows, creating an appearance from the outside of a single large window in a high-ceilinged room. These features were deliberately designed to give the illusion that Monticello was just one story high when one approached the entrance (McLaughlin 1988, 7–8). William Beiswanger noted that this design was Jefferson's "effort to suggest a one-story house by the use of a mezzanine level, just what was being perfected in cities such as Paris" (Beiswanger 1984, 168–171, 2000, 596).

Conversely, the rear of Monticello is the "ancient" architectural elevation, dominated by the octagonal dome. Though the rear octagonal dome is sometimes erroneously linked to the dome of the Hotel du Salm, it most directly inspired by the Roman Temple of Vesta, illustrated in Palladio's *Four Books of*

*Architecture* (Palladio 1965; Beiswanger 1993, 51). That Jefferson would deliberately create his architectural masterpiece with "two faces," the modern to the front and the ancient to the rear, may go far toward explaining his landscape design for Poplar Forest.

Unlike the temple-room dome in the rear of Monticello, at Poplar Forest the house itself is essentially the temple. However, significant architectural distinctions can still be made between the front and rear elevations. Travis McDonald believes that the north and south elevations of Poplar Forest subtly represent two faces of architecture in the same manner as those at Monticello. He notes the modern element of a single-story front elevation and the two-story rear elevation with ancient Roman-style arches on the basement story (McDonald, personal communication 2010). It is only natural that this subtle architectural dichotomy would be carried into the landscape, given that Jefferson clearly viewed architecture and landscape as intimately related parts of the same whole.

Jefferson deliberately chose to intermix different classical orders on the interior entablature of the central room, explaining, "In my middle room at Poplar Forest I mean to mix the faces and ox skulls, a fancy which I can indulge in my own case, altho in a public work I feel bound to follow authority strictly."[7] At his private retreat, Jefferson's freedom to "indulge his fancy" by mixing traditionally separated decorative elements according to his own taste was carried into the landscape. The architectural precedent of the modern/ancient elevations of Monticello and Poplar Forest provides the perfect corollary to the natural/geometric split of the design of the ornamental landscape at Poplar Forest. Indeed, it may be more accurate to term the north core area the "modern" garden, a garden that reflected Jefferson's interpretation of the English picturesque style, and the southern core area as the "ancient" garden, one that framed Jefferson's view from the south portico and was grounded in neoclassical Palladian geometry. The landscape at Poplar Forest appears to have been a similar mixture of naturalness and artifice. The blend was an appropriately sophisticated creation for Jefferson—a design that reflected his complex tastes, his enjoyment of the landscape, and his time and place in the history of garden design.

## Notes

1. Joseph Slaughter, *Map of Tomahawk Creek Lands,* September 1813, Thomas Jefferson Papers, Albert and Shirley Small Special Collections Library, University of Virginia, Charlottesville, Virginia.

2. Thomas Jefferson to Hugh Chisholm, June 5, 1807, Coolidge Collection of Thomas Jefferson Manuscripts, Massachusetts Historical Society, Boston, Massachusetts (hereafter Coolidge Collection, MHS).

3. Thomas Jefferson to Madame de Corny, October 18, 1787, in Boyd (1955, 246–247).
4. Thomas Jefferson to John Page, May 4, 1786, in Boyd (1954, 444–446).
5. Thomas Jefferson to William Hamilton, March 1, 1808, Coolidge Collection, MHS.
6. Jefferson to William Hamilton 1806, in Maccubbin and Martin (1984, 182).
7. Jefferson to William Coffee, July 10, 1822, Coolidge Collection, MHS.

# 5

# Ceramics and Jefferson's Aesthetic Philosophy

JACK GARY

The architectural and landscape designs for Poplar Forest are covered with the metaphorical fingerprints of Thomas Jefferson (Brown 1990; Chambers 1993; Heath 2007; McDonald 1994; Trussell this volume). Imbued with an Enlightenment aesthetic philosophy that Jefferson embraced from his earliest studies, Poplar Forest can be seen as a personal statement by which architectural and landscape elements came together in an attempt to create nothing less than beauty itself (Heath 2007, 141). Jefferson used different elements and designs that he felt conformed to a universal ideal that all (European-descended) individuals could recognize as beautiful. These elements often recalled the designs of classical antiquity or the naturalistic gardens and landscapes of England. Jefferson believed that designs that used the classical styles that had "received the approbation of men of all epochs" could educate and instill virtue in his American countrymen, leading them to imitate these designs and create buildings and landscapes that were intrinsically beautiful (Hafertepe 2000, 222–224; Quinby 1982, 339). This philosophy is most obviously seen in Jefferson's architecture and landscapes, but did this sentiment translate into other aspects of the material world of Poplar Forest? This chapter will examine how archaeologically recovered ceramics can provide a glimpse into the ways Jefferson's aesthetic philosophy and personal identity carried over to the material world of everyday objects used at Poplar Forest. Examining ceramic style and decoration suggests that Jefferson purchased particular vessels because they contained imagery evocative of landscapes, architecture, and concepts closely aligned to his vision for Poplar Forest.

## Consumer Decisions

This chapter examines the Jefferson-era ceramics at Poplar Forest within the framework of consumer studies. Understanding the reasons behind consumer choices and decisions can elucidate the thought process of the purchaser and give insight into an individual's personal or projected identity. Suzanne Spencer-Wood states that decisions to acquire certain goods revolve around a number of interrelated factors within the cultural system, including the ability to afford those goods, the functional utility of the goods, the use of the goods for socioeconomic status display, and behaviors related to ethnicity, political status, religion, family size, and life cycle (1987, 323). Similarly, in choosing which goods to purchase, the consumer makes decisions that "forecast" how the object will actually perform, both functionally and symbolically (Walker and Schiffer 2006, 74–75). The "forecast" may depend on how well the consumer thinks the object will represent his or her identity and interests to him or herself or to others in certain situations. In the case of ceramic vessels used in social dining contexts, the purchaser of the vessels imposes the object on others, having a captive audience for whatever messages the consumer might feel are embedded in his or her purchase. Thus the decision to acquire vessels may be guided by numerous factors that could include the desire to project the perceived or real cost of the vessels or, as argued here, to make a connection with certain imagery, styles, or themes found in the vessels' decoration.

Prior to discussing the ceramic assemblage itself, this study will examine some of the factors that may have influenced the acquisition of certain ceramic vessels, such as Jefferson's access to goods and the role of dining at Poplar Forest. Ceramic vessels are further placed in context by examining the interior furnishings known to have existed at Poplar Forest. Study of these factors makes Jefferson's decisions and choices as a consumer more obvious within the ceramic assemblages recovered from two sites most directly connected to his occupation: the Wing of Offices and Site B (see map 1.2). These objects provide added insight into the ways Jefferson projected his identity into almost every aspect of Poplar Forest.

## Access to Goods

Understanding a consumer's acquisition of certain goods must take into consideration his or her financial and physical access to markets. Choice of goods may be constrained or dictated by the materials available in certain areas or the economic status of the individual making the purchase. Thomas Jefferson, who was a member of the upper economic tier of consumers in the United States by the time he was regularly visiting Poplar Forest, likely had few limits on his access to goods or the credit to purchase goods. While his debts continued to mount in the years after his presidency, Jefferson had several connections with merchants in Richmond, Lynchburg, and Milton (outside Charlottesville) who not only provided goods for his plantations but also acted as creditors able to make advances of cash when needed.

Despite Jefferson's lack of money, a number of these merchant creditors seemed willing, if perhaps begrudgingly, to extend credit almost indefinitely. Credit was given on crops of wheat and tobacco and seemingly on good faith, as the cost of running the plantation was not always met by the returns on the crops. Jefferson drew on his credit accounts with these different merchants to pay his taxes, plantation costs, and debts to numerous individuals, including his Poplar Forest overseers (Bear and Stanton 1997, 1292–1293; Marmon 1991, part 1, 66–72). By 1810 Jefferson had several primary business relationships with merchants in Richmond and Lynchburg (Chambers 1993, 67; Marmon 1991, part 1, 64–73). For the less exotic items needed to outfit the Poplar Forest main house and plantation, Jefferson used his contacts in Lynchburg. While he frequented several businesses in the city, his primary factor was Archibald Robertson, a merchant to whom he was indebted for over $6,000 when he died in 1826 (Malone 1981, 511; Winner 1992, 37–39).

Robertson's store regularly provided a variety of materials for the Poplar Forest plantation such as nails, leather, corn, beef, and clothing for the slaves. He also supplied the main house with candles, molasses, sugar, rice, coffee, and tea.[1] Robertson's store also acted as the shipping destination for the goods Jefferson ordered that came up the James River from Richmond (Chambers 1993, 67). No inventory of Robertson's exists to give an indication of specific items or level of quality for the merchandise he carried in his store, but advertisements for contemporaneous Lynchburg merchants suggest they were all tapped into goods from the larger trading centers on the East Coast and in England.

No longer a frontier town, Lynchburg in the early nineteenth century was growing into the major center of commerce for Central Virginia (Chambers 1993, 99; Scruggs 1978, 16). Advertisements for Lynchburg merchants and businesses from 1814 to 1822 show that a range of merchandise was available, including mahogany, watches, jewelry, plated coffee and teapots, French wallpaper, Queensware, and Chinaware, as well as some specialty foods (*Lynchburg Press,* April 4, 1817). Jefferson's instruction to let his grown granddaughters purchase—on his account—anything that might strike their fancy on a shopping excursion to Archibald Robertson's in 1823 may be additional evidence that fashionable items could be found in Lynchburg.[2]

Some things that Jefferson desired to have at Poplar Forest were not available or of a sufficient quality in Lynchburg. For these items, he was able to call on merchants in Richmond who had extensive connections with northern and European markets or on acquaintances in other cities (Marmon 1991, part 1, 70). Richmond merchants could procure specialized objects, including groceries, as evidenced by Jefferson's attempt to alleviate a boring diet at Poplar Forest with an order for cod tongues and air bladders, crackers, raisins, and imported cheese placed with merchant Bernard Peyton in 1819.[3] Peyton procured these goods and a year later was also able to obtain strings for a harpsichord that had been sent to Poplar Forest.[4]

Jefferson also had access to markets outside Virginia through his extensive network of friends and family. Jefferson's desire for quality foods often required him to request locally unavailable groceries from acquaintances in East Coast cities as well as in Europe (Wilson 2005, 47–53). He asked consuls in France to ship him wine, pasta, and Smyrna raisins, while he asked his granddaughter in Boston to send more cod tongues and bladders, all for the Monticello table (Wilson 2005, 51, 129). Jefferson's horticultural pursuits also gave him access to different markets, and he routinely traded plants with acquaintances not only in the neighborhood around Poplar Forest but also with friends who lived in the larger East Coast cities and overseas (Betts 1944, vi–vii, 305–306, 317, 379, 504–505; Hatch 1992, 8–16).

By 1809, when Jefferson began making regular visits to Poplar Forest, he would have been able to tap into any number of avenues to procure goods, both local and further afield. His choice of particular goods was hardly constrained by availability in one place, and no doubt he had the luxury of choosing objects that he wanted instead of settling for what was available.

## Social Life at Poplar Forest

Thomas Jefferson designed the main house at Poplar Forest as a personal retreat, constructing it between 1806 and 1809 and adding a row of service rooms, called the Wing of Offices, between 1813 and 1816. Jefferson visited the property regularly after his retirement in 1809, using the retreat as a private place to get away from the social pressures of Monticello. Here he engaged in the things he most enjoyed, such as reading and studying topics that interested him. Often accompanied only by his body servant Burwell Colbert or select family members or friends, Jefferson claimed to be "in the solitude of a hermit" while in residence (Chambers 1993, 70).

While this claim may have been mostly true, Poplar Forest served as a site of entertainment and company on numerous occasions. Dining was the primary social activity at Poplar Forest on these occasions, and the only social space within the house itself was the dining room in the center. Enlightenment philosopher Lord Kames had prescribed that the largest room in a house should serve as the locus of social activity (Hafertepe 2000, 221). Not only was the dining room at Poplar Forest the largest room in the house, it also occupied the very middle of the structure and indeed was the very center of the retreat landscape (figure 1.3).

Jefferson was keenly aware of the benefits of social dining, and he may have tried to impart this value to his granddaughters, Ellen, Cornelia, and Virginia, who began traveling with their grandfather to the retreat after 1816. While at Poplar Forest, these young women often bore the responsibility for entertaining guests, even though their letters suggest a reluctance to invite the women and families of the neighborhood for meals or tea. Jefferson, however, insisted that they host "lady dinners."[5]

Jefferson himself was on many occasions a similarly disgruntled host of dinner parties in his many public roles, perhaps most intensely when he served as president (Scofield 2006). However, he also realized the value of entertaining guests, friends, politicians, and enemies as a way to exert power and influence. This was Jefferson's primary mode of political communication with members of Congress, and as Merry Ellen Scofield (2006, 459) suggests, the almost-daily dinners he held as president made it clear to him that persuasion came "not in public debate but in private conversation . . . cloaked in the informality and congeniality of an intimate dinner." While he recognized the importance of dining, by 1804 Jefferson was ready to pass the torch. He wrote, "I wish much to turn it over to younger hands and to be myself but a guest at the table, and free to leave it as others are" (ibid., 468).

Those younger hands at Poplar Forest were his granddaughters. Jefferson was always aware of opportunities to instruct his grandchildren, and his insistence upon "lady dinners" may have served to continue the education they received at Monticello to make them into good hostesses and household managers. Under the guidance of their mother, Jefferson's granddaughters rotated through monthly turns managing Monticello's enslaved laborers, provisions, and hostess duties (Chew 2005, 29–35). It appears that their grandfather did not allow for a break from these duties even on their trips to Poplar Forest.

Entertaining may have also served as a way to exert influence in a fashion similar to the presidential dinners. While the guests at Poplar Forest did not carry the same political weight as those at the presidential table, individuals invited to dine were members of the local community who were important to Jefferson's familial, financial, and intellectual interests. Such guests included principals and teachers at the New London and Lynchburg academies where Jefferson's grandson Francis Eppes attended school and several merchants, including Archibald Robertson, to whom Jefferson constantly owed money.[6] Other guests of note included Abbé Joseph Francis Correa de Serra and Francis Gilmer, two intellectuals on a botanical tour of the southern states; John Wood, a Scottish immigrant and onetime master of the Trustees' Drawing Academy at

Edinburgh; and George Tucker, a Virginia state representative whom Jefferson appointed to become the first professor of moral philosophy at the University of Virginia in 1825.[7]

It appears that while dining was one of the primary social activities at Poplar Forest, it was not an extravagant affair in terms of the food served, despite Jefferson's attempts to procure quality groceries through his merchants in Richmond. Guests were often invited with a warning that all he had to serve them was a simple "plantation" or "family" dinner.[8] These meals may have consisted of poultry purchased from the enslaved residents, bacon, and whatever produce could be procured from the garden or from neighbors.[9] The simplicity of these meals may have been the result of Jefferson's absentee status; he would have been unable to directly oversee many of the operations that made it possible for him to maintain a well-stocked table at his Monticello home. The lack of an icehouse, for instance, caused difficulty in maintaining fresh meat such as lamb, while there are also indications that the vegetable garden was not particularly productive and may have even been raided by at least one of the enslaved residents (Chambers 1993, 123, 142–144).

## Evidence of Furnishings

No historic inventory of the furnishings of the main house exists, but tax records; passing references by visitors, Jefferson, and his granddaughters; and, to a more limited degree, archaeological remains provide some indication of how the house was furnished. When reminiscing in 1856 about her time spent at Poplar Forest with her grandfather, Ellen Randolph Coolidge claimed: "It [the main house] was furnished in the simplest manner, but had a very tasty air; there was nothing common or second-rate about any part of the establishment, though there was no appearance of expense" (Randall [1857] 1970, 342). One visitor wrote in his journal after an 1816 visit that the house resembled a French chateau where "floors of polished oak, lofty ceilings, [and] large mirrors betokened [Jefferson's] French taste, acquired by his long residence in France" (Nichols 1984b, 32). Style was not lost on his visitors, and because of Jefferson's almost-mythical status at the time—one woman seeing him at a Lynchburg party was disappointed to see that he ate like a normal human (Cabell 1879, 75)—visitors to Poplar Forest may have been particularly attuned to the types of objects they encountered once they were admitted into the house.

Documentation of specific furnishings for the main house supports Ellen's description. Among some of the items used at Poplar Forest were an octagonal mahogany dining-room table, dumbwaiters, a harpsichord, three dozen Windsor chairs, tea tables, a large map to hang on a wall, bookcases, a portable polygraph for copying letters, and a "campeachy," or siesta chair, that Jefferson found conducive to relieving pain in his back (Chambers 1993, 85–89, 127, 130, 135–36). Archaeological remains of specific furnishings that are not ceramic vessels are limited, however. Elements of a mantle clock and the possible arm for a portable "lap" desk were recovered from the Wing of Offices excavations (Kelso, Patten, and Strutt 1991, 93).

Objects such as the octagonal dining-room table, which mirrored the shape of the house and rooms, suggest that architectural themes were carried over into the material world of the retreat and that furnishings may have been selected to fit within the larger vision for Poplar Forest. Other furnishings, such as the wall maps, polygraph, and bookcases, are indicative of how the house actually functioned; not like a rustic retreat, filled with only what was needed for survival, but like a large study or office. The letters of the granddaughters provide accounts of Jefferson delving into various studies or academic pursuits that the more social and formal atmosphere of Monticello prohibited (Chambers 1993, 113, 117, 122, 125).

## Documentary Evidence of Ceramics at Poplar Forest

While there is some mention of ceramic vessels in the documentary record during Jefferson's residence at Poplar Forest, the vague nature of these references makes it difficult to draw accurate conclusions about the use and presence of specific vessels, much less to ascribe meaning to their uses. The earliest mention comes in 1807, when Jefferson was still president. As he was shipping trunks of books and other items from Washington back to Monticello through his cousin George Jefferson, who was a merchant in Richmond, he mentioned that among the trunks was a box containing a load of "crockery ware for my use in Bedford" that should be delivered to Poplar Forest.[10] This shipment may be among the first of Jefferson's preparations for his impending retirement and may also suggest that ceramic vessels used at the White House served a second life at Poplar Forest. The use of the word "crockery" may indicate that the shipment contained utilitarian earthenware vessels.

Jefferson's account book contains two instances of ceramic purchases associated with Poplar Forest. Either Jefferson or a slave purchased patty pans in 1812 and Cate, an enslaved woman, was given two dollars to buy milk pans in 1815 (Bear and Stanton 1997, 1284, 1309). The purchase of two coffee pots was also recorded, but it is unclear if these were plated metal or ceramic vessels (Bear and Stanton 1997, 1284, 1295). A final reference to ceramics associated with Poplar Forest came in the Campbell County estate inventory taken in 1826, after Jefferson's death.[11] The inventory lists six crocks and a tin pan valued at fifty cents. The main house and Wing of Offices fell within Bedford County however, so it is likely that these objects were related to and used in outbuildings that stood to the east, across the county line. No inventory for Bedford County and the main house has been located, and archaeologically recovered ceramics provide the most detailed view of the types of vessels associated with Jefferson's residence.

The Sites and Assemblages

Ceramics recovered from the Wing of Offices and Site B, the location of the ornamental plant nursery, comprised the assemblages for this study. These two sites were the loci of deposition for the materials most directly related to the Jefferson occupation of the main residence. The excavation of the Wing of Offices has produced the most material that can be attributed to the domestic functions of the house itself. This functional space housed four rooms, including a possible storeroom, the kitchen, a third room that may have doubled as a laundry and sleeping quarters for the cook Hannah, and a smokehouse (figures 1.3 and 1.6). The functions of this space make it the most likely repository of ceramics used by the Jefferson household. However, the Wing of Offices was also a space of labor and part-time residence for enslaved workers when Jefferson was staying in the house. Thus, categorical attributions of Thomas Jefferson's use or ownership of all the materials found at this site are difficult to make. Similarly, the Wing was used by two other families after Jefferson's death before it was torn down in the following decades and rebuilt as a disconnected kitchen and smokehouse.

The second assemblage came from the area believed to have been the ornamental plant nursery, located approximately 150 yards southeast of the main house. Crossmends have been discovered between several ceramic vessels found at this site and the ceramics recovered from the Wing of Offices (Gary and Paull 2008). This direct connection between the two areas suggests that trash from the main house was deposited here, possibly in an attempt to create better drainage in the soil of the nursery (Gary 2008). In the decades after Jefferson's death, this site also became the location of housing for enslaved residents and was later plowed extensively. These disturbances created a highly fragmented assemblage that contains a wide temporal range of materials.

Minimum vessel counts were conducted for both sites (Brooks 1994; Gary and Paull 2008). Because both sites were used, plowed, or disturbed extensively in the decades following Jefferson's death, only ceramics with production dates that coincided with Jefferson's residence in the main house were examined (1809–1823). Ware types included Chinese export porcelain, creamware, pearlware, black basalt, and refined red-bodied stoneware. Coarse stoneware and utilitarian redware vessels have been omitted from this study because of the difficulty of dating these ware types.

A total of 220 vessels from the Wing assemblage and 211 from Site B have been attributed to the Jefferson era (table 5.1) (Brooks 1994). Some of these vessels may overlap, as direct crossmends between the two sites show that fragments of the same vessel could be located in both places (Gary and Paull 2008, 157). At both sites pearlware is the dominant ware type, followed by creamware at Site B and Chinese export porcelain at the wing. The larger number of creamware vessels at Site B may indicate a depositional history that began before the construction of the Wing.

Tableware recovered from the two sites came predominantly in the form of undecorated creamware, shell-edged pearlware, and transfer-printed pearlware (table 5.2). Only four Chinese-export porcelain plates were identified at the Wing and none were identified from Site B, suggesting that porcelain vessels did not constitute a large portion of the vessels used for table settings. Blue and green shell-edged ware was prevalent at both sites, although blue-edged vessels were found in larger quantities. The only green shelled-edged vessels found were plates, platters, or unidentified flatware. The blue-edged assemblage contained a slightly wider range of vessel forms, including plates, platters, saucers, tureens, and chamber pots. For both colors, plates were the dominant form. The edge-molding style was diverse for both colors and included both scalloped and unscalloped rims combined with curved and straight lines and embossed and impressed patterns. The rim of one chamber pot was painted blue to imitate a molded shell-edge design.

Creamware and pearlware industrial slipware also constitutes a small portion of the tableware assemblages from these sites (table 5.2). Nine pearlware and one creamware vessel were recovered from the Wing of Offices, while nineteen pearlware and six creamware vessels were found at Site B. Dendritic mocha patterns, annular banding, rouletting, and slip trailing comprise the decorative techniques. Because the Site B assemblage is highly fragmented, the only vessel type identified for that site was hollowware. The Wing assemblage contained

Table 5.1. Number of Jefferson-era vessels recovered from Site B and the Wing of Offices

|  | Site B | Wing of Offices |
|---|---|---|
| Pearlware | 140 | 172 |
| Creamware | 49 | 20 |
| Chinese export porcelain | 19 | 24 |
| Refined stoneware | 3 | 4 |

Table 5.2. Jefferson-era vessels identified at Poplar Forest by type, decoration, and form

| Site Ceramic Type | Decoration/Subtype | Vessel Form | | | | | | | | | |
|---|---|---|---|---|---|---|---|---|---|---|---|
| | | Plate | Saucer | Platter | Unid. Flat | Cup | Bowl | Other Hollow | Chamberpot | Teapot | Misc./Unid. |
| **Wing of Offices** | | | | | | | | | | | |
| Pearlware | Transfer prints | 20 | 6 | 5 | 1 | 2 | 5 | 10 | | | 5 |
| | Green shell edge | 13 | | 1 | | | | | | | 2 |
| | Blue shell edge | 22 | 3 | 2 | | | | | 1 | | 1 |
| | Handpainted | | 15 | | | 16 | 8 | 3 | | | |
| | Industrial slipware | | | | | | 6 | 4 | | | |
| | Undecorated | 7 | | | | 3 | 1 | 3 | 6 | | |
| Creamware | All types | 5 | 2 | | 2 | 2 | 3 | 1 | | | 2 |
| Chinese export porcelain | Undecorated | | | | | | 1 | 4 | | | |
| | Handpainted | 4 | 10 | | | 3 | 1 | 3 | | | 2 |
| Refined stoneware | Black basalt | | | | | | | | | 3 | |
| | Rosso antico | | | | | | | | | 1 | |
| **Site B** | | | | | | | | | | | |
| Pearlware | Transfer prints | 16 | 1 | 5 | 17 | | | 11 | | | 5 |
| | Green shell edge | 2 | | | 3 | | | | | | |
| | Blue shell edge | 8 | | | | | | | 7 | | |
| | Handpainted | | 15 | | 6 | 2 | 2 | 2 | | 1 | 3 |
| | Industrial slipware | | | | | | | 17 | | | |
| Creamware | All types | 1 | | 1 | 14 | | 4 | 19 | 5 | | |
| Chinese export porcelain | Undecorated | | 3 | | 1 | 3 | 1 | 22 | | | |
| | Handpainted | | 9 | | | 2 | | | | | |
| Refined stoneware | Black basalt | | | | | | | | | 2 | |
| | Rosso antico | | | | | | | | | 1 | |

seven bowls, one pitcher, and two mugs. The popularity and prevalence of slip-decorated ware during the early nineteenth century in conjunction with the small number of vessels of this type found in Jefferson-era contexts at Poplar Forest may indicate that they were not chosen as a primary component of the table assemblage or that meals requiring bowls were not often served (Miller, Martin, and Dickinson 1994, 241, 244). Enslaved residents may have also owned these vessels.

One black and fifty-three blue transfer-printed vessels were identified at the Wing and fifty-five blue transfer-printed vessels were identified at Site B (table 5.2). Numerous patterns are evident, including the widely manufactured and popular willow pattern. Second in prevalence to willow are vessels in the Oxford and Cambridge College series (figure 5.1) (Coysh and Henrywood 1982, 271). Three border series are also present at the two sites, including the Foliage, Foliage and Scroll, and Bluebell border series (figure 5.2) (Coysh and Henrywood 1982, 46, 142). The remaining assemblage is composed of single vessels from different patterns, such as the Coronation pattern, a scene from

Figure 5.1. Transfer-printed pearlware plates in the Oxford and Cambridge College series by J & W Ridgway, Radcliffe Library depicted. Partial plates recovered from the Wing of Offices, whole plate donated to Poplar Forest. Plate courtesy of Randy Peckham; image by permission of Thomas Jefferson's Poplar Forest, Bedford County, Virginia.

the Caramanian series, the Boy Piping pattern, and miscellaneous unidentified floral, chinoiserie, and pastoral patterns (table 5.3) (Coysh and Henrywood 1982, 53, 70, 94). In the absence of a large quantity of porcelain tableware, the transfer-printed vessels represent the most expensive ceramics found at Poplar Forest.

Typical for the early nineteenth century, the teaware assemblage is distinctly different from the tableware, and the two assemblages do not share any decorations (Miller, Martin, and Dickinson 1994, 241). Porcelain vessels are more numerous; however their numbers do not suggest that porcelain was the pri-

Table 5.3. Jefferson-era transfer-printed series and patterns recovered from the Wing of Offices and Site B

| Site | Series | Pattern | Maker |
|------|--------|---------|-------|
| Wing of Offices | | | |
| | Bluebell border | Unidentified | Clews, Adams |
| | Caramanian | Colossal Sarcophogus | Unknown |
| | Foliage | Wistow Hall | Unknown |
| | Foliage | Blenheim | Unknown |
| | Foliage and Scroll | Melrose Abbey | Clews, Adams |
| | Oxford and Cambridge College | Theater Printing House | John and William Ridgway |
| | Oxford and Cambridge College | Christ Church | John and William Ridgway |
| | Oxford and Cambridge College | Radcliffe Library | John and William Ridgway |
| | Unknown | Boy Piping | Unknown |
| | Unknown | Rural Cottage | Unknown |
| | Unknown | Building with multiple windows | Unknown |
| | NA | Tuscan Rose | John and William Ridgway |
| | NA | Willow | |
| | NA | Coronation | Clews |
| | NA | Fruit Basket | William Smith and Co. |
| | NA | Tower in Ruins? | John and George Alcock? |
| Site B | | | |
| | Foliage | Unidentified | |
| | Foliage and Scroll | Unidentified | |
| | Oxford and Cambridge College | Theater Printing House | John and William Ridgway |
| | Oxford and Cambridge College | Christ Church | John and William Ridgway |
| | Oxford and Cambridge College | Wadham | John and William Ridgway |
| | Oxford and Cambridge College | St. Peter's | John and William Ridgway |
| | NA | Willow | |
| | NA | Tuscan Rose | John and William Ridgway |

Source: Coysh and Henrywood 1982, 46, 53, 90, 94, 142, 148, 271, 372.

Figure 5.2. Fragments of transfer-printed pearlware plates from different border series found at the Wing of Offices. Foliage series on the top left, Foliage and Scroll series on the bottom left, and Bluebell series on the right. Used by permission of Thomas Jefferson's Poplar Forest, Bedford County, Virginia.

mary ceramic type acquired for Poplar Forest. Based on amounts, hand-painted pearlware vessels appear to have composed the tea service used at Poplar Forest in Jefferson's time. Polychrome and monochrome floral designs compose the Wing assemblage (figure 5.3). Site B is similar but also includes some teaware with hand-painted geometric and chinoiserie designs that were produced in the late eighteenth century and early nineteenth centuries (Miller, Martin, and Dickinson 1994, 223). Like the larger number of creamware vessels found at Site B, these may also suggest a slightly earlier deposition into the nursery, before the Wing was constructed. The highly fragmented nature of the Site B assemblage makes it difficult to distinguish between bowls, cups, and saucers. Ceramic teapots found at the Wing are also typical for the early nineteenth century in that they did not match the cups and saucers (Ibid., 241). All teapots identified from the Wing were refined stoneware; they included engine-turned rosso antico, black basalt, and Jackfield-type vessels.

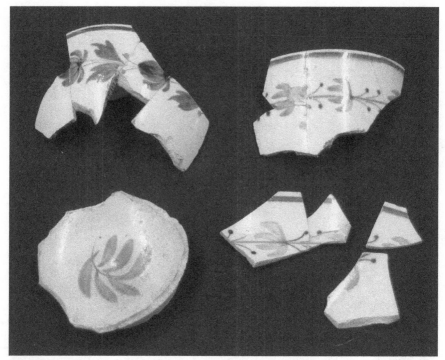

Figure 5.3. Fragments of hand-painted polychrome pearlware teacups and saucer recovered from the Wing of Offices. Used by permission of Thomas Jefferson's Poplar Forest, Bedford County, Virginia.

## A Timeline for the Poplar Forest Ceramic Assemblage

The refined earthenware and refined stoneware assemblage from the Jefferson residence at Poplar Forest reflects many of the trends of the early nineteenth century with regard to the types of decoration and vessels produced for the market. The lack of matching sets and the almost hodgepodge nature of the Poplar Forest assemblage would have been common in the homes of most middle- and upper-class consumers. This was due to the types of ceramics being produced by the English potters, who partly dictated the market, as well as the social separation of tea drinking from dining (Miller, Martin, and Dickinson 1994, 238; Wall 1994, 262–64).

Different types of ware and decoration accompanied different eating and drinking activities. Assembling matching sets of ware to serve all functions was not common until the mid- to late nineteenth century (Brooks 1994; Miller, Martin, and Dickinson 1994, 238, 243). Teaware would have been distinctly different than tableware, and as Wall (1994, 264) argues, was more likely to act in a status display function because of the social role of the tea ceremony in the late eighteenth and early nineteenth century. Tableware, on the other hand, was part of the more private realm of family dining during this time period and was therefore embedded with social meanings different from those that teaware displayed.

As the role of the family and domestic life changed in the early nineteenth century to include more focus on family dining, the decorative techniques of tableware changed to follow suit as a way to highlight and enhance meals and the dining experience (Wall 1994, 273). While teaware remained relatively static in terms of decoration, tableware changed rapidly and went through a progression of elaboration from molded-rim creamware in the last decades of the eighteenth century to shell-edged pearlware in the early nineteenth century and finally to transfer-printed ware by the 1820s (Miller, Martin, and Dickinson 1994, 244; Wall 1994, 270–273).

These changes coincide approximately with the time frame of the Jefferson residence at the main house at Poplar Forest and the archaeologically recovered ceramic tableware assemblage. As Jefferson began inhabiting the house after 1809, shell-edged vessels may have comprised most of the tableware used for both private and social dining.

The construction of the Wing from 1813 to 1816, which made the house more habitable for guests, and the beginning of Jefferson's granddaughters' visits to Poplar Forest in 1816 signaled a change in the operation of the retreat. The granddaughters' presence added a different dimension to Poplar Forest; after they began visiting, Jefferson regularly dined with family members. The presence of these young women also resulted in more frequent visits from neighbors and friends. These changes may have necessitated the acquisition of new sets of tableware, which was readily available in a multitude of English transfer-printed designs that glutted the North American market after the War of 1812.

The increased range of tableware available on the market and Jefferson's almost universal access to goods allows for an exploration of the possible reasons why he acquired certain transfer-printed ware by examining the potential messages embedded in their designs. For the Poplar Forest assemblage, these messages may be seen most clearly in the images found on the transfer-printed tableware. Perhaps the most overt examples are ware in the Oxford and Cambridge College series and tableware in specific border series that contain romantic imagery.

## Transfer-Printed Pearlware

The Oxford and Cambridge College series, which was produced from 1814 to 1830 by John and William Ridgway, consisted of central images depicting different buildings associated with the English cities of Oxford and Cambridge. An octagonal frame surrounded each image, and the rim was decorated with vegetation and four medallions showing cherubs feeding and milking goats. Typical for the early nineteenth century, the vessels came in a wide variety of tableware forms, including platters, plates, tureens, and specialized pieces such as a fish strainer and a pickle dish. Six vessels from this series have been recovered from the Wing and thirteen from Site B. The vessel forms found at Poplar Forest include plates, platters, and a pickle dish.

Five different scenes have been identified within the assemblage, including the Theater Printing House, Christ Church, Radcliffe Library, Wadham College, and St. Peter's College. The themes in this series of ceramic tableware resonate so closely with Jefferson's personal interests that it is hard to believe that he did not acquire them because they represented these images. The octagonal border is the most recognizable connection to the Poplar Forest design; the octagon is seen in the shape of the house, the rooms in the house, and even the dining room table, while the combination of architecture and education is closely connected to Jefferson's personal interests (Heath 2007). The Poplar Forest collection includes the image of Radcliffe Library in Oxford, a Palladian-style rotunda with a domed roof that served as a repository for books dealing with medicine and natural science (figure 5.1). During Jefferson's retirement and his time at Poplar Forest, he began his plans for the University of Virginia, which ultimately included as its centerpiece a library in the form of a domed rotunda that was inspired by neoclassical and Palladian designs (figure 5.4) (Vaughan and Gianniny 1981, 14–15). While the individual images in the Oxford and Cambridge College series were primarily confined to a single vessel form, two small plates were produced with different images, Radcliffe Library and a scene called "Senate House, Cambridge." It is interesting to note that only Radcliffe Library is found at Poplar Forest.

Other transfer-printed ware that likely made up the Jefferson household assemblage may have been chosen for similar reasons as the Oxford and Cambridge College series. The romantic imagery seen on many of the other printed tableware, most notably the patterns in the Foliage and Foliage and Scroll border series, highlight buildings, either real or fanciful, set within naturalistic landscapes. Jefferson had even toured one of the subjects, Blenheim Palace, during his tour of English gardens with John Adams in 1786. While not necessarily impressed by the gardens of Blenheim, Jefferson admired the English style of naturalistic landscapes and incorporated many elements of their design in the Poplar Forest landscape (Betts 1944, 114; Trussell this volume). The other two images of identifiable places found at Poplar Forest include Wistow Hall and Melrose Abbey. No direct connection to Jefferson is known to exist for

Figure 5.4. The Rotunda at the University of Virginia. This building served as a library and was the center of the Academical Village, which Jefferson designed. Photograph by Travis McDonald, by permission of Thomas Jefferson's Poplar Forest, Bedford County, Virginia.

these places, but Melrose Abbey's strong connection to Scottish history could relate to Jefferson's strong preference for Scottish Enlightenment philosophers.

Overall the strongest connection between Jefferson and these printed ceramics exists in the romantic imagery and the entwining of architecture and landscape. In these examples a scene is created through a frame of vegetation with a building in the background and water elements and pastoral settings usually in the foreground (figure 5.5). The creation of "scenes" with trees, shrubs, and buildings was a primary element of the picturesque and naturalistic landscape movement of which Jefferson was particularly fond (Trussell 2000, 95–112). This style was certainly incorporated into the landscape of Poplar Forest, and indeed Jefferson's vision for his retreat was a place that incorporated architecture and landscape elements in a seamless whole (Trussell this volume).

The fact that multiple vessels from these transfer-print series have been found at Poplar Forest suggests that Jefferson used them together. The singular examples of transfer-printed vessels, such as the plate from the Caramanian series or the plate with the Boy Piping image, may have been intermixed into the other sets or they could have been purchased by enslaved residents for their own use. The large number of willow-pattern transfer prints suggests that they

Figure 5.5. Fragments of a transfer-printed pearlware plate in the Foliage and Scroll series found at the Wing of Offices. The central image is unidentified, but it is an example of the romantic imagery of landscapes and buildings framed by vegetation that was typical of pearlware of this period. Used by permission of Thomas Jefferson's Poplar Forest, Bedford County, Virginia.

were used as a set, and most likely the shell-edged ware comprised another, possibly earlier set of tableware. What situation called for which set is unclear, but perhaps the larger number of willow vessels indicates that they were used for social occasions, while the more personal messages of the other sets may have been reserved for family or private dining. However, it is also possible that sets were intermixed for social dining, creating a unique combination of vessels containing imagery associated with landscapes, architecture, and education, all elements that Jefferson felt his countrymen needed help improving in the newly formed republic (Hafertepe 2000).

Conclusions

Determining potential reasons for acquiring consumer goods can provide a deeper understanding of how people use materials to construct and display identities in both social and private contexts (Mullins 2001; Olsen 2003, 91–93).

Jefferson's acquisition of certain consumer goods allowed him to construct the material world of Poplar Forest to suit his vision. This vision incorporated a unique blend of personal experiences, neoclassicism, and naturalistic designs in the landscape and architecture of the retreat in pursuit of something universally beautiful (Heath 2007; McDonald 1994). At Poplar Forest, Jefferson may have acquired certain ceramic vessels because they tied into this personal aesthetic philosophy, something that was then related to others or to himself in a reflexive capacity, through the use of this specific tableware in dining situations.

It should be noted that the ceramic assemblage includes few higher-priced items such as Chinese-export porcelain. This contrasts with the finely painted porcelain vessels recovered archaeologically from Monticello and with the documentary evidence of the porcelain that was used as the dinner service at Jefferson's primary residence (Stein 1993, 86–87, 348–349; Kelso 1997, 87–88). This may be a temporal difference however, as recent research suggests that transfer-printed ware was also present in abundance on Jefferson's Monticello table in the years after his retirement (Chew and Bon-Harper 2007). Perhaps the use of shell-edged and transfer-printed vessels at Poplar Forest and Monticello was a necessity given Jefferson's awareness of the staggering debt that he had accrued. He may have felt that it was unwise to expend large amounts of money on ceramic vessels that would be used only three to four times a year. This may have been the case when Jefferson first constructed the main house and he journeyed to Poplar Forest with only his body servant. After construction of the ornamental landscape and house were largely finished and family members began to visit regularly, Jefferson may have thought it important to use dinner settings that tied into the larger vision of Poplar Forest. He could accomplish this goal quite successfully with the types of transfer-printed ceramics that had become affordable after 1812. Not only was the acquisition of printed ware economically possible, this ware also contained imagery that was more directly associated with his aesthetic sensibilities and interests than porcelain vessels. Jefferson may have also been able to exploit his extensive commercial and personal connections to gain access to particular vessels with specific imagery instead of settling for what was available.

These objects reinforced many of the themes visitors encountered and Jefferson created at Poplar Forest. Like the landscape and the architecture, the use of ceramic vessels helped contribute to the creation of something Jefferson hoped would be universally beautiful. As objects of personal choice the ceramics also functioned in a reflexive capacity for Jefferson, reaffirming his personal identity (Smith 2007). To the extent that he was able to do so, Jefferson surrounded himself at Poplar Forest with the themes, landscapes, architecture, imagery, and people that were important to him.

## Notes

1. Marmon (1991, part 1, 67–69); Thomas Jefferson to Archibald Robertson, August 27, 1813, Thomas Jefferson Papers, Albert and Shirley Small Special Collections Library, University of Virginia, Charlottesville, Virginia; Thomas Jefferson to Archibald Robertson, August 11, 1817, Coolidge Collection of Thomas Jefferson Manuscripts, Massachusetts Historical Society, Boston, Massachusetts (hereafter Coolidge Collection, MHS).

2. Thomas Jefferson to Archibald Robertson, May 21, 1823, Coolidge Collection, MHS.

3. Thomas Jefferson to Bernard Peyton, July 17, 1819, Coolidge Collection, MHS.

4. Bernard Peyton to Thomas Jefferson, October 5, 1820, Coolidge Collection, MHS.

5. Cornelia Randolph to Virginia Randolph, September 8, 1819, Nicholas Philip Trist Collection, Southern Historical Collection, Louis Round Wilson Special Collections Library, University of North Carolina, Chapel Hill, North Carolina.

6. Chambers (1993, 103, 136); Tyler (1915, 341); Thomas Jefferson to Thomas Holcomb, August 28, 1813, Coolidge Collection, MHS.

7. Chambers (1993, 91–94); Koch (1963, 504); Tyler (1915, 309); Thomas Jefferson to John Wood, August 16, 1816, Thomas Jefferson Papers, 1606–1827, Library of Congress, Washington, D.C.; Thomas Jefferson to George Tucker, August 24, 1822, Tucker-Coleman Papers, The College of William and Mary, Special Collections Research Center, Earl Gregg Swem Library, Williamsburg, Virginia.

8. Thomas Jefferson to Charles Clay, May 6, 1813, Thomas Jefferson Papers, Albert and Shirley Small Special Collections Library, University of Virginia, Charlottesville, Virginia; Thomas Jefferson to Mr. Holcomb, August 28, 1813, Coolidge Collection, MHS; Thomas Jefferson to Archibald Robertson, May 25, 1822, Coolidge Collection, MHS.

9. Charles Clay to Thomas Jefferson, May 1, 1813, Coolidge Collection, MHS; Chambers (1993, 125); Bear and Stanton (1997, 1313).

10. Thomas Jefferson to George Jefferson, November 7, 1807, Coolidge Collection, MHS.

11. Albemarle County Will Book 9, 1826–1829, 7, Library of Virginia, Richmond, Virginia.

# 6

## Slave Housing, Community Formation, and Community Dynamics at Thomas Jefferson's Poplar Forest, 1760s–1810s

BARBARA J. HEATH

In the 1660s, hereditary slavery began to develop in tidewater Virginia. Sixty years later, slavery was central to the economic, legal, and social organization of the colony, and planters had begun to send African and native-born slaves west to establish tobacco plantations in the Virginia piedmont. The movement of enslaved laborers and the importation of West and Central Africans into the region resulted in a fundamental shift in the geography of slavery. Within fifty years, slaves in the piedmont outnumbered those in the Tidewater (Kulikoff 1986, 92–96; Morgan and Nicholls 1989, 215–217).

Poplar Forest plantation, located in the foothills of the Blue Ridge Mountains in Bedford County, was at the western edge of piedmont expansion into the 1760s (Kulikoff 1986, 141–143). For more than twenty years, archaeologists have studied the material lives of people who were enslaved on the property (Heath and Bennett 2000; Heath 1999a, 1999b, 2001, 2004, 2008b; Kelso, Patten, and Strutt 1991; Lee 2008; Raymer 2003). While Lee has recently considered late antebellum slavery (Lee 2008, this volume), our principal focus has been on the conditions of slave life during the period from 1773 to 1826, when Thomas Jefferson owned and developed Poplar Forest. Using household and community archaeology, this research illuminates the development and maturation of slavery in the Virginia piedmont in the period during and just after the Revolutionary War. In this chapter, I review the evidence of slave dwellings and domestic landscapes and their relationship to household and community formation from the late 1760s to the early 1810s, responding to models proposed by Garrett Fesler (2004b) and Fraser Neiman (2008). Before turning to the specifics of their studies and my own, it is important to situate my research within the broader scholarship of households, communities, and enslavement in Virginia.

Household and Community Archaeology

Household archaeology has its roots in studies of Mesoamerican settlement patterns carried out in the 1970s. In this research, households formed the smallest unit of analysis for investigating subsistence, craft production, divisions of labor, and status (Flannery 1976). Historical archaeologists quickly recognized the utility of this approach, and over the past four decades they have used a variety of theoretical models and analytical methods to understand the complex relationships that people who shared a living space formed and sustained (Barile and Brandon 2004; Beaudry 1999; Groover 2003, 2004; King 2006; Wilkie 2010). This space can be a dwelling shared by all residents at a site or it can be a building that is divided into individual housing units (Ashmore and Wilk 1988, 6, as cited in Fesler 2004b, 40).

Household membership has been variously conceived and is not necessarily synonymous with family membership. Cohabitation within a housing unit is the defining factor for some researchers (Wilk and Rathje 1982, 618). For others, the level of cooperation between residents has been seen as crucial to defining households; in this research model, members of non-cooperating groups are categorized as co-residents (Ashmore and Wilk 1988, 6 as cited in Fesler 2004b, 40; Bender 1967, 495). More recently, households have been seen as groups of social actors "differentiated by age, gender, role, and power" whose interrelationships among themselves and across multiple households reflect and shape the economic and political norms of the broader society in which they live (Hendon 1996, 46, 49). In this chapter, I use the first definition of a shared space. The historical record indicates that most enslaved households at Poplar Forest were kin-based and thus largely cooperative. Many were headed by single women or women whose mates were absent.

Archaeologists are increasingly careful to distinguish between "family" and "household," since members of a family can be accommodated in multiple places, while members of a household, by definition, live together. Typically, families form households, but historically, non-kin such as servants, slaves, orphans, or wards might share a living space (Bender 1967, 495–496). In the early years of Chesapeake slavery, unrelated slaves and indentured servants were housed together. By the mid-eighteenth century, enslaved men and women began to form families. While their unions were not legally recognized in Virginia, many slaves married informally. Planters condoned this practice, recognizing the profit to be gained from the children of these marriages and the community stability that long-term relationships between enslaved men and women engendered. Over time, as the degree of interrelatedness within plantation populations grew, men and women often sought spouses off the plantation on which they lived

(Heath 2006; Kolchin 1993, 123; Morgan 1998, 508–509). Men participating in these "abroad" marriage lived apart from their wives and children.

While studies of households offer micro-scale evidence of the choices and actions of members (King 2006, 299), community-scale analysis provides the opportunity to study how household members interacted in a broader cultural context. In this study, I define the Poplar Forest community as the group of people, enslaved and free, whose regular interactions constituted, maintained, and challenged the racial, economic, social, and material orders of the plantation (Yaeger and Canuto 2000, 3). The term "slave community" refers to the majority of the resident population who were enslaved and the non-resident slaves (mostly men) with whom residents had formed bonds of real or fictive kinship. Community ties extended beyond plantation borders, where people created and maintained economic, social, and religious ties both locally and regionally. Studying this broader community from an archaeological perspective is challenging, although useful comparisons can be drawn between the extended slave communities living at Thomas Jefferson's Poplar Forest and Monticello plantations.

Moving between household and community scales of analysis is especially helpful in plantation settings. Historical data often exist at the community rather than the household level. Issues of research funding, site access, and data comparability frequently limit archaeologists to examining the material remains of a single household or a small sample of a larger community. By reconstructing community histories and combining community- and household-level scales of analysis, archaeologists can explore the material, spatial, and social dynamics of enslaved groups within their historical contexts (Fesler 2004b; Franklin 1997, 2004; Kern 2010).

## The Material Culture of Slavery

A substantial body of archaeological literature examines evidence relating to the emergence of racialized slavery and its effect on identity formation; the invention, maintenance, or loss of ethnic identities by the enslaved; conditions of daily life; and material strategies for responding to enslavement in Virginia (Edwards-Ingram 2001; Epperson 1990, 1999, 2001; Fesler 2004a, 2004b; Franklin 1997, 2001, 2004; Galle 2006; Hatch 2009; Heath 1999a, 1999b, 2004, 2008b, 2010; Kelso 1984a, 1986; Kern 2010; Lee 2008; Mrozowski, Franklin and Hunt 2008; Pogue and White 1991; Samford 1996, 2007; Sanford 1994, 1995). From the late 1990s, a handful of historical archaeologists working in Virginia have explicitly structured their research to study household dynamics through the interplay between changing household composition and material culture (Fesler 2004a, 2004b; Franklin 1997; Galle 2004, 2006; Heath 2004a; Lee this volume; Neiman 2008).

When discussing households in the context of slavery, some contextual housekeeping is in order. Historians and archaeologists use the term "quarter" somewhat ambiguously to refer to individual structures that slaves inhabited, clusters of slave houses, and productive units of larger plantations where agriculture was carried out, enslaved people and overseers lived, livestock were kept, and agricultural outbuildings stood. To avoid confusion, in this chapter I use the term "house" or "houses" rather than "quarter" or "quarters" to refer to single or multiple slave dwelling(s) and "duplex" to refer to two housing units under a single roof. I use the phrase "quarter farm" to refer to the larger plantation unit to which enslaved workers were assigned.

Garrett Fesler (2004b) examined the development of the Utopia quarter farm, which was located in the Virginia tidewater, from the 1670s to the 1770s. He used a combination of surviving historical documentation and archaeological evidence of houses, landscapes, and consumer goods to study the quarter farm over time. Fesler concluded that changes in house size, declining numbers of interior storage features (known as subfloor pits), and the emergence of new gendered consumption patterns pointed to a transition from co-residential to family-based households for most quarter farm residents in the Virginia Tidewater by the mid-eighteenth century.

Fraser Neiman acknowledges that enslaved people formed families in increasing numbers between 1700 and 1750 and built more "kin-based coalitions" by the last quarter of that century (Neiman 2008, 180). However, he attributes changes in the architecture of slave housing at Monticello to changing management strategies brought about by a shift in the base of agricultural production there. Specifically, Neiman argues that Jefferson profited from providing positive incentives to enslaved workers who met standards of productivity. Although enslaved families existed quite early in the history of Monticello, they were housed alongside co-residents in barracks. Neiman asserts that it was not in Jefferson's interest to accommodate their wishes for kin-based housing prior to the 1790s. At that time, Jefferson changed his cash crop from tobacco to wheat. This transition placed greater demands on laborers and increased the difficulty of supervising their work. Wheat cultivation required that slaves accept a new system for organizing their labor, adopt new time management practices, and learn new skills, and it provided them with greater autonomy in their daily work routines. These changes provided an incentive for Jefferson to motivate members of his enslaved workforce to be more productive by providing them with something they wanted—small houses shared by kin (ibid., 178–182).

To support this argument, Neiman compares housing that predated 1793, the year Jefferson introduced wheat to his Albemarle County plantation, with housing that is dated after this transition. The earlier structures, constructed in the 1770s, were larger buildings with one to four subfloor pits each. Houses dating to the 1790s were significantly smaller and had either one or no subfloor pits (Neiman 2008, 175–176). After 1800, no pits are associated with excavated buildings. Although he does not explicitly say so, Neiman's study (ibid., 175, table 1) suggests that Monticello slaves intentionally abandoned pit use sometime after 1800. This abandonment relates to changes in household composition.

Neiman's argument is not based on an analysis of the particulars of kin relations at Monticello. His sample size was small, and he noted that the model's relevance to the broader history of Atlantic slavery needs to be tested (2008, 182).

In the following discussion, I introduce data on the plantation labor force, the demographics of the enslaved community, and the architecture of slave houses from Jefferson's Poplar Forest plantation and look at demographic data from Monticello to test the strength of Fesler's and Neiman's models as they pertain to house size and changes in the numbers of subfloor pits. Poplar Forest offers evidence from three domestic sites over a period of nearly fifty years and is a good laboratory for testing Fesler's model in a different region. Because Jefferson owned both Monticello and Poplar Forest, many enslaved men and women from the same families had lived at both places. In addition, Jefferson introduced wheat as a cash crop at close to the same time at both plantations. Thus, the Poplar Forest dataset is a logical starting point for testing Neiman's model as well.

The Plantation Labor Force at Poplar Forest

Scholars have pieced together various types of historical and archaeological evidence over the last two decades to study the development and maturation of the enslaved community at Poplar Forest (Marmon 1991, part 1, 3; Heath 2006; Monticello Plantation Database 2008; Stanton 2000). This work makes it possible to explore slavery from the 1770s through the 1820s by examining the intersection of the material world of plantation housing and changing demographic patterns at that site.

In 1773, Thomas Jefferson's wife Martha was apportioned almost 11,000 acres of land divided between plantations in Amherst, Bedford, Cumberland, and Goochland counties from the estate of her father, John Wayles. She also received 135 enslaved individuals from the estate (Bear and Stanton 1997, 329n15). That year, the people she inherited lived and worked on a number of plantations spread across the Virginia piedmont, including Poplar Forest. When Jefferson first recorded his Bedford County slaveholdings in 1774, Poplar Forest consisted of approximately 5,000 acres and the slaves who lived there worked on two quarter farms (Bear and Stanton 1997, 330; Jefferson in Betts 1987, 7). He likely established one of these, which he called Wingos, in 1773, in compliance with instructions in the codicil to his father-in-law's will (Marmon 1991, part 1, 27).

During the 1770s and 1780s, Jefferson sold the remaining land from the Wayles estate (map 6.1). He integrated many of the inherited slaves into existing plantation communities at three properties he owned: Poplar Forest, Monticello, and Elk Hill. He sold thirty slaves formerly owned by Wayles in 1785; sixteen others ran away during the American Revolution and either escaped or died.[1] During the 1790s, Jefferson sold the Elk Hill property (Bear and Stanton 1997, 468–469n14, 524n43). He also sold additional enslaved people and moved a substantial number of former Wayles slaves from Monticello to Poplar Forest. These actions created a twenty-year period of instability for enslaved individuals and families during which some people were relocated and others experienced the loss of family members and friends through sales and death.

Wayles had established the oldest quarter farm at Poplar Forest sometime between 1764, when he purchased the property, and 1769, when county court records first referred to slaves living at the plantation (Marmon 1991, part 3, 2). This early settlement was the primary place of residence at Poplar Forest for the people Wayles owned, and it came to be known as "the Old Plantation" or "Old Quarter" within thirty years. The settlement included a house for the overseer, a large barn, and forty years of slave housing.[2] We know part of this area archaeologically as the North Hill site, which has been dated to the 1770s–1810; the subsequent Quarter Site has been dated to 1790–1813. Although the "Old Plantation" was abandoned and the buildings dismantled in the winter of 1812/1813, this part of the property continued to be intensively used for agriculture, light industry, and domestic space. A quarter farm known as Tomahawk was established somewhere on the property next to the branches of Tomahawk Creek after the "Old Plantation" was abandoned.

Jefferson named the Wingos quarter farm, located in the northeast quadrant of the property, for John Wingo, whom he hired to oversee operations from 1773 until about 1777 (Marmon 1991, part 1, 28). In 1790, Jefferson gave the 1,000-acre Wingos quarter lands, along with its residents, structures, and plantation livestock, to his daughter Martha and Thomas Mann Randolph as part of their marriage settlement (Boyd 1961, 189–191).

Beginning in the 1760s, enslaved men, women, and children at Poplar Forest grew tobacco for sale and tended livestock and a variety of other crops for domestic consumption. While we do not know the exact date when Jefferson's farm managers introduced wheat as a cash crop at Poplar Forest, carbonized

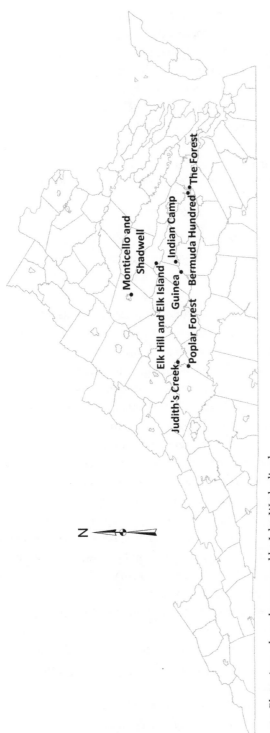

Map 6.1. Plantations where slaves owned by John Wayles lived.

wheat fragments recovered from sealed deposits at the North Hill quarter pre-date the mid-1780s (Raymer 2003, 41,43), indicating that it was being produced and consumed on the plantation by that time. The earliest written evidence of the cultivation of wheat for sale refers to the 1789/1790 winter crop that was at market in Richmond by April 1790.[3] By July 1790, Jefferson was pressing his steward to go "into that culture [of wheat] as much as you think practicable," and that autumn the harvest was 200 bushels.[4]

By about 1800, after twenty-five years of reorganization of people, crops, and landscape, Poplar Forest began to assume the organization it would retain throughout much of the rest of the period that Jefferson owned the property.

## Demographic Data

A rich documentary record that begins in the 1770s and continues through the 1820s makes a community-level analysis of the Poplar Forest population pos-sible.

A partial history of enslaved residents is preserved in lists of tithables, wills, deeds, and other documents that survive from the period when they were owned by John Wayles.[5] After Wayles's death, Jefferson kept detailed lists of his slaves from 1774 to 1819 in a document which he referred to as the Farm Book (Jefferson in Betts 1987). While he wrote some lists to capture information about births, deaths, allotted provisions, or other useful information, he used a core group of lists—which I'll call "slave rolls"—to record the names, birth years (when known), and location (by quarter farm or larger plantation) of separate groups of slaves. On these rolls, Jefferson used spacing, lines, or brackets to group or separate the names of the enumerated individuals. He organized these rolls on the basis of family membership, with fathers and/or mothers typically at the head of each grouping and children or dependents listed below. Jeffer-son followed this practice in 1774, when he first began to systematically record information about the enslaved people in his possession. Only two compre-hensive slave rolls that include Poplar Forest survive from the 1770s, both from 1774. These rolls and one made in 1783 indicate that only one generation existed for most families living within the fledgling community. Beginning in the 1790s, Jefferson separated adult sons and daughters and their children from parents on his Poplar Forest rolls. His consistent use of this very specific way of recording information remained unchanged from the 1770s through the 1810s, a period of more than forty years.

If Jefferson wrote explicit instructions for organizing particular enslaved households at Poplar Forest, none survive from the eighteenth century. How-ever, the slave rolls provide essential clues about his organizational plans when examined over time. A nineteenth-century exchange of letters between Jefferson and his overseer provide details about new housing arrangements for recently married slaves and support my interpretation that Jefferson's practice of segmenting and bracketing names on rolls made between 1800–1812/13 was linked to the formation of new kin-based households.[6] These households accommodated new families in different housing units from those that they had occupied prior to marriage or the birth of a first child. Based on the consistency of his record-keeping, we can assume that Jefferson used lines, bracketing, or segmentation to convey the same type of information—the development of new households—in his earlier record-keeping as well.

Thus, while the slave rolls do not provide enough level of detail to assign people to specific houses, they do provide direct information about approximately when intergenerational families segmented to form new households—by definition, groups that shared a living space. They also convey aspects of the spatial relationships between households in cases where people moved from one quarter farm to another.

It may be helpful to consider the specifics of a few early lists. As we have seen, the enslaved communities that had been part of John Wayles's estate were fragmented in the 1770s and 1780s. The resulting disruptions and changes are evident in the housing arrangements in the slave quarters of Poplar Forest in the 1770s. In early 1774, Jefferson recorded that the Old Plantation was occupied by one family, and a single male artisan, while the Wingos quarter farm was occupied by a group of young, mostly unrelated men and women. He moved slaves from other plantations to Poplar Forest so that later in the year, each of these sites was occupied by two nuclear families and between three and five unrelated adults (Jefferson in Betts 1987, 7, 16). Jefferson did not distinguish between Wingos and the Old Plantation quarters in his 1783 list, but everyone enumerated on that list belonged to one of eight kin-based households (Jefferson in ibid., 24).

Further dispersal of the community took place in 1790 at the time of Martha Jefferson's marriage, when Jefferson transferred five families at the Wingos quarter farm and one at the Old Plantation to her ownership, and in 1791 and 1792, when he sold another group of enslaved individuals and families.[7] Despite these interruptions, the size of the enslaved work force at Poplar Forest in the period 1790 to 1819 (the last year for which we have comprehensive population data) grew steadily from fifty-six to ninety-four people (figure 6.1; table 6.1).

The Farm Book lists also indicate that the first generation of slaves to live at Poplar Forest occupied a social landscape populated by individuals brought together from the Forest, Elk Hill, Elk Island, Indian Camp, Guinea, Bridge Quarter,[8] and Judith's Creek plantations, all of which John Wayles had owned (map 6.1). These properties were located in Charles City County, east of the

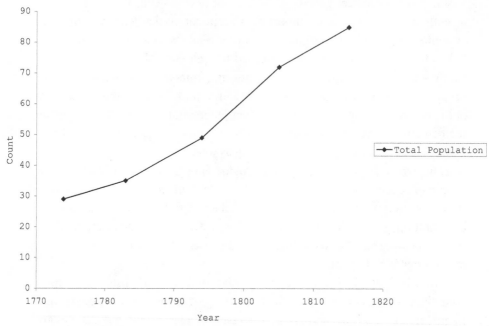

Enslaved Population

Figure 6.1. Population growth at Poplar Forest (including Wingos and the Old Plantation), 1774–1819. From Jefferson in Betts 1987, 16, 24, 30, 57, 60, 129, 166–167.

Table 6.1. Enslaved population at Poplar Forest, 1774–1819 (available years)

| Year | Total |
|------|-------|
| 1774 | 28 |
| 1783 | 35 |
| 1792 | 56 |
| 1794 | 49 |
| 1796 | 46 |
| 1798/1799 | 60 |
| 1805 | 72 |
| 1810 | 85 |
| 1812 | 75 |
| 1815 | 85 |
| 1819 | 94 |

*Source*: Jefferson in Betts 1987, 16, 24, 30, 57, 60, 129, 166–167; Bowling Clarke to Thomas Jefferson Randolph, ca. 1792, Thomas Jefferson Papers, Albert and Shirley Small Special Collections Library, University of Virginia, Charlottesville, Virginia ; Christie's New York 2004; Oberg 2001, 97–98; Slave Lists, Jefferson Papers, Rosenbach Museum and Library.

*Note*: In documents for this period, Poplar Forest refers to the entire property; statistics from Poplar Forest, Wingos, and Bear Creek have been combined as appropriate.

fall line, and in the Virginia piedmont counties of Goochland, Cumberland, Amelia, Amherst, and Bedford (Bear and Stanton 1997, 329–330). Despite the geographical diversity of Wayles's landholdings, most enslaved people at Poplar Forest could trace their lineage to Bermuda Hundred in Chesterfield County, the home of Martha Jefferson's grandparents, Francis and Sarah Eppes and their descendants.[9] A significant number of individuals were also descendants of men and women enslaved by Peter and Jane Jefferson (Jefferson's parents) at their Shadwell plantation in Albemarle County (Kern 2010).[10] By 1819, nearly everyone living at Poplar Forest was either biologically related to or married to women with kin ties that had been formed decades earlier (table 6.2). To avoid

Table 6.2. Enslaved women and their descendants living at Poplar Forest in 1819

| Name and Birth and Death Dates | Owners (in chronological order) | Grand-children | Great-grand-children | Great-great-grandchildren | Total |
|---|---|---|---|---|---|
| Aggy (b. before 1733, d. 1798)[a] | Francis Eppes<br>John Wayles<br>Thomas Jefferson | 5 | | 1 | 6 |
| Bess (b. 1747, d. after 1822[b] | John Wayles<br>Thomas Jefferson | 6 | 9 | 1 | 16 |
| Cate Hubbard (b. 1747, d. after 1822)[b] | Peter Jefferson<br>Thomas Jefferson | 18 | 5 | | 23 |
| Dinah (b. before 1733, sold 1785)[c] | Francis Eppes<br>John Wayles<br>Thomas Jefferson<br>Tandy Rice | 7 | 1 | 3 | 11 |
| Island Betty (b. 1749, d. after 1822)[b] | John Wayles<br>Thomas Jefferson | 15 | 1 | | 16 |
| Judy (b. ca. 1728, d. 1811)[b] | Francis Eppes<br>John Wayles<br>Thomas Jefferson | 7 | 15 | 1 | 23 |
| Molly (b. ca. 1749, d. 1811)[d] | Peter Jefferson?<br>Thomas Jefferson | 5 | 1 | | 6 |

a. Jefferson in Betts 1987, 9, 18; Bear and Stanton 1997, 391n64.
b. Jefferson in Betts 1987, 131.
c. "Negroes alienated from 1784 to 1794, inclusive," page 25 of Thomas Jefferson's Farm Book, in Sol Feinstone Collection of the American Revolution, David Library of the American Revolution, Washington Crossing, Pennsylvania.
d. Jefferson in Betts 1987, 130.

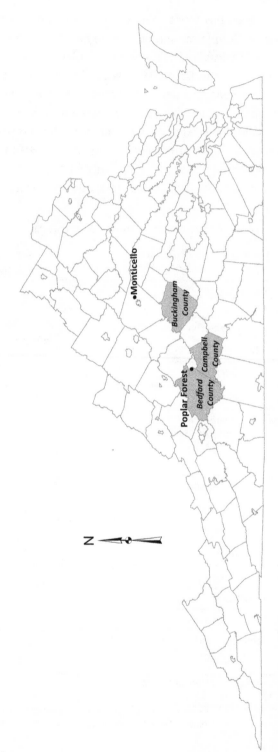

Map 6.2. Location of neighboring counties where relatives of Poplar Forest slaves lived.

marrying siblings or first cousins, Poplar Forest women often participated in abroad marriages. It is difficult to know where their husbands lived.

Documents confirm that as a result of Jefferson's slave sales, the transfer of slaves to his daughters when they married, and his movement of individuals between plantations, enslaved people at Poplar Forest had children, siblings, parents, grandparents, aunts, and uncles living ninety miles away at Monticello. Many also had relatives who lived in Bedford, Buckingham, and Campbell Counties (map 6.2).[11] In addition, the enslaved women Jefferson transferred to Poplar Forest in the 1770s and 1780s after Wayles's death likely left spouses, children, or other kin behind on plantations in the counties where they had previously lived.

## The Archaeology of Slave Spaces

Archaeologists have explored two slave housing areas, the North Hill and the Quarter Site, that formed part of the Old Plantation quarter farm complex, and research is currently under way at the Wingos quarter farm. Each site was occupied for thirty years or less, and when work at Wingos is complete, it will be possible to study the physical remains of discrete slave domestic spaces spanning a fifty-year period from the 1770s through the early 1810s.

The residents at Wingos (occupied 1770s–1790s) and the North Hill (occupied ca. 1770s–1810) lived at a satellite plantation with a nonresident owner. Enslaved people lived at the Quarter Site both before and during the time when Jefferson's retirement retreat was being built. The site was torn down in the winter of 1812–1813, during Jefferson's redesign of the plantation landscape after he retired (Heath 1999b). The Tomahawk quarter farm complex that provided housing for slaves during Jefferson's retirement has not yet been found.

## Housing

Jefferson intended slave houses on his plantations to be only temporary features of the landscape. Put into practice, this intention resulted in ephemeral structures that were vulnerable to fire and rot and that enslaved carpenters put together quickly. In his Farm Book, Jefferson recorded that at Monticello it took Davy, Lewis, and Abraham six days to build Bagwell's house, "getting the stuff & putting it together" (Jefferson in Betts 1987, 67). With the exception of temporary living spaces for enslaved people incorporated into Jefferson's dependency wing and in the basement of his octagonal house, accommodations at Poplar Forest were no better (Heath 1999b; Kelso, Patten, and Strutt 1991). Jefferson's instructions to overseer Jeremiah Goodman indicate that significant repairs to

Poplar Forest slave housing were necessary on an annual basis. By the 1810s, the prevalence of abroad marriages meant that Goodman was coordinating maintenance activities for the dwellings of women who were household heads (Betts 1944, 466–467, 493).

While several references exist to houses for enslaved men and women, none explicitly detail the materials or methods used for construction at Poplar Forest. Other structures on the property, however, are described as being built of logs, including a "log house"—likely a circa 1770 tobacco house or barn—and an existing log dwelling that Jefferson contemplated modifying for a prospective overseer's use.[12] If the structure Jefferson anticipated renovating was an existing house for slaves, it was a single-story lofted building that did not include plaster, glazed windows, or a masonry chimney.

Late eighteenth-century accounts of slave housing at Mulberry Row at Monticello confirm the use of log construction there as well.[13] Archaeologists found a single sill log of southern yellow pine at a house known as Building s and numerous fragments of well-preserved daub chinking associated with a duplex structure known as the "Negro Quarter" (Sanford in Kelso et al. 1985, 26, 37–41; Sanford 1995, 180). Daub is associated with other Mulberry Row houses and with recently discovered late eighteenth-century houses for field hands located along the eastern slope of Monticello Mountain (Bon-Harper 2006).

The remains of five Poplar Forest slave houses have been excavated to date: one each at Wingos and the North Hill and three at the Quarter Site (table 6.3). Few architectural features have been located. However, many nails and fragments of daub recovered from plow zone and from subfloor pits indicate that carpenters assembled each of these buildings using logs, sided some of them with clapboards, and roofed them with wooden shingles or slabs. Chimneys constructed fully or partially of wood and daubed with clay provided each dwelling with heat.

Archaeologists interpret the presence of subfloor pits as evidence that enslaved people altered living spaces to meet their needs (Heath 2010b, 164–168; Neiman 2008; Samford 2007). On piedmont sites where log architecture predominated and agricultural plowing usually followed the razing of houses, these features are often the only surviving in situ evidence of individual structures.

How slaves used subfloor pits varied over time and between groups, but archaeologists agree that many pits served as storage places for root crops and personal belongings (Fesler 2004b; Franklin 1997; Kelso 1984, 1986; Samford 1996, 2007; Singleton 1991, 1995; Sprinkle 1991; Young 1997). The rate of occurrence of subfloor pits has been attributed to changing social relationships within the households, while their size, morphology, incorporation of secondary materials, and placement within houses varied according to the particular needs of quarter residents (Fesler 2004b; Neiman 2008; Samford 2007). A few subfloor pits that have been found in slave cabins in Virginia and North Carolina contained sacred objects or symbolic arrangements of objects. Patricia Samford argues that these pits were created by imported Igbo slaves or their descendants to serve as shrines (Samford 2007).

## Archaeological Evidence of Slave Housing at Poplar Forest

The excavations at Wingos have located a single structure sited atop a hill that sloped down to two natural springs. Archaeologists excavated two subfloor pits in an east-west alignment. They were separated by four feet. Together, they indicate that the house that contained them measured at least 10.5 feet by 18 feet and enclosed a minimum of 180 square feet of living space (table 6.3).

The western pit was roughly circular in plan, measuring 6 by 6.5 feet. Slaves had to cut through soft greenstone bedrock to create the pit, an indication that this pit was not excavated to collect the clay they used to chink the cabin. Due to later disturbances to the site, the feature's original depth is not known. However, archaeologists found that the pit reached a depth of approximately 1.7 feet below the modern ground surface. The bottom of the feature was covered by soil mixed with ash that was likely deposited while the house was occupied. Secondary fill included a thick deposit of daub. Many of the larger fragments of daub preserved lath and stick impressions on their surfaces and straw, stick, and plant impressions on their interiors. Intermixed with the daub were burned

Table 6.3. House sizes and subfloor pit frequencies, Poplar Forest

| Structure | Occupation Span | Size | Square Feet | Subfloor Pits |
|---|---|---|---|---|
| North Hill, Structure 1 | Late 1760s/early 1770s–1780s | Unknown | Unknown | 1 |
| Wingos, Structure 1 | 1770s–1780 | 10.5′ × 18′ (minimum) | 189 sq. ft. (minimum) | 2 |
| Quarter Site, Structure 1, Housing unit 1 | 1790–1813 | 12.5′ × 15′ | 187.5 sq. ft. | 1 |
| Quarter Site, Structure 1, Housing unit 2 | 1790–1813 | 12.5′ × 15′ | 187.5 sq. ft. | 2 |
| Quarter Site, Structure 2 | 1790–1813 | 13′ × 13′ | 169 sq. ft. | 0 |
| Quarter Site, Structure 3 | 1790–1813 | 18.5′ × 18.5′ or two rooms at 9.25′ × 18.5′ each | 342 sq. ft. or 2 rooms at 171 sq. ft. each | 0 |

wrought nails and quantities of charred wood. A fill layer made up almost entirely of flat stones of local origin sealed the daub deposit. Twenty-five percent of the stones measured between 1 foot and 1.3 feet in length; the average length was 0.65 feet (8 inches). Household members may have built a dry-laid hearth or a base for the chimney to improve its efficiency and its ability to transfer heat inside the building. The chimney apparently burned and collapsed or was pushed into the pit when the structure was razed sometime after 1773, the year that documents suggest the site was first settled. Creamware from the pit provides a *terminus post quem* (*tpq*) date of 1762 for the fill of the feature (Miller et al. 2000, 12; Noël Hume 1980, 126–128). The absence of pearlware from the fill of the pit—and indeed from any context yet excavated at the site—suggests that this area of the site was abandoned before the 1780s.

The eastern subfloor pit was oval in shape, measuring 6 by 4.4 feet. The walls were relatively vertical with evidence of intermittent slumping and were cut 1.5 ft into bedrock. Compared to its western neighbor, this pit contained a much lower density of architectural material and no large stones or concentrated daub. Instead, layers of fill with few artifacts (mostly animal bone, eggshell, and wrought nails) alternated with layers of dense ash and charcoal. Artifacts were more frequent in the northern half of the feature than in the southern half but were few in number overall. The pit has a *tpq* of 1720 based on the presence of white salt-glazed stoneware in the fill (Noël Hume 1980, 114). A white metal button also found in the pit that is likely dated after 1760 brings the fill date more in line with the historical occupation dates of 1773 to the 1790s. The uneven distribution of artifact types between the two subfloor pits indicates that household members filled the eastern pit during the occupation of the dwelling, while the western pit remained open until the building was torn down.

Artifacts were scattered down slope (south) of the house, and work to date suggests a much lower density in the level ground north of the building. The building footprint seems to represent the northernmost extent of historic occupation of this portion of the site. A slight depression running northeast to southwest across the field directly north of the house may be the trace of a road that created a boundary for the site's development. Whether or not this was the case, artifact densities and differences in soil chemistry indicate segregated uses of space around the dwelling (Heath, Breen, and Ptacek 2011; Wilkins 2011).

At the North Hill, archaeologists excavated several features and collected artifacts and soil samples from plow-zone deposits associated with two phases of occupation. The first, dating from the late 1760s or early 1770s and extending until about 1800, represents the earliest period of occupation at the Old Plantation and includes a subfloor pit 4.7 feet square. Within the fill of the subfloor pit, daub, wrought nails, and a small quantity of brick were concentrated in the upper layers and are associated with the destruction of the building. A *tpq* of 1775 is based on the presence of light-colored creamware in the deepest stratum of the feature (Miller et al. 2000, 12). No other architectural features survived to indicate the size or orientation of the dwelling that contained the pit. Other phase-one deposits include the bottom fill layers of a deep erosion gully located down slope from the structure and a shallow exterior pit located in the adjacent yard. The second occupation phase, which dates as late as 1810, consists of yard scatter, upper layers of gully fill, and a narrow fence containing molds from a wattle fence. No features associated with a dwelling have been located for this phase.

Artifact concentrations at the site indicate a fairly distinct boundary that trends southwest to northeast approximately fifteen feet north of the house. No evidence of a fence line or other barrier was found in this area, but artifact frequencies dropped off precipitously here. No such clean spaces were located to the east, west, or south of the house. Artifact densities peaked along the southeast edge of the excavations.

The three Quarter Site structures represent a later generation of housing at the Old Plantation (map 6.3). They are located on a slope approximately 160 feet south of the North Hill site. Structure 1 measured 15 by 25 feet. It was elevated above the surface by haphazardly placed support posts that appear to represent an effort to raise log sills off the ground to prevent rot. The combination of the slope of the terrain and the presence of these postholes indicates that the structure had a wooden floor. Irregularly spaced postholes within the building site point to the presence of a central dividing wall that created a duplex with two 12.5 by 15 foot rooms that served as separate housing units and provided each household with 187.5 square feet of living space (map 6.3, table 6.3).

Jefferson's overseer Jeremiah Goodman noted the presence of such a house at Tomahawk in 1814, when he suggested to Jefferson that a newly married couple should be housed in "one end of Dick's house" and that a new house should be built for Aggy, who lived with Dick at this time. Both the bride and Aggy were Dick's adult daughters. It is significant that the bride was Dick's daughter and Aggy was her sister; this suggests a practice of housing extended families in side-by-side units.[14] The letter also indicates Jefferson's practice of providing new families with housing units separate from their parents.

The western room of Structure 1 contained a single subfloor pit. Within its fill were small amounts of architectural material, including daub, wrought nails and hand-headed cut nails, and a few grams of window glass. Polychrome painted pearlware provided a *tpq* of 1795 (Miller 1991, 8). Two subfloor pits, one of which cut into the other, sat in the middle of the eastern room. While there

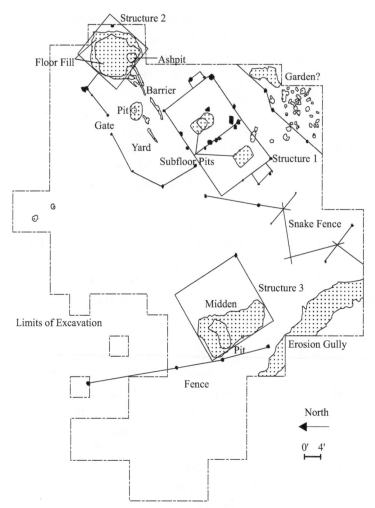

Map 6.3. Plan of house locations and yard features at the Poplar Forest Quarter Site.

were few artifacts in either pit, each contained small numbers of wrought nails and only tiny amounts of brick or daub and window glass. The earlier of the two pits had a *tpq* of 1790 based on the presence of a cut nail with a wrought head, while the later pit's *tpq* of 1795 was assigned because of the presence of polychrome painted pearlware (Miller 1991, 8; Nelson 1968, 6; Wells 1998, 323).

In addition to the duplex, archaeologists found evidence of two sets of features that likely were associated with other structures. Structure 2, located thirteen feet northeast of the duplex, was square in plan. When excavated, it consisted of a shallow depression with inward-sloping walls. A separate ash-filled pit was located within its limits. While this evidence is difficult to interpret, the larger feature's square shape and size (13 feet) and the location of the smaller pit within it make it likely that these features were related to a building. The *tpq* for its fill is 1800 based on the presence of even-scalloped blue shell-edged pearlware (Miller et al. 2000, 12). If this feature does represent a house, it provided 169 square feet of living space. It shared yard space with the duplex.

Structure 3 was located fourteen feet northwest of the duplex. Part of its footprint lay within a portion of the site that had never been plowed. Immediately beneath the topsoil, excavators uncovered a thick deposit of organic, charcoal- and artifact-rich sediment. This deposit appears to be the remains of trash and organic material that accumulated under the raised floor of a house that stood above it, although the eastern and northern portion of the deposit have been lost to plowing that was done after the structure was abandoned. The *tpq* for the fill is 1807 based on the presence of stippled blue transfer-printed pearlware (Coysh and Henrywood 1982, 9). A structural posthole marked its eastern corner. The building, which was 18.5 feet square and appears to have rested on stone piers and a single wood post, had a wood floor (Heath 1999b, 40). If Structure 3 was internally divided into two living spaces, each would have consisted of 171 square feet, a size between the floor space available in Structure 2 and the floor space of the duplex. If the structure was not divided, its 342 square feet provided nearly twice as much space to occupants as each half of the duplex or Structure 2 (table 6.3).

Evidence of a segmented landscape included a fence line that connected Structures 1 and 2 and enclosed a shared yard. This space embodies a cooperative relationship between three households (two in Structure 1 and one in Structure 2) that may have been kin-based, given the extent of interrelatedness among Poplar Forest residents by the time the site was occupied. Residents not only shared a yard but apparently also shared a midden (trash pile) just outside the yard. Although the midden was disturbed by later plowing, its location can be inferred by high artifact densities and changes in soil chemistry along the outer northern line of the fence enclosing the yard.

Postholes, evidence of planting activity, and low artifact densities immediately south of Structure 1 mark the probable location of a garden. Its size is unknown, since some of the features of this site extended beyond the modern Poplar Forest property line, and neighboring landowners did not grant permission for further excavations. Pollen and macrobotanical evidence from feature fill at the site indicates that enslaved residents harvested a variety of domestic and wild plants from the surrounding landscape, some of which may have been grown on this site (Heath and Bennett 2000; Heath 2008b; Raymer 2003). Household-level production of vegetables, fruits, poultry, and eggs allowed residents to supplement plantation rations and brought some variety to monotonous diets. Slaves might have grown vegetables here for barter or sale, as they did at Monticello. Documentary evidence indicates that Poplar Forest slaves sold poultry and eggs that they raised in their quarters to the Jefferson family (Heath 2004). By producing surplus goods, enslaved people created important opportunities to engage with the growing consumer economy of the late eighteenth and early nineteenth centuries (Heath 1997a, 2004; Martin 2008, 174–181; Penningroth 2003).

Structure 3 was not connected to the other two houses or to the garden. It was situated down slope from Structure 1 and was separated from that building by a fence. This landscape evidence indicates that the residents of this structure did not form a cooperative bond with their neighbors, or at least not one that was expressed and maintained by shared domestic space.

Beyond size, over which households had little control, the evidence for variability in construction materials (which is limited) indicates that enslaved people used different strategies to improve their dwellings. For example, small numbers of bricks scattered in plow zone at the Quarter Site and a deposit of stone associated with the burned remains of a chimney at the Wingos site are indications that residents may have used leftover or available materials to create masonry hearths or chimney bases. The fact that only three small fragments of flat glass have been found to date at the Wingos quarter suggests that the house found at that site did not have glazed windows. While window glass was found at the North Hill, it appeared only in plow zone and second-phase deposits. Its absence from the fill of the subfloor pit casts doubt on whether earlier occupants of the site used it. However, the ubiquity of window glass in plow zone and feature fill associated with all three structures at the Quarter Site provides evidence of improvements to housing there (DAACS 2004).

These small clues attest to the efforts of household members to improve the basic structures that Jefferson had provided. While a dry-laid masonry hearth was attainable for most households whose members had the time to collect the materials and possessed the skills to construct it, glazed windows were another matter. For his own houses, Jefferson ordered imported German and English glass from merchants in Boston and Philadelphia. Flat glass was expensive to purchase and transport and often suffered significant breakage in transit. Beyond the expense involved, Jefferson found delivery to be slow and inefficient; it took several months for glass to be delivered to the property (McDonald 2000, 182–183).

Given the cost and effort involved to glaze his own windows, it is unlikely that Jefferson supplied window glass to residents of the Quarter Site, whose houses were old and in poor repair by the time that he was engaged in building his retreat. It is probable that residents of that site supplied themselves with glass. This surely involved substantial effort to locate sources, produce goods or offer labor for sale or exchange, and transport materials to Poplar Forest. The presence of window glass in association with all three Quarter Site structures indicates that at least by the early nineteenth century, members of enslaved households had the capacity to devote considerable resources to improving their dwellings and felt that such improvements were important.

## Discussion and Conclusions

How do demographic and archaeological data from Poplar Forest help us assess Fesler's and Neiman's models? Table 6.3 summarizes current archaeological findings relating to house dimensions, square footage, and the frequency of subfloor pits at Poplar Forest. The sample is too small to challenge Neiman's argument that the size of slave houses trended downward over time, although variability within the Quarter Site does not indicate unidirectional change.

The Poplar Forest data support Fesler's and Neiman's arguments that the number of subfloor pits used by residents of slave households in the late eighteenth century was low, a phenomenon that may relate to communal strategies of sharing resources within households that made multiple pits unnecessary (Fesler 2004b, 333–338; Hatch 2009, 41–44). However, at Poplar Forest, the number of pits did not change that much from the 1770s through the 1810s. The North Hill house (likely the earliest structure) and the Quarter Site duplex each have one pit per living unit, although thirty or more years separated the time that these two dwellings were occupied. The Wingos quarter, which was occupied during a period that overlapped with the occupation of the North Hill site, is the only site researched to date that had two pits in a single living space.[15] Neiman's argument that pits had disappeared by 1800 and that their disappearance correlates with the introduction of wheat agriculture does not hold up at Poplar Forest.

To better understand house sizes and the number of subfloor pits within houses over time at Poplar Forest, it is helpful to review historical evidence of family structure and likely household composition at that plantation. The slave lists demonstrate that the overwhelming majority of enslaved people at Poplar Forest lived with close family members by 1783 and that many did so as soon as they arrived at the property in the late 1760s and 1770s. Barracks-style housing sheltered some unrelated people during this earliest period, but kin groups occupied single and multiple household units as early as 1774. The documentary evidence suggests that Jefferson accommodated slaves' desires for kin-based living arrangements from his earliest period of ownership. This practice supports Fesler's argument that slave owners recognized the importance of family formation and rewarded it by accommodating families in kin-based houses even at a time when tobacco cultivation dominated the working lives of slaves.

Neiman argues that the onset of single-family dwellings for slave laborers was linked to changes in the agricultural base of plantation production. The evidence at Poplar Forest does not support this thesis. Jefferson housed families in single-family dwellings ten to twenty years before he introduced wheat as a commercial crop at Poplar Forest, where the size and number of housing units seem to be largely tied to changes in family composition. New households were formed as children matured and started families of their own, and the formation of new households was not linked to changes in agricultural practices.

A brief detour to examine the Monticello community supports this challenge to Neiman's model. A comparison of the 1783 slave roll, taken before the transition to wheat agriculture at Monticello, and the 1794 roll, taken just after the change, is particularly helpful in understanding community dynamics during this period. In 1783, Jefferson recorded that twenty-seven kin groups lived at Monticello, of which five constituted members of the extended Hemings family (Jefferson in Betts 1987, 24). Another eight men on the list appear to be unrelated; three or four had recently come to Monticello from Bedford. Jefferson's 1794 list (Jefferson in Betts 1987, 30) is not organized by kin groups, necessitating some work to establish family relationships. The transfer of three large families to Poplar Forest fragmented the Monticello community, and the sale or transfer of twenty-eight additional individuals from 1785 to 1794 divided or completely erased households.[16] It is difficult to argue that Jefferson came to recognize the need to encourage cooperation within his labor force through family-based housing as a result of changes in the agricultural base of his plantation. During the first year he produced wheat at Monticello, he sold individuals and transferred others to other properties he owned. These actions, far from supporting family life, split families apart.

At Monticello, as at Poplar Forest, as individuals who were children or teenagers in the 1780s matured, they formed families of their own. For example, by 1787, Critta Hemings had a child. In that year, Bagwell married Minerva and they had their first child. In 1790, Thamar and Phill had a daughter. In 1793, Isaac and Iris had their first son. In most cases, these changes in life stage resulted in the formation of a new household that occupied its own housing unit. However, Thamar and Phil, and Iris and Isaac, worked in different places on Jefferson's Albemarle County holdings; the men labored on the Monticello mountaintop and the women (and their children) lived and worked on the outlying quarter farms of Lego and Shadwell.

This separation of families is perhaps what is most striking about the 1794 list (Jefferson in Betts 1987, 30). Smiths, carpenters, spinners, and nailers, all skilled workers, constituted the majority of the population at Monticello mountain. Some of these men and women could return home to their families at night; for others, family members lived on separate quarter farms (Shadwell, Lego, and Tufton) owned by Jefferson that were adjacent to Monticello but not a short walk away. At Monticello, the transition to wheat production may have created family divisions instead of leading to kin groups living under one roof. It may have been the case that artisans and specialized servants (who were mostly men) were housed at Monticello and agricultural workers (many of whom were women) and their children lived at separate quarter farms.

Understanding the relationship between house size, subfloor pit frequency, agricultural continuity or change, and other material aspects of the lives of slaves in the late eighteenth and early nineteenth centuries in the piedmont region will necessitate further research and a larger database. However, this analysis must be grounded in an understanding of the demography and household composition of plantation communities. Understanding trends in age groups and sex ratios within slave communities and how and to what degree such communities were interrelated, both within and among plantations, will form a strong basis for interpreting observed differences in material culture.

## Notes

1. "Negroes alienated from 1784 to 1794, inclusive," page 25 of Thomas Jefferson's Farm Book, Thomas Jefferson Papers, Sol Feinstone Collection of the American Revolution, David Library of the American Revolution, Washington Crossing, Pennsylvania; Jefferson in Betts 1987, 29.

2. Boyd (1961, 190); Heath (2008b, 126); Nicholas Lewis Account Book, November 1790, Albert and Shirley Small Special Collections Library, University of Virginia, Charlottesville, Virginia (hereafter Lewis Account Book); Nichols (1984a, 39).

3. Mary Lewis to Thomas Jefferson, April 14, 1790, Thomas Jefferson Papers, Albert and Shirley Small Special Collections Library, University of Virginia.

4. Betts (1944, 152); Lewis Account Book, 1790.

5. In seventeenth- and eighteenth-century Virginia, a head tax was levied each year at three levels: colony, county, and parish. Each household head was required to provide a list of free white males, African American slaves, and Native American slaves over the age of 16 in his household. The tax levied against the household head was based on the number of people (or "tithables") on this list.

6. Jeremiah Goodman to Thomas Jefferson, December 30, 1814 and Thomas Jefferson to Jeremiah Goodman, January 6, 1815, Thomas Jefferson Papers, Albert and Shirley Small Special Collections Library, University of Virginia, Charlottesville, Virginia; Thomas Jefferson to Joel Yancey, November 19, 1818, Coolidge Collection of Thomas Jefferson Manuscripts, Massachusetts Historical Society, Boston, Massachusetts.

7. Boyd (1961, 189–191); "Negroes alienated from 1784 to 1794, inclusive."

8. The location of Bridge Quarter is presently unknown.

9. Heath (2006); Henrico County Deeds and Wills 1725–1737, Number 1, Part 2, 459, 612, and Henrico County Deed Book, ca. 1744–1748, 132, both Library of Virginia, Rich-

mond, Virginia. Francis Eppes was Martha Jefferson's maternal grandfather. He entailed land and gave slaves to Martha Jefferson's mother (also named Martha), who married John Wayles in 1746. When Martha Wayles died in 1748, the Eppes property she had inherited fell under the management of John Wayles, Martha Jefferson's father.

10. Shadwell later became a quarter farm in Thomas Jefferson's Albemarle County holdings. It is located at the base of Monticello Mountain, on the east side of the Rivanna River.

11. "Negroes alienated from 1784 to 1794, inclusive."

12. Thomas Jefferson to Jeremiah Goodman, October 10, 1812, Thomas Jefferson Papers, 1775–1825, American Philosophical Society, Philadelphia, Pennsylvania; Thomas Jefferson to William P. Newby, January 20, 1815, Thomas Jefferson Papers, Library of Congress, Washington, D.C.

13. Betts (1987, 27–28); Kimball (1968, 136); Thomas Jefferson to Clarkson, September 23, 1792, Thomas Jefferson Papers, Albert and Shirley Small Special Collections Library, University of Virginia, Charlottesville, Virginia (hereafter Jefferson Papers, University of Virginia); Thomas Jefferson to Thomas Mann Randolph, May 19, 1793, Thomas Jefferson Papers, Library of Congress, Washington, D.C.

14. Jeremiah Goodman to Thomas Jefferson, December 30, 1814, Jefferson Papers, University of Virginia.

15. In fact, as Lee discusses elsewhere in this volume, a late antebellum log house and a brick duplex that together span the late antebellum and postbellum periods each contain a single subfloor pit, suggesting that the practice of using a single subfloor pit continued throughout the nineteenth century at Poplar Forest (Table 6.3) (Heath et al. 2004; Kelso, Patten, and Strutt 1991, 33–35; Lee this volume).

16. "Negroes alienated from 1784 to 1794, inclusive."

# 7

## Carved in Stone

Stone Smoking Pipes at Historic Sites in Central Virginia

LORI LEE

Smoking pipe fragments are common finds on archaeological sites dating from the seventeenth through the nineteenth centuries. In addition to being fragile and easily broken, historic clay pipes were relatively cheap and replaceable, making them ubiquitous in the archaeological record. The assemblage from Poplar Forest plantation is not unique because of the variety or number of clay pipes found there, but rather because of the historic stone pipes found on the property. Enslaved African Americans likely made the stone pipes at Poplar Forest in the late eighteenth and early nineteenth centuries. African Americans also likely made, and they certainly used, stone pipes at other historic sites in central Virginia dating from the same time period. This essay describes these pipes and the contexts they came from with the goal of documenting them for future comparative research.

The Poplar Forest Quarter Site was the location of a slave quarter that was occupied from circa 1790 to 1812 (Heath 1999b; Heath this volume). Prior to the completion of Jefferson's retreat home in 1809, this location was the core of the plantation. By the 1790s, enslaved individuals comprising seven families lived and worked at Poplar Forest (Heath 1999b, 8, 13). Archaeologists have recovered the remains of three houses where some of these people lived at the Quarter Site (Heath 1999b; see map 6.2). No documentary evidence that identifies the particular inhabitants of each cabin has been discovered. Archaeological evidence provides some clues regarding the gender, social relations, and skill sets of some of these men and women. Particularly compelling is the archaeological signature of a pipe maker, or pipe makers, found in the topsoil, the plow zone, the middens, and within the fill of a subfloor pit at the Quarter Site.

Table 7.1 Description of stone pipes recovered at historic sites in central Virginia

| Site | Subsite | Context | Deposit Type | Material | Pipe Type | Decoration | Completeness |
|------|---------|---------|--------------|----------|-----------|------------|--------------|
| Poplar Forest | Quarter Site | 1123A/2 | Plow zone | Schist | Type 1 | no | Bowl form and stem form |
| Poplar Forest | Wing of Offices | 285C | Debris layer of robbed brick floor | Schist | Type 1 | no | Bowl |
| Poplar Forest | Quarter Site | 829C | Subfloor pit inside Structure 1 | Schist | Type 1 | no | Bowl |
| Poplar Forest | Quarter Site | 831 | Topsoil | Schist | | no | Bowl |
| Poplar Forest | Quarter Site | 1003D | Subfloor pit inside Structure 1 | Schist | | no | Stem |
| Poplar Forest | Quarter Site | 1006A/3 | Plow zone | Schist | Type 1 | no | Stem, bowl |
| Poplar Forest | Quarter Site | 1009A/2 | Plow zone | Schist | | no | Bowl |
| Poplar Forest | Quarter Site | 1103A/1 | Accumulation above paving | Schist | | no | Bowl |
| Poplar Forest | Quarter Site | 1103A/3 | Accumulation above paving | Schist | | no | Bowl |
| Poplar Forest | Quarter Site | 1124C/2 | Transition from paving to plow zone | Schist | Type 1 | no | Stem, bowl |
| Poplar Forest | Quarter Site | 1128A/3 | Plow zone | Schist | | no | Bowl |
| Poplar Forest | Quarter Site | 1129A/3 | Plow zone | Schist | | no | Bowl |
| Poplar Forest | Quarter Site | 1180A/3 | Wash | Schist | | no | Bowl |
| Poplar Forest | Quarter Site | 1184A/3 | Wash/Bottom of topsoil | Schist | | no | Bowl |
| Poplar Forest | Quarter Site | 1184A/3 | Wash/Bottom of topsoil | Schist | | no | Bowl |
| Poplar Forest | Quarter Site | 1184A/3 | Wash/Bottom of topsoil | Schist | | no | Stem, bowl |
| Poplar Forest | Quarter Site | 1185A/4 | Plow zone | Schist | | yes | Bowl |
| Poplar Forest | Quarter Site | 1186A/3 | Plow zone | Schist | | no | Bowl |
| Poplar Forest | Quarter Site | 1186A/4 | Plow zone | Schist | | no | Bowl |
| Poplar Forest | Quarter Site | 1187L | Plow scar | Schist | | yes | Bowl |
| Poplar Forest | Quarter Site | 1188A/2 | Plow zone | Schist | | no | Bowl |
| Poplar Forest | Quarter Site | 1188A/2 | Plow zone | Schist | | yes | Stem |
| Poplar Forest | Quarter Site | 1189A/2 | Plow zone | Schist | | no | Bowl |
| Poplar Forest | Quarter Site | 1207B/2 | Plow zone | Schist | | no | Bowl |
| Poplar Forest | Quarter Site | 1207H | Plow scar | Schist | | yes | Bowl |

| Site | Location | Context ID | Context | Stone | Type | | Form |
|---|---|---|---|---|---|---|---|
| Poplar Forest | Quarter Site | 1213A/1 | Plow zone | Schist | | no | Bowl |
| Poplar Forest | Quarter Site | 1250A/1 | Plow zone | Schist | | yes | Bowl |
| Poplar Forest | Quarter Site | 1254A/1 | Plow zone | Schist | | no | Stem |
| Poplar Forest | Quarter Site | 1255A/2 | Plow zone | Schist | | no | Bowl |
| Poplar Forest | Quarter Site | 1297A/2 | Plow zone | Schist | | yes | Bowl |
| Poplar Forest | Quarter Site | 1297A/3 | Plow zone | Schist | | yes | Bowl |
| Poplar Forest | Quarter Site | 1299A/3 | Plow zone | Schist | | no | Bowl |
| Poplar Forest | Quarter Site | 1299A/3 | Plow zone | Schist | | no | Bowl |
| Poplar Forest | Quarter Site | 1300 | Topsoil | Schist | | no | Bowl |
| Poplar Forest | Quarter Site | 1300A/1 | Midden associated with Structure 3 | Schist | | no | Stem |
| Poplar Forest | Quarter Site | 1375A/4 | Plow zone | Schist | Type 2 | yes | Bowl? |
| Poplar Forest | Quarter Site | 1375D/2 | Midden fill associated with Structure 3 | Schist | | no | Tube pipe |
| Poplar Forest | Quarter Site | 1385A/3 | Plow zone | Schist | | no | Bowl |
| Poplar Forest | Wing | Unidentified | Backfill | Schist | Type 1 | possibly | Bowl and stem |
| Poplar Forest | Garden | 1026 | Garden | Schist | | no | Stem |
| Poplar Forest | Ornamental Nursery | 2361A/4 | Plow zone | Schist | | no | Bowl |
| Point of Honor | Structure 1 | 118L9 | Pit fill | Schist | | yes | Bowl |
| Sweet Briar | Domestic Site | | Unidentified | Schist | | yes | Stem, bowl |
| Shadwell | Slave Quarter | | | Candler phyllite | | no | Blank |
| Monticello | Privy Tunnel | 1195E/4 | | Steatite | | yes | Bowl |
| Monticello | Stewart-Watkins House | 1349A | Destruction Layer | Steatite | | yes | Stem |
| Monticello | MRS 2 Mulberry Row | 223C | | Steatite | | no | Stem, bowl |
| Monticello | West Kitchen Yard | 464/465A | Upper plow zone | Steatite | | no | Rim, bowl |
| Monticello | West Kitchen Yard | 265B | Lower plow zone | Steatite | | yes | Stem |
| Monticello | Home Farm Quarter Site 6 | 014A | Plow zone | Steatite | | yes | Bowl |
| Monticello | Home Farm Quarter Site 8 | 396A | Brush pile fill | Unidentified stone | | no | Bowl form and stem form |
| Monticello | Buildings Mulberry Row | 831E/3 | Occupation/Destruction layer | Unidentified stone | | yes | Bowl |
| Free State | | | Plow zone | Steatite | | yes | Bowl |
| Canada | | | | Steatite | | yes | Stem, bowl |

## Material

All of the stone pipes at Poplar Forest were made of schist, a metamorphic rock common to central Virginia. It is found in the piedmont and in the Blue Ridge Mountains, and it is scattered in the fields and creek beds at Poplar Forest (Canel 1996, 4). The color of the stone pipes is not uniform. Some of the pipe fragments are dark green, some are gray, and others have a slight pink hue. The variation in color is due to the use of different types of schist with different mineral inclusions. Most of the Poplar Forest pipes and manufacturing by-products were made from local green chlorite schist, others were made from hematite schist, and the mineral components of a few have not yet been analyzed (ibid.). Color variability and the underlying divergent mineral composition suggests that the source stone may have come from different locations in the region, but this hypothesis has not yet been tested through sourcing studies.

In total, thirty-six fragments of schist pipes and seventeen fragments of modified schist have been recovered from several different contexts at the Quarter Site (Heath 1999b). Based on archaeological evidence, it is probable that the schist pipes found at Poplar Forest were made by one or more laborers who lived or stayed at the site in the late eighteenth and early nineteenth centuries.

## Manufacture

The exact method used to produce the stone pipes is unknown, but marks on the stone provide clues. In addition to pipes and pipe fragments, archaeologists recovered several worked pieces of schist that were the by-products of pipe manufacture. Eight fragments of stone wasters and nine blanks, or possible blanks, were found at the Quarter Site. Blanks represent the first phase of production, when stone is rough-hewn to the approximate shape of the final form. Wasters are unintentional by-products of the stone-carving process. Several wasters and blanks exhibit clear evidence of processing with a steel toothed implement such as a saw blade or file.

A squared, elbow-shaped, reed-stem pipe blank found at the Quarter Site provides evidence of the second phase of production (Heath 1999b, 56). The pipe blank broke when the pipe maker drilled a hole for the stem or bowl (figure 7.1). This evidence indicates that the sequence of pipe production was preparing a pipe blank, drilling a hole for the bowl, and then drilling the hole for the stem. A small metal tool, such as an awl or gimlet, was probably used to drill these holes. Finished pipe fragments bear evidence of carving with a sharp tool, perhaps with a folding knife, to hollow out the bowl and refine the exterior shape. Finished pipes were burnished to create a smooth surface.

Figure 7.1. Schist pipe blank from the Poplar Forest Quarter Site. Used by permission of Thomas Jefferson's Poplar Forest, Bedford County, Virginia. Drawing by Hannah Canel.

Incised decorations were carved on some pipes with a sharp tool, completing the production process.

## Typology

A minimum of six stone pipes is represented at the Quarter Site, based on the use of stem/bowl junctures and unique shape to determine the count. Among the three pipes that are complete enough to determine the form, there are two types. Type 1 is an elbow-shaped reed-stem pipe with a rounded bowl and a rounded stem. The bowl-to-stem angle is approximately ninety degrees (figure 7.2). Type 2 is a tapered tubular pipe with a hole drilled on top in the area just before the pipe begins to taper (ibid.). Two Type 1 smoking pipes and one Type 2 pipe were recovered at the Quarter Site. Other distinct types are present in the assemblage, but only nearly complete pipes were included in the typology because of the difficulty of determining whether or not separate bowls and stems came from the same or different pipes.

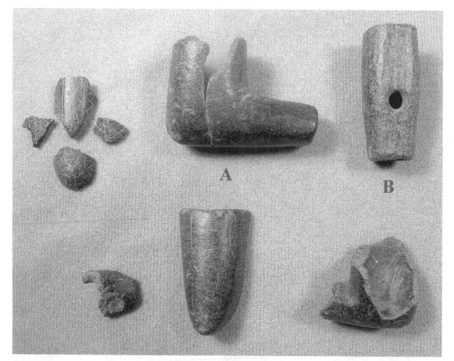

Figure 7.2. Six schist pipes from the Poplar Forest Quarter Site. A) Type 1 pipe; B) Type 2 pipe. Used by permission of Thomas Jefferson's Poplar Forest, Bedford County, Virginia.

### Decoration

Two schist pipes from Poplar Forest have incised decoration on the bowls. These two pipes differ in both style and execution. One pipe has simple, light incisions that form wide crosshatching and intersecting lines (figure 7.3). The second pipe bowl is carved into a polygon shape. Each vertical panel has rows of incised X's separated by thin bands created by two parallel incised lines (figure 7.4). The latter pipe may have had an octagonal stem or the bowl and stem may represent two different pipes. One pipe blank has a polygon bowl, although it is unclear if the final shape was intended to be a polygon or if this was part of the refining process. One additional Type 1 pipe has five notches cut into the body of the pipe (figure 7.5). It is unclear whether these marks were intentional.

### Context

The preponderance of worked stone, schist pipe blanks, and wasters was found in a trash midden under the cabin known as Structure 3, in an erosion layer that sealed that midden, and in a layer of plow zone immediately north, west, and east of that cabin (N = 13 of 20). The midden was formed while people were

Figure 7.3. Pipe-bowl fragment from the Poplar Forest Quarter Site with wide cross-hatching and intersecting lines. Image used by permission of Thomas Jefferson's Poplar Forest, Bedford County, Virginia. Drawing by the author.

Figure 7.4. Polygon bowl fragment from the Poplar Forest Quarter Site with incised X's and vertical bands. Image used by permission of Thomas Jefferson's Poplar Forest, Forest, Virginia. Drawing by the author.

living there (Heath 1999b, 40–41). Therefore it seems that the pipe maker lived in Structure 3 and produced pipes there. Several tools found in the midden beneath Structure 3 and in the area surrounding the cabin suggest that an artisan lived there. These tools include a brass hinge from a carpenter's ruler, a gimlet, a croze iron, a wedge, two files, a pocketknife, and possibly a hardy (ibid., 48). Although evidence of pipe production is centered on Structure 3, the remains of completed pipes are more widely dispersed at the Quarter Site, suggesting that stone pipe use was not restricted to the manufacturer.

The contexts of completed but subsequently broken stone pipe fragments found at the Quarter Site include topsoil, a plow-zone layer, middens at the edge of a fenced yard, and the fill of a subfloor pit. Stone pipe remains are particularly concentrated in the yard between Structure 1 and Structure 2 and in the plow zone across the fence line to the northwest of the yard (see map 6.2). Structure 1 was a duplex cabin measuring approximately fifteen by twenty-five feet that was connected by a fenced-in yard to Structure 2 (Heath 1999b, 35; this volume; see map 6.2). Structure 2 was a log cabin that measured about thirteen feet square (ibid., 39; this volume).

The most complete Type 1 pipe found at the Quarter Site was found in the subfloor pit inside the west half of the Structure 1 duplex cabin, although it was broken into two pieces. One completed stone pipe was found in association with Structure 3. This was the Type 2 tubular pipe that was recovered in the midden beneath the cabin. A nearly complete, small Type 1 pipe was found about fifteen feet west of Structure 3. Nine other stone pipe fragments were found in the ten by ten foot excavation units surrounding the cabin.

The pipe bowl with light crosshatching was recovered approximately ten feet northeast of Structure 3. Bowl fragments of the polygon bowl with rows of X's separated by incised, vertical, parallel bands were distributed outside the fence for the northwest yard between Structures 1 and 2, northwest of Structure 3 in the excavation unit that contained the pipe bowl with light crosshatching, and in the unit where the southwest corner of Structure 3 once stood. All of these pipe remains were recovered in a layer of plow zone except one fragment, which was recovered in a plow scar (map 7.1)

Although fence lines at the Quarter Site created a physical boundary that separated Structures 1 and 2 from Structure 3, the presence of pipes in Structure 1 and in the yard northwest of it suggests that a close relationship existed between the pipe maker and the inhabitants of Structure 1. This relationship may have been practical, based on trade, rather than familial, which could explain the social boundaries implied by the fence. Alternatively, the pipe maker may have moved into Structure 3 at the Poplar Forest Quarter after the fences were already established.

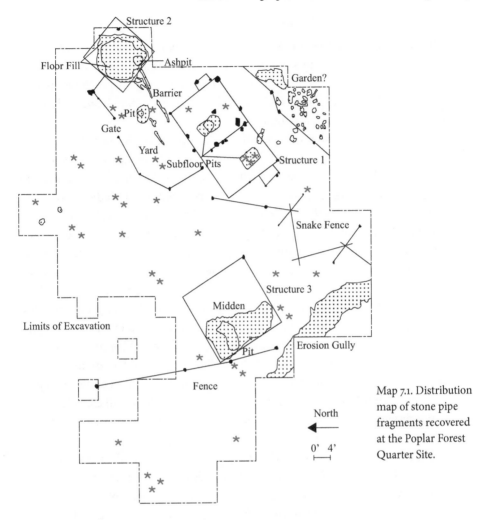

Map 7.1. Distribution map of stone pipe fragments recovered at the Poplar Forest Quarter Site.

Comparison of the dates of ceramics associated with each structure support the hypothesis that Structure 3 was built later than the other two cabins. Further, schist pipes are absent at two earlier slave-quarter sites excavated at Poplar Forest—Wingos and the North Hill site (Heath this volume; Gary and Heath this volume). The North Hill slave cabin was occupied during the 1770s and 1780s and was located approximately 175 feet north of the Quarter Site. The absence of schist pipes at Wingos and the North Hill slave quarter site suggests that the pipe maker moved to Poplar Forest, or learned how to manufacture pipes at some point, after these sites were abandoned. Since the Quarter Site was occupied immediately after the North Hill cabin was abandoned, the pipe maker likely arrived or learned how to manufacture stone pipes after the initial settlement of the Quarter Site.

Quarter Site Pipe Assemblage

Schist pipes were not the only kind of smoking pipes found at the Quarter Site. A minimum of three long-stemmed white clay pipes and two clay reed-stem elbow pipes were also recovered. The reed-stem elbow pipes include one anthropomorphic green-glazed white clay pipe with an Indian head design and one locally produced red clay pipe.

The minimum number of three white clay pipes is based on the number of bowl/shank junctures. Two white clay pipes were decorated with molded designs. These designs are consistent with decorations that manufacturers began using in the late eighteenth and early nineteenth centuries (Bradley 2000, 114).

Two white clay pipe-bowl fragments have impressed decoration or marks. One has wheel rouletting along the lip, next to the rim. This feature is more common on seventeenth-century pipes than on later pipes. One white clay bowl fragment bears a cartouche with an impressed "TD" maker's mark and a curvilinear scroll beneath the letters. Impressed initials on the back of the bowl are a hallmark of English manufacture. Unfortunately for identification purposes, the TD mark is ubiquitous; it is thought to have originated from a quality pipe manufacturer whose trademark was appropriated for profit (Bradley 2000, 112).

One partial, undecorated white ball clay-bowl fragment has an undecorated spur. Spurs became common pipe features in the eighteenth century (Bradley 2000, 114). Thus in form and decoration, most of the white ball clay pipes used by the enslaved at the Quarter Site were typical of the time period in which they were being used.

The number of clay pipes found at the Quarter Site is small. The presence of a pipe maker living at the Quarter Site provides the possibility that new stone pipes may have been produced to replace broken clay ones. Because both clay pipes and stone pipes have been recovered from the Quarter Site, it is possible that handcrafted stone pipes had a different significance to the pipe maker and pipe users or that they may have been used in a different way. Stone pipes, for example, may have been used to smoke something other than tobacco, such as hemp or wild plants. Chemical and forensic tests were conducted to test this hypothesis. Resin samples were sent to the Virginia State Police Forensic Lab to test for plant hairs or fibers, but none were detected (Canel 1996, 7). Chemical tests were conducted to search for evidence of nicotine or hemp by-products, but the results were inconclusive (ibid.).

Schist Pipes in Other Poplar Forest Contexts

Two additional schist pipes, a schist pipe stem, a schist pipe-bowl fragment, and a schist pipe blank were recovered within the ten-acre core of Poplar Forest plantation outside the Quarter Site. One complete pipe was recovered from backfill during excavations of Jefferson's east dependency wing. The second complete pipe was recovered in a debris layer within the robbed out brick floor of Jefferson's kitchen. Both of these are Type 1 pipes. The pipe stem was recovered in a disturbed layer in a historic garden. This stem is rounded. The round pipe bowl fragment and rectangular stone blank were recovered in a plow-zone layer of Jefferson's ornamental nursery.

The pipe recovered in the backfill has no exact provenience. The pipe recovered from the kitchen floor and the stem recovered from the historic garden both come from disturbed contexts. The *terminus ante quem* of the kitchen assemblage containing the pipe is somewhere between 1840 and 1845, when William Cobbs or Edward Hutter dismantled Jefferson's kitchen. The *terminus post quem* for deposition of this pipe (although not for production) is 1813, when workmen started digging to create a foundation for the kitchen.

The historic garden layer contains artifacts from the eighteenth through the early twentieth centuries. The pipe-bowl fragment recovered in Jefferson's ornamental plant nursery comes from a plow-zone context with a *terminus post quem* of 1889. The rectangular schist blank comes from a plow-zone layer with a *terminus post quem* of 1845. This area of the property continued to be used as living and working space long after Jefferson's death, which is why later artifacts are found in the plow zone there. Most of the artifacts recovered in association with the pipe fragments date from the era of Jefferson's ownership of the property.

The Quarter Site was abandoned around 1812 when Jefferson reorganized the plantation. At that time he established homes for some of his enslaved labor force closer to the main house, which was constructed during the Quarter Site occupation. Discovery of a stone pipe-bowl fragment and a pipe blank at Jefferson's ornamental nursery suggests that the pipe maker may have begun working or living at the nursery-stable-quarter complex when it was established. However, numerous crossmends between ceramics found at the dependency wing and ceramics found in the ornamental plant nursery suggest that the schist pipe fragments found at the nursery site may have been redeposited there, like the ceramics (Gary this volume).

The two nearly complete pipes, which were recovered during the excavation of Jefferson's Wing of Offices, indicate that the pipe maker may have worked on the construction of or within that structure or may have had a personal relationship with a person(s) working in the Wing (figure 7.5). Distribution of historic stone pipes at other African American sites in central Virginia may also be indicative of social relationships between pipe maker(s) and users, regional stone-working traditions, or both.

Figure 7.5. Schist pipes recovered from excavations of Jefferson's Wing of Offices. Used by permission of Thomas Jefferson's Poplar Forest, Bedford County, Virginia.

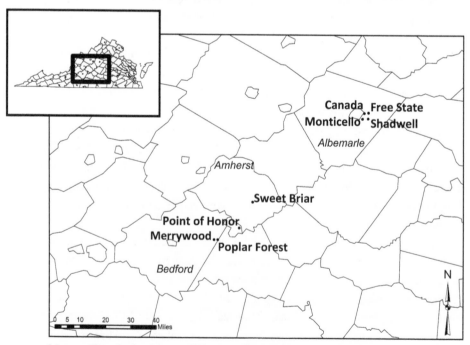

Map 7.2. Historic sites in central Virginia where archaeologists have recovered stone pipes and worked stone.

## Other Stone Pipes from Central Virginia

Carved schist pipes and modified schist fragments have been found at several other historic sites associated with African Americans in central Virginia (map 7.2). Stone pipes, pipe fragments, and worked stone have been found at Merrywood, Point of Honor, Sweet Briar plantation, Shadwell, Monticello, Free State, and Canada. Unfortunately, in contrast to the stone pipe remains from the Quarter Site at Poplar Forest, most of these other schist pipe remains have been located in poor archaeological contexts. Sites that produced evidence of historic stone working and historic stone-pipe production are discussed first, followed by a discussion of sites that contained only completed stone pipes.

### Merrywood

Evidence of historic stone working and stone-pipe production is limited to Poplar Forest, Merrywood, Shadwell, and Monticello. The Merrywood plantation was located on the southeastern boundary of Poplar Forest in the late eighteenth and early nineteenth centuries. Jefferson's friend, Richard Walker, owned Merrywood during the occupation of the Quarter Site. Several pieces of cut schist, similar to the wasters recovered at the Quarter Site, were recovered by the present owners of Merrywood plantation in the 1990s while working in their garden. While they did not report finding any pipe fragments, the presence of worked schist on an adjacent plantation suggests the possibility that stone working was practiced locally during the late eighteenth or early nineteenth centuries.

### Shadwell

Shadwell plantation was the birthplace of Thomas Jefferson. It is located in Albemarle County near Monticello. Shadwell was the home of Peter and Jane Jefferson, their eight children, and over sixty enslaved laborers from the 1730s through the 1770s (Kern 2010). Archaeologists working at the location of the slave quarter near the kitchen and main house recovered a worked object made of Candler phyllite that may represent a stone pipe blank (figure 7.6). This stone is very specific to the ridge between Charlottesville and Lynchburg (ibid., 102). Although the possible pipe blank is the only potential evidence of stone pipe production at Shadwell, when considered in the context of the assemblage of other pipes and pipe fragments from Albemarle County, its presence is significant.

This object may be the earliest evidence of stone pipe production by enslaved laborers in Virginia. Jefferson inherited a number of enslaved laborers from his father's estate. Some of these individuals eventually went to live at Poplar Forest. These same individual(s) may have practiced stone working at Shadwell and

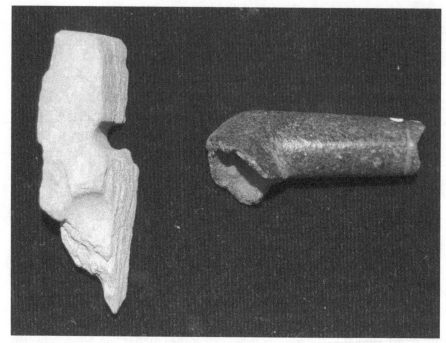

Figure 7.6. Possible Candler phyllite pipe blank from the slave quarter at Shadwell next to a steatite pipe from MRS-2 at Monticello. Used by permission of Monticello/Thomas Jefferson Foundation, Inc., Charlottesville, Virginia.

Poplar Forest or the stone-working tradition may have been passed on within the family or community.

## Monticello

Evidence of stone-pipe production and use was also found during excavations at another site associated with Jefferson and his enslaved laborers—Monticello, Jefferson's Albemarle County plantation. One complete stem with a partial bowl, four bowl fragments, two partial stems, and a pipe blank were found.

Evidence of pipe production at Monticello comes from Site 8, a slave quarter on the ridge of Monticello Mountain that was occupied from circa 1770 to 1800. During this time it served as the home for most of the enslaved field workers who labored on the Monticello home farm. The remains of four houses have been excavated at Site 8 to date (Bon-Harper et al. 2004; Bon-Harper 2009). Archaeologists recovered a chlorite schist pipe blank in 2009 with an elbow-shaped form (figure 7.7). It broke vertically as the bowl was being carved. It was found in a disturbed plow-zone layer beneath a modern brush pile, although the mean ceramic date for the assemblage from this layer is 1795.

The most complete Monticello schist pipe is a Type 1 elbow-shaped reed-

Figure 7.7. Stone pipe blank from Home Farm Site 8 at Monticello. Used by permission of Monticello/Thomas Jefferson Foundation, Inc., Charlottesville, Virginia.

stem pipe (figure 7.6). The stem has an incised band parallel to the distal end. The stem opening is broken off and unfinished. Most of the bowl is missing. Archaeologists recovered this pipe during excavations of Mulberry Row Structure 2 (MRS-2). Mulberry Row was the location of housing for enslaved African Americans and free white workers, iron and woodworking shops, a dairy, a smokehouse, a washhouse, storage space, and a stable (Kelso1997, 51–81). These buildings were not all standing simultaneously. The earliest were built in the 1770s. Mulberry Row activity peaked in the 1790s and then dropped off again by the 1820s (ibid.). MRS-2 was a probable slave cabin that was occupied in the late 1780s and early 1790s (Sawyer and Smith 2011). The stone pipe was found in a modern utility trench that cut into Jefferson period deposits, about fifteen feet down slope of the subfloor pit associated with MRS-2. The mean ceramic date for the ceramics recovered inside the utility trench is 1809 (E. Sawyer, personal communication 2011).

Four schist pipe-bowl fragments were also recovered at Monticello. One is a polygon-shaped bowl with two parallel rows of incised squares adjacent to the rim (figure 7.8). This bowl fragment was found in a layer of fill inside Building s, a slave cabin on Mulberry Row built in the early 1790s. This structure was a

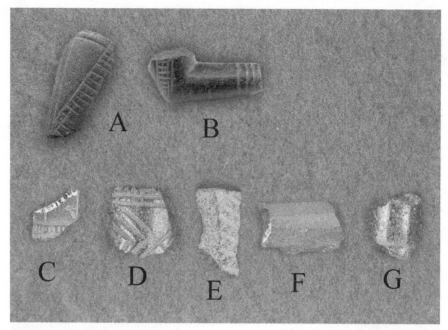

Figure 7.8. Decorated stone pipes from Albemarle County sites: A) pipe bowl from Free State; B) pipe from Canada; C) pipe bowl from Building s at Monticello; D) pipe bowl from Home Farm Site 6 at Monticello; E) pipe bowl from the Privy Tunnel at Monticello; F) pipe stem from the West Kitchen Yard at Monticello; G) pipe stem from the Stewart-Watkins House at Monticello. This figure is a composite image; objects are not in true relative scale. Photos A and B by the author; photos C–G by permission of Monticello/Thomas Jefferson Foundation, Inc., Charlottesville, Virginia.

log cabin measuring twelve by fourteen feet with a wood chimney and dirt floor (Hill 2003; Kelso 1982, 1997).

The second schist bowl fragment is round. Like the fragment from Building s, this fragment has a double row of incised squares adjacent to the rim (figure 7.8). The surface of the bowl is also decorated with incised lines that form an X in the center with intersecting V's, triangles, or diamonds radiating out from this, though the complete pattern is indiscernible because the fragment is broken. This bowl fragment came from a layer of plow zone at Home Farm Quarter Site 6, a slave quarter. The site is currently being excavated and analyzed, but preliminary occupation dates are circa 1790s to after 1826 (Monticello Archaeology 2011).

The third schist bowl fragment is broken but retains evidence of two panels. One panel is undecorated and the second has incised crosshatching, creating embossed diamonds (figure 7.8). The stem is polished and also exhibits one undecorated panel and a second with incised crosshatching, creating raised diamonds. The pipe is polished, indicating that the pipe was finished when it broke. This stem fragment was recovered during excavations of a privy tunnel associated with the main house (K. Smith, personal communication 2010).

The fourth pipe-bowl fragment is undecorated and was possibly broken before the pipe was finished. This fragment came from a plowing or leveling layer in the West Kitchen Yard (Clites and Bates 2008; Kelso 1997, 38–44). A stem fragment was also recovered from this location. It has a polygon form and was broken during the carving process (figure 7.8). The mean ceramic date for this layer is 1809 (Clites and Bates 2008).

Archaeologists recovered a second schist pipestem fragment from another Monticello site. It is a polished, round stem with an incised line creating a raised band adjacent to the end of the pipe (figure 7.8). The fragment is broken 13 mm below the end, precluding evidence of additional decoration. This stem fragment comes from an occupation layer in the Stewart-Watkins house, named for two white artisans who lived at the site, which is located on the side of Monticello Mountain (Heath 1991a, 1999c, 193–217). William Stewart was a hired blacksmith and whitesmith who occupied the 18-by-24-foot dwelling from 1801 to 1807; Elisha Watkins was a carpenter who lived at the site in 1809 (Heath 1991b, 1999c, 196).

### Point of Honor

Evidence of historic stone working is limited to Poplar Forest, Merrywood, Shadwell, and Monticello. However, archaeologists have found fragments of finished historic stone pipes at two additional plantations—Point of Honor in Lynchburg and Sweet Briar in Amherst County—and the free black communities of Free State and Canada in Albemarle County.

A broken schist pipe bowl was recovered at Point of Honor, a plantation on the south bank of the James River built and owned by Dr. George Cabell from 1815 to 1830. Cabell was a prominent Lynchburg physician. The pipe-bowl fragment was recovered during excavation of a stable near the Point of Honor mansion, just above the stable floor in a layer that was deposited during the Cabell occupation period (Heath 1995). The rounded pipe-bowl fragment was polished on the exterior and the rim was cut to create a crenellated design (figure 7.9) (ibid., 28). This is the only stone-pipe bowl examined for this study that exhibits this kind of decoration.

### Sweet Briar

Sweet Briar plantation was located northeast of Poplar Forest in Amherst County. Elijah Fletcher, a businessman, newspaper publisher, and former mayor of neighboring Lynchburg, purchased the land in 1830. He built a profitable

Figure 7.9. Schist pipe-bowl fragment from the Point of Honor plantation. Used by permission of the Lynchburg Museum System, Lynchburg, Virginia.

plantation, and upon his death in 1858 he owned 110 slaves that included both African Americans and Native Americans from the Monacan Confederacy. Archaeological surveys and shovel testing on the Sweet Briar property have identified over 350 sites from the eighteenth into the late twentieth centuries. Artifact processing from the shovel tests is incomplete and to date no results have been published (L. Rainville, personal communication 2010).

Excavations at Sweet Briar have produced a schist pipe similar to those recovered at Poplar Forest. The pipe was found, associated with several antebellum artifacts, above a stone foundation for an unidentified structure believed to have been occupied in the mid-nineteenth century. Further analysis of the artifacts and features from the site will refine the dates of occupation and provide additional evidence about the site's function.

The Sweet Briar pipe is a reed-stemmed, elbow-shaped pipe. Unlike the Type 1 pipes from Poplar Forest, the angle between the reed and stem of the Sweet Briar pipe is slightly obtuse. Most of the bowl is missing. The pipe stem is decorated with incised lines (figure 7.10). Three parallel bands are incised adjacent to the distal end of the stem. Wide-spaced diagonal incisions connect the innermost of these bands to another incised band ten centimeters closer to the bowl. A parallel band is incised adjacent to that band. The Sweet Briar pipe is not polished and the schist is a lighter gray than the schist used to produce the Poplar Forest pipes.

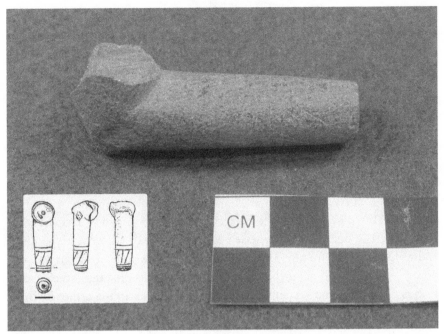

Figure 7.10. Schist pipe from the Sweet Briar plantation. Used by permission of Sweet Briar College, Sweet Briar, Virginia. Drawing by Lynn Rainville, photograph by Keith Adams.

## Free State

A steatite pipe bowl was recovered during excavations of the Free State site in Albemarle County. Free State was a rural African American community that was occupied from the late eighteenth century into the twentieth century (Thompson 2010). In the late eighteenth and early nineteenth centuries, Free State was owned and occupied by free blacks beginning with the purchase of the property by Amy Farrow in 1788 (ibid., 10).

The Free State steatite bowl fragment was recovered in a plow-zone layer within the confines of a concentration of late eighteenth- and early nineteenth-century artifacts associated with a domestic site (Thompson 2010). The pipe-bowl fragment recovered from Free State has an incised acute V shape composed of three or four rows of incised lines with crosshatching that create embossed squares (figure 7.8). This V is intersected in the center by four parallel lines that are not crosshatched. Two incised lines parallel to the rim of the bowl create a raised band.

## Foster Family Site

Archaeologists recovered a steatite pipe, similar in decoration to the pipe from Free State, at the Foster Family site, another free black site in Charlottesville

(Ford 2008). In 1833, Kitty Foster, a free black woman, purchased 2 1/8 acres and a house near the University of Virginia. She and her descendants lived there until the first decade of the twentieth century (ibid., 12). Within a few decades of this purchase, the area surrounding the Foster residence grew into a predominantly black neighborhood known as Canada (ibid., 39).

The steatite pipe was recovered next to the Foster/Canada cemetery during excavations undertaken to determine the extent of the cemetery. Unfortunately, the area it was recovered in was disturbed by the presence of a large root system from an extant tree stump overlying the excavation unit. Archaeologists dated the excavation layer the pipe was found in to the first or second quarter of the nineteenth century (ibid., 76).

The steatite pipe found at the Foster Family site is an elbow-shaped reed-stem pipe. The stem has three incised concentric bands adjacent to the distal end of the stem (figure 7.8). The front of the pipe has an acute V shape composed of four incised parallel lines with crosshatching, creating three rows of embossed squares and rectangles. This V is intersected in the center by three incised lines with crosshatching, creating two rows of embossed squares.

## Pipe-Making Traditions

The question remains how the pipe maker(s) began making stone pipes. Was this talent honed independently using artisanal skills on a locally available stone or was this a craft taught by someone else? If the latter is the case, what pipe-making or stone-working traditions were available in central Virginia in the late eighteenth to early nineteenth centuries?

When the first fragments of schist pipes were recovered at Poplar Forest, archaeologists initially thought they were probably associated with previous Native American activity on the land. Hannah Canel began research into prehistoric stone pipes and consulted with archaeologists familiar with Native American material culture from central Virginia (Canel 1996). She determined that the forms of these particular pipes were common to the historic period and were too crudely executed to be prehistoric Native American pipes. In addition, although some Woodland Period sites and artifacts have been identified on the museum's current property (Adams 2008), no evidence of schist pipes has been recovered anywhere except from the historic contexts of the Quarter Site, the Wing of Offices, a historic garden, and a Jefferson-era plant nursery.

The Quarter Site occupation period coincides with a low population point for Native Americans in the region (J. Hantman, personal communication 2002) However, the discovery of what seems to be Late Woodland or protohistoric pottery at Wingos, at sites on the modern Poplar Forest property, and in the surrounding neighborhood suggests some level of Native American presence in the immediate area (Adams 2008; Heath, personal communication 2009; Proebsting this volume). Contextual and production evidence at Poplar Forest indicates that the schist pipes were manufactured and used by enslaved laborers, yet the degree of influence of Native American stone-working traditions is not resolved.

Although the late eighteenth and early nineteenth centuries may have been a low point for the presence of Native American groups at Poplar Forest, they were present in Amherst, Nelson, and Albemarle counties. Native Americans were enslaved alongside African Americans at Sweet Briar plantation in Amherst County (L. Rainville, personal communication 2004). Therefore, Native American pipe production merits consideration. The Cherokee of North Carolina are well known for historic stone-pipe manufacture (Schroedl 1986, 375–379; Witthoff 1949). Evidence suggests that Native Americans were also producing stone pipes in Albemarle County into the eighteenth century (E. Bollwerk, personal communication 2009).

Fragments of prehistoric chlorite schist tobacco pipes with incised designs have also been recovered at the Fout Site in Frederick County, Virginia (MacCord 1996, 16–17). Intriguingly, a pipe identified as a Woodland/Archaic prehistoric pipe that is similar in form to Type 1 pipes was recovered along the Rivanna River in Albemarle County at site 44AB22 (Canel 1996, 3). This site is located six-tenths of a mile from the confluence of Town Branch stream. Free State is located at the headwaters of Town Branch (S. Thompson, personal communication 2011).

Archaeologists recovered two stone pipes identified as "aboriginal," one made of limestone and the other from serpentine or soapstone, during excavations of Liberty Hall in Lexington, Virginia (McDaniel, Russ, and Potter 1979, 88). The archaeologists defined aboriginal pipes as those "that are similar to those used by prehistoric populations in the area" (ibid., 83). The Liberty Hall site includes remains associated with nine structures of the historic academy that became Washington and Lee University. The occupation dates of these buildings range from the late eighteenth century into the late nineteenth century (ibid.). McDaniel and his colleagues believed that the stone pipes "were probably collected as artifacts," in contrast to clay aboriginal pipe fragments, which they thought "were manufactured locally in a primitive kiln" (ibid., 88). Additional research may reveal that the stone pipes at Liberty Hall are historic rather than prehistoric pipes.

Elizabeth Bollwerk, a University of Virginia graduate student, is currently researching prehistoric and historic Native American stone and clay pipes in central Virginia (E. Bollwerk, personal communication 2010). When her research is complete, comparison with the stone pipes produced and used by African Americans in Central Virginia may indicate more conclusively whether or not Native American pipe production traditions influenced African American pipe production, directly or indirectly.

Determining whether these pipes were the result of particular pipe-making or stone-working traditions proves problematic, partly because elbow-shaped reed-stem smoking pipes are intercultural artifacts. Africanist archaeologist Thurstan Shaw notes that "it seems likely that when slaves in the Americas had the opportunity to make pipes for themselves, their form might be influenced by what they had been accustomed to in their African homeland" (Shaw 1960, 281). Yet Native American and European pipe traditions also influenced the African traditions that enslaved people were familiar with.

Historically, Africans chewed tobacco, inhaled it as snuff, and smoked it in pipes (Handler 2008, 2). Africans used imported European pipes and produced clay and stone pipes of their own. Stone-pipe production seems to have been limited to the San of South Africa (Philips 1983, 315). Several West African cultures produced clay elbow-shaped reed-stem pipes (DeCorse 2001; Gijanto 2010; Handler and Norman 2007; Handler 2008; Kelly 2001; Ozanne 1962, 1976; Philips 1983; Shaw 1960; Stahl 2001).

Pipes produced by Africans and African West Indians have been recovered from a few sixteenth- and seventeenth-century archaeological sites in the Caribbean. Four reed-stemmed elbow-shaped clay pipes were recovered at a seventeenth-century runaway slave site, José Leta, in the Dominican Republic (Deagan and Macmahon 1995). Incised geometric motifs that form triangles and diamonds decorate the body of the pipes and parallel bands are incised along the stem of one pipe (Arrom and García Arevalo 1986, 64–65). Handler and Lange recovered an African clay elbow-shaped reed-stem pipe in a late seventeenth- or early eighteenth-century burial at Newton Plantation in Barbados (Handler and Lange 1978). Yet these sites are significantly earlier than those examined for this study, and the particular African origins of the pipe makers are unknown.

Historians have recently begun to trace the African origins of slaves trafficked to Virginia during the Atlantic slave trade (Chambers 1999, 2000; Walsh 1999, 2001). These studies suggest that the Igbo formed a significant part of the African component of slavery in central Virginia in the late eighteenth century (Chambers 1999; Samford 2007; Walsh 1999, 2001). Chambers argues that the presence of the Igbo in the interior tidewater and piedmont counties had a transformative impact on colonial and early national African American culture in Virginia (Chambers 2000; Samford 2007, 11).

Design elements on the stone pipes are consistent with documented West African iconography. Geometric designs and incised X's are frequently attributed to various African antecedents (for examples, see Emerson 1988, 1994; Ferguson 1992; Klingelhofer 1987). These designs were common among the Igbo and had iconographic significance to them (Samford 2007, 166). Samford noted that "alternating plain and crosshatched space was significant to the Igbo" (ibid., 168). This pattern is common on the decorated pipes from Poplar Forest, Monticello, Free State, and the Foster Family site. However, without additional evidence, particularly from good archaeological contexts, it is not possible to determine whether there were particular Native American or African influences on the intercultural stone pipes produced and used by African Americans in central Virginia.

## Conclusions

Evidence of stone pipes that were produced and used by enslaved laborers living at Poplar Forest plantation in the late eighteenth and early nineteenth centuries is a significant finding, demonstrating a skill developed by enslaved people to produce objects for their own use and to share with or sell to others. Discovery of these pipes led to a search for similar historic stone-pipe production and use at other African American sites in the region. Evidence of stone-pipe production or use or working schist was found at seven other locations in central Virginia. Although provenience is poor for a number of the recovered pipes and pipe fragments, most of these sites date from the late eighteenth and early nineteenth centuries.

Intriguingly, all but possibly one of the historic archaeology sites in central Virginia that have evidence of stone-pipe production or use have ties with the slaves of Peter or Thomas Jefferson. This includes all of the historic sites where stone pipes were produced (Shadwell, Monticello, and Poplar Forest). Merrywood plantation, where evidence of stone working was found, also has ties to the enslaved laborers of Thomas Jefferson.

A letter Ellen Randolph (Jefferson's granddaughter) wrote to her mother, Martha Randolph, in 1819 describes the generosity of Mrs. Walker, the wife of Richard Walker, the owner of the Merrywood plantation. Mrs. Walker sent several gifts of food via a "tidy mulattoe girl," whom Martha later refers to as a "maid."[1] At the end of the letter Martha notes that actually two women sometimes came from Merrywood with food, but one came more often than the other. This letter establishes movement of enslaved people between the two adjacent plantations. Given the close proximity of the two properties, it is probable that friendship, marriages, and other kin relationships existed among the enslaved residents of these two plantations.

These relationships would mean that resources as well as people circulated between the two plantations. These may have been material resources, such as food, and nonmaterial resources, such as knowledge or services, possibly including lapidary skills. The worked stone at Merrywood, Poplar Forest, Shadwell, and Monticello may represent a regional practice of stone working among enslaved African Americans. This practice may have been shared among friends, family members, or acquaintances and in this way spread across central Virginia.

All of the sites that produced only evidence of pipe use in the form of used stone-pipe fragments had some connection to Thomas Jefferson's slaves, with the possible exception of Sweet Briar plantation. Convenient access to the James River led to a successful shipping business at Cabell's Point of Honor. Jefferson was among the group of planters who shipped some of his agricultural products through Cabell, and his slaves brought the tobacco to Cabell for shipment. Interaction between Jefferson's slaves and Cabell's slaves as a result of these shipping transactions may have provided an opportunity to exchange a stone pipe, offer it as a gift, or teach lapidary skills. Two free black sites, Free State and Canada, in Charlottesville, Virginia, may have been the location of similar opportunities.

The inhabitants of Free State were associated with two people who worked for Jefferson at Monticello, one free black and one enslaved laborer. Amy Farrow purchased Free State in 1788. Through this purchase, she initiated a free black community. She eventually divided Free State between her sons Thomas Farrow Jr. and Zachariah Bowles. Bowles married Critta Hemings, the daughter of Betty Hemings, the enslaved matriarch of the Hemings family, and John Wayles, Thomas Jefferson's father-in-law. Critta Hemings was an enslaved house servant at Monticello. After Jefferson's death, his grandson Francis Eppes purchased Critta's freedom in 1827. She was already married to Zachariah Bowles. Zachariah and Critta may have met when Zachariah worked as a seasonal laborer at Monticello in the early 1790s (Thompson 2010, 15–19). The stone pipe recovered at Free State may have been crafted by one of Thomas Jefferson's slaves who had ties with Critta Hemings and Zachariah Bowles.

Kitty Foster's family, who lived at the Canada site, were also related to Thomas Jefferson's slaves through marriage. Eston Hemings and Elizabeth Ann Fossett, both former slaves of Thomas Jefferson, married members of the Foster Family (Ford 2008: 14). In 1857, Jefferson's grandson, Thomas Jefferson Randolph, testified on behalf of Kitty Foster's grandchildren, Susan and Clayton Foster, to support their claims that they were "not negroes" in a legal sense (ibid.). This legal ruling enabled them to avoid the restrictions placed on free blacks and mulattoes. These facts demonstrate that the Foster family had several ties to Jefferson's slaves, his former slaves, and Jefferson's family.

These connections may be linked to the presence of the stone pipe recovered at the Foster site.

Evidence of stone working found at Peter Jefferson's Shadwell suggests that someone there may have also engaged in pipe production. These stone-working skills may have been taken to Poplar Forest or passed on to someone who eventually moved there. Two of Peter Jefferson's slaves, Bella and Cate, ended up at Poplar Forest (Jefferson in Betts 1987, 24–30; Monticello Plantation Database 2008). Although Cate and her husband Jame Hubbard lived at Jefferson's Bear Creek quarter farm, Cate's daughter, Hannah, was one of Jefferson's cooks. She lived in and worked at the Wing of Offices when Jefferson was in residence and most likely lived at the Poplar Forest quarter when Jefferson was away. Her presence in the kitchen would make her the recipient of gifts of food for the plantation that enslaved servants from Merrywood brought.

Hannah's stepbrother, Nace, worked as a headman and shoemaker at Poplar Forest (Heath 1999b). He or his nephew, also called Nace, worked as a gardener. One of these men is known to have had a subfloor pit in his cabin because John Hemings complained to Jefferson that Nace stole vegetables from the garden and buried them in the floor in his cabin.[2] This documentation of a subfloor pit is interesting because remains of stone pipes and by-products of their manufacture were found in subfloor pits at Poplar Forest's Quarter Site. This letter, however, was written a few years after the Quarter Site was abandoned. Other Monticello-based enslaved laborers moved to Poplar Forest and some people, particularly artisans and carters, traveled between the two sites as needed (Heath 1999b). Therefore the list of individual(s) potentially involved in pipe production at Poplar Forest is long, although some patterns are emerging. Stone-pipe evidence from other historic central Virginia sites suggest that some of Jefferson's slaves were involved not only in production of stone pipes but possibly also in their distribution.

The ties between Jefferson's slaves and stone-pipe production and use may not be relevant at all of the sites discussed, but they do not seem coincidental. However, sites associated with Thomas Jefferson and his enslaved workers have been subjected to extensive historical archaeology investigations. Additional research at other sites associated with African Americans in central Virginia in the relevant time frame may produce additional stone pipes suggesting that stone-pipe production and use at sites associated with Jefferson's slaves is only a small part of a larger, complex picture. Research on the ties between Native Americans and African Americans in this region should also prove fruitful for determining whether stone-working traditions were shared between these groups. Social networks between Native Americans and African Americans and among African Americans may prove more relevant for understanding stone-pipe production and use than the ties that bound the enslaved to Jefferson.

It is intriguing that evidence of stone pipes was found in association with enslaved African Americans, a white artisan's household, and free blacks. If stone-pipe production was regional, this may indicate that using a stone pipe was associated with class. If stone-pipe production was limited to a few individuals or a particular social group, that would suggest social relations between these social groups. Further research into historic stone-pipe production, distribution, and use will help define the geographic boundaries of pipe production and the social boundaries involved in the use of stone pipes.

## Notes

1. Ellen Randolph to Martha Jefferson Randolph, August 24, 1819, Coolidge Papers, Accession #9090, Albert and Shirley Small Special Collections Library, University of Virginia, Charlottesville, Virginia.

2. John Hemings to Thomas Jefferson, November 29, 1821, Coolidge Collection of Thomas Jefferson Manuscripts, Massachusetts Historical Society, Boston, Massachusetts.

# 8

## Social Dimensions of Eighteenth- and Nineteenth-Century Slaves' Uses of Plants at Poplar Forest

JESSICA BOWES AND HEATHER TRIGG

Poplar Forest's extensive program of macrobotanical sampling and analysis over the last fifteen years has provided a wealth of data about the plantation's enslaved peoples (Bowes and Trigg 2009; Heath 2008b; Raymer 1996, 2003). Macrobotanical remains recovered from the areas that slaves occupied allow us to explore the complexities of the slaves' use of plants throughout the history of Poplar Forest as a working plantation. Plants played a prominent role in the slaves' lives as food, as utilitarian items like brooms or floor mats, as medicine, as fuel, and perhaps in rituals. Archaeobotanical remains thus provide a window into the lives of the enslaved community (Heath 2001; Mrozowski, Franklin, and Hunt 2008). Choices made by and for slaves regarding their diet and subsistence went beyond mere caloric satisfaction and were imbued with social relations of power and resistance (Gibbs et al. 1980; McKee 1999; Mrozowski, Franklin, and Hunt 2008). Slaves' diets reflect, in part, negotiation between slaves and plantation owners as well as the owners' management decisions. We can use archaeobotanical remains to explore the social context in which the enslaved African Americans and owners of Poplar Forest operated. Changes in plantation management during the tenure of two owners, Thomas Jefferson and Edward Hutter, reflect the shifting attitudes towards slavery in colonial and antebellum society and the economic pressures facing owners.

These social relationships were set within a changing environmental context as plantation grounds were landscaped and agricultural fields were cleared, planted, and abandoned. Jefferson was well known for agricultural experimentation and landscaping, including the introduction of ornamental and useful plants to Poplar Forest (Betts 1944, 1987; Jones 2002; Raymer 1996, 2003; Trussell 2000). Throughout the eighteenth and nineteenth centuries, Virginia's farmers struggled to maintain the fertility and productivity of their lands as cash crops stripped vital nutrients from the soil (Nelson 2007). Plantation owners coped with depleting soil fertility by diversifying their crops (Proebsting this volume; Sanford 1994, 128), and they implemented these farming practices using the labor of enslaved African Americans, engaging the slaves in the changing environment.

Changing trends in the treatment and management of slaves may be visible in how owners provisioned slaves and how slaves provisioned themselves (Bowes 2009; Heath 2004a; McKee 1999; Mrozowski, Franklin, and Hunt 2008). The habitats at Poplar Forest, which include the grounds around the plantation buildings, agricultural fields, slaves' gardens, managed lawns, forests, and successional fields, provided slaves and owners with a variety of plant resources. We focus on the macrobotanical remains recovered from features associated with slaves' cabins (Bowes 2009; Bowes and Trigg 2009; Heath 2008b; Raymer 1996, 2003) and use the botanical materials as indications of slaves' subsistence activities. We explore the range of habitats enslaved people used as an indication of the ways they met their subsistence needs. These different habitats represent variations in the slaves' control and mobility, but they may also provide information about how Poplar Forest's slaves were treated throughout the eighteenth and nineteenth centuries.

## Historical and Environmental Contexts

Thomas Jefferson and his wife, Martha Wayles Skelton Jefferson, inherited the 5,000-acre Poplar Forest from her father in 1773. Along with the property, the Jeffersons also received 135 enslaved African Americans, who formed the core of the enslaved work force at Poplar Forest over the five decades of Jefferson's occupation (Heath 1999b; Heath et al. 2004; Heath this volume). Jefferson was largely absent during the earliest period of ownership, when he relied completely on overseers to manage the land and slaves. Jefferson became more active in the administration of the plantation during and after the construction of the main house from 1806 through 1810 (Heath 2004c). Although he did not visit Poplar Forest regularly until 1810, the home's construction did elicit increased concern for the management of Poplar Forest. Once the mansion was finished, the estate remained Jefferson's retreat property, a place he visited periodically.

Jefferson died in 1826 and his grandson, Francis Eppes, inherited Poplar Forest along with thirteen slaves. In 1828 Eppes sold the 1,075 acre plantation to William Cobbs before relocating his own family to Florida. Although most of Eppes's slaves moved with his family, it is possible that a few of his slaves were included in the sale of the plantation to William Cobbs. Although Cobbs had stopped managing the plantation by the 1840s, he lived at Poplar Forest with his wife, daughter, and son-in-law, Edward S. Hutter, until his death. Edward Hutter took over managing Poplar Forest for Cobbs in 1842 to well beyond 1865, when slavery was abolished (Chambers 1993, 178–179; Heath et al. 2004; Lee 2008). Each owner (and manager, in the case of Hutter) added slaves to the community already established at Poplar Forest and sold and moved others. This created almost two decades of frequent additions to—and losses from— the slave community, which had to adjust repeatedly to the instability (Heath et al. 2004).

Poplar Forest is located in a mixed southern hardwood forest, and the area around the plantation supported stands of old-growth oak, chestnut, and hickory before Anglo Americans settled in the area. Virginia's piedmont contained a large variety of hardwood species that included beeches and tulip poplars. Sycamores, elms, maples, and box elders grew along rivers (Gemborys 1974). The understory contained a diverse array of small trees and shrubs that included dogwoods, rhododendrons, and blueberry bushes. Before Anglo American settlement, Native peoples used fire to clear lands for hunting and agriculture (Druckenbrod and Shugart 2004), and the vegetation may have adapted to fire to some extent. While Native peoples' use of fire and their agricultural activities may have structured vegetation communities (Delcourt and Delcourt 1997), by the mid-eighteenth century, the area was largely an anthropogenic landscape (Nelson 2007; Proebsting this volume).

Before Jefferson arrived, Poplar Forest lands were under tobacco cultivation for about a decade, and the soils may have already been negatively affected. Some farmers' attempts to amend similarly depleted soils made problems worse (Nelson 2007). Changes in soil fertility and chemistry encouraged certain weeds that were more tolerant of extreme environmental conditions than most native vegetation or crops. When productivity was severely compromised, fields were abandoned. These areas underwent ecological succession, which provided a dynamic habitat. Ruderal plants and those adapted to lower fertility were first to grow, then grasses, then light-tolerant shrubs, and eventually small trees such as red cedars and pine (Druckenbrod and Shugart 2004). Disturbed areas and lands undergoing succession provided a variety of plant communities. Some successional areas may have included portions of the plantation core; one area, the Quarter Site, was thought to be located on an abandoned field (Heath 2004c).

Documents, archaeology, and palynology have revealed that Jefferson actively managed the curtilage, which comprised the ten-acre core area of the plantation along with fifty-one acres surrounding the core (Jones 2002; Trussell 2000). In addition to physically modifying the land, he installed new decorative and useful plants. Ornamental trees such as Lombardy poplars, paper mulberries, and additional tulip poplars were planted. Jefferson also ordered the planting of fruit trees in the nursery, orchards, and kitchen garden. Ornamental flowering shrubs such as lilacs and roses and ornamental herbs such as lilies and tulips were grown in pleasure grounds. Kitchen produce, small vegetables, and fruits such as strawberries were grown in vegetable gardens. The curtilage also housed plantation outbuildings, the main house, and some slave quarters and their gardens. These highly disturbed areas supported a variety of ruderal plants—those encouraged by human activities and disturbance—in addition to the desired plants in lawns and gardens.

Outside of the immediate area of the plantation core (but most likely within the curtilage), orchards of peaches, cherries, and apples were grown. Beyond the curtilage lay the plantation's agricultural fields, where cash crops of wheat and tobacco as well as crops intended for use on the plantation were planted, tended, and harvested by the slaves. During Jefferson's time, flax, hemp, and cotton were grown sporadically to provide fibers for clothing (Betts 1987, 247–254; Raymer 2003). Fertility of the soil was always a problem with these types of crops. A common method of maintaining soil fertility was to rotate grains such as maize and wheat with a green manure such as clover or alfalfa (Nelson 2007), and Jefferson discusses these types of rotation regimes in his farm journal (Betts 1987, 310–319).

While Hutter was not as adventurous as Jefferson in his landscaping ambitions, he maintained Poplar Forest as a working plantation with fields of wheat and other crops.[1] Beyond the plantation's core and its active and abandoned agricultural fields lay forest margins and then forested areas that housed a variety of nut trees as well as useful understory plants. This patchwork of habitats was the source of plants that were useful to the slaves and provided food, firewood, medicine, and utilitarian items.

## Archaeological Contexts and Archaeobotanical Analysis

The macrobotanical remains from three areas associated with slaves' dwellings have been analyzed: the North Hill quarter and Anderson's Garden, the Quarter Site, and Site A (map 8.1). Wingos quarter has been sampled but has not yet been analyzed (Breen and Heath 2010). The North Hill Site (Heath 2004b) is divided into two phases. Phase 1 dates from 1770 to the mid-1780s and includes a subfloor pit, several short trenches, an exterior pit, and the deepest layers of an erosion gully. This phase corresponds to the early period, from 1770 to 1785, before Jefferson's investment in the plantation house and grounds (ibid.). Phase 2, dating from 1790 to 1810, includes the upper fill of the gully, narrow trenches, and another exterior pit. Nearby is the Anderson's Garden site, where a possible

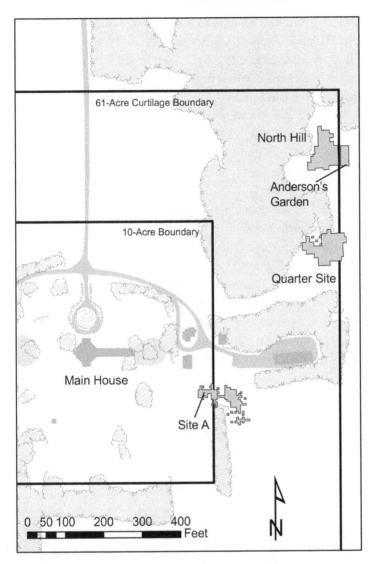

Map 8.1. Poplar Forest sites where samples have been taken for macrobotanical analysis.

subfloor pit that may or may not be related to the North Hill occupation was sampled for macrobotanicals.

A second slave living area is the Quarter Site, which dates from 1790 to 1812 (Heath 1999b, 2004c; McDonald 2000). A variety of features were excavated, including several structures, subfloor pits, post molds, and the remnant of a midden. Raymer (1996, 2003) analyzed the macrobotanical remains from the Jefferson-period areas.

Site A, which dates to the period when the Hutters owned the plantation, includes a slave cabin with a stone-filled feature that has been interpreted as a chimney base and a subfloor pit that is three feet by three feet (Heath et al.

2004). The pit (feature 2352R-DD/4) dates to between 1840 and 1858 and possibly as late as 1865. The pit is composed of eleven lenses and layers, which produced about 300 liters of floated soil. Of 123 light fractions, 61 were examined for charred plant remains and charred wood (Bowes 2009; Bowes and Trigg 2009).

The plant remains at the three analyzed sites were collected using two recovery strategies. Flotation samples were taken from most contexts, but some samples from the Quarter and North Hill sites were water-screened through 1/16-inch (1.6 mm) mesh (Heath and Lee 2008; Raymer 1996). While the differences in techniques may alter the types of seeds collected (in the latter technique, seeds smaller than 1.6 mm will not be recovered), the flotation samples from these two sites provide comparable data. In addition, most taxa recovered in the float samples have seeds larger than 1.6 mm. Large numbers of charred and uncharred seeds were recovered at all three locations. Because of preservation conditions (Miller 1989; Raymer 1996), the uncharred seeds were considered to be recent contaminants. Thus, our discussion focuses on charred plant parts. Raymer attempted to identify all charred wood greater than 2 mm, while Bowes identified a 25-piece subsample of wood.

Because the taxa recovered from features may relate to how that feature functioned, we used only the data from subfloor pits, external pits, and structures that provide the best evidence of domestic plant use and comparability among sites. We also chose these features because they typically contained the widest variety and highest density of plant remains. The North Hill features analyzed here are the subfloor pit (feature 1546) and an exterior pit (feature 1476). The Quarter Site features consist of Structure 2 (feature 1206) and one subfloor pit (feature 829) associated with Structure 1. Plant remains relating to Hutter's slaves come from the subfloor pit in Site A (feature 2352R-DD/4).

## Jefferson-Era Contexts

A wide variety of plants constitute the botanical remains from the North Hill Site: nutshells and nutmeats, cultivated grains, fruit (both wild and cultivated), edible and medicinal herbs, weeds, and charred wood. Raymer (2003) found 796 seeds and related plant parts from earlier Phase 1 features and seventy-two seeds and related plant parts from later features. Overall, the North Hill assemblage includes thirty-nine taxa of seeds and fruit and twenty-one taxa of wood. Plant remains from Anderson's Garden were from a smaller number of taxa but included domesticated fruit, maize, millet, nutshell, and a few weeds and grasses; the most notable plant remain was a large number of peach pits (ibid.). From the Quarter Site, Raymer (1996) found twenty-one taxa of seeds and fruit and four taxa of wood. Below, we examine the taxa recovered from the features we analyze further (tables 8.1 and 8.2).

Table 8.1. Seeds and fruits identified from archaeological remains at Poplar Forest slave quarter sites

| Common Name | Scientific Name | North Hill | | Quarter Site | | Site A/Hutter |
|---|---|---|---|---|---|---|
| | | 1546 | 1476 | 829 | 1206 | ER2353/4 |
| Acorn | Quercus sp. | | X | | | X |
| Amaranth | Amaranthus sp. | X | | | | |
| Aster family | Asteraceae | X | | | | |
| Bean | Phaseolus sp. | | X | | | |
| Bean family | Fabaceae | | | | | X |
| Bedstraw | Galium sp. | X | | | X | |
| Blueberry | Vaccinium sp. | | | | | X |
| Carpetweed | Mollugo sp. | X | | | | |
| Chenopod family | Chenopodiaceae | | | | | X |
| Cherry | Prunus sp. | | | X | | X |
| Cinquefoil | Potentilla sp. | | | | | X |
| Cocklebur | Xanthium sp. | | | | | X |
| Corn | Zea mays | X | X | X | X | X |
| Dock | Rumex sp. | X | | | | |
| Elderberry | Sambucus sp. | X | | | | X |
| Fanpetals | Sida sp. | X | | | | |
| Foxtail | Setaria lutescens | | | | | X |
| Goosefoot | Chenopodium sp. | X | | | X | |
| Goosegrass | Eleusine sp. | X | | | | |
| Grain | | X | | | X | |
| Grape | Vitis sp. | X | | X | | X |
| Grass family | Poaceae | X | | | X | X |
| Ground Cherry | Physalis sp. | | | | | X |
| Hazelnut | Corylus sp. | | | | | X |
| Hickory | Carya sp. | X | X | X | | |
| Huckleberry | Gaylussacia sp. | | | | X | |
| Jimsonweed | Datura stramonium | X | | | | X |
| Knotweed | Polygonum sp. | X | | | X | X |
| Mallow family | Malvaceae | | | | | X |
| Medick/clover | Medicago sp. | | | | | X |
| Millet | Panicum miliaceum | | | | | X |
| Mint | Mentha sp. | | | | | X |
| Nightshade | Solanum sp. | X | | | | X |
| Oat | Avena sativa | X | | | | |
| Panicgrass | Panicum sp. | | | | | X |
| Paspalum | Paspalum sp. | | | | | X |
| Peach | Prunus persica | X | | X | X | X |
| Persimmon | Persimmon sp. | | X | X | | |
| Pink family | Caryophyllaceae | | | | | X |
| Plantain | Plantago sp. | | | | | X |
| Poppy | Papaver sp. | X | | | | |
| Privet | Ligustrum vulgare | | | | | X |
| Purslane | Portulaca sp. | X | | | | X |
| Ragweed | Ambrosia sp. | X | | | | |
| Raspberry | Rubus sp. | X | | | X | X |
| Rose family | Rosaceae | | | | | X |
| Rye | Secale sp. | X | | | | |
| Ryegrass | Lolium sp. | | | | | X |
| Sedge | Carex sp. | | | | | X |
| Sorghum | Sorghum sp. | X | | | | X |
| Sorrel | Oxalis sp. | | | | | X |
| Strawberry | Fragaria sp. | X | | | | |
| Sumac | Rhus sp. | X | | | | |
| Sunflower | Helianthus sp. | | X | | X | |
| Vervain | Verbena sp. | X | | | | |
| Violet | Viola sp | X | | | | |
| Walnut | Juglans sp. | | | X | | X |
| Walnut family | Juglandaceae | X | X | | | |
| Watermelon | Citrullus lanatus | | | | | X |
| Wheat | Triticum sp. | X | | | X | X |
| Wheatgrass | Agropyron sp. | X | | | | |

Table 8.2. Wood species identified from archaeological remains at Poplar Forest slave quarter sites

| Common Name | Scientific Name | North Hill | | Quarter Site | | Site A/Hutter |
|---|---|---|---|---|---|---|
| | | 1546 | 1476 | 829 | 1206 | ER2353/4 |
| Ash | Fraxinus sp. | | | | | X |
| Beech | Fagus sp. | X | X | | | |
| Birch | Betula sp. | X | | | | X |
| Black Locust | Robinia pseudoacacia | X | X | | | X |
| Chestnut | Castenea sp. | | | | | X |
| Dogwood | Cornus sp. | | X | | | |
| Elm | Ulmus sp. | | | | X | X |
| Hickory | Carya sp. | X | X | X | X | X |
| Hophornbeam | Ostrya sp. | X | X | | | |
| Maple | Acer sp. | | X | | | X |
| Oak | Quercus sp. | X | X | X | X | X |
| Pine | Pinus sp. | X | X | X | X | X |
| Red Mulberry | Morus rubra | | | | X | |
| Red Oak | Quercus rubra | X | X | | | X |
| Sycamore | Platanus sp. | X | X | | | |
| Tulip Poplar | Liriodendron tulipifera | | | | | X |
| Walnut | Juglans sp. | | X | | | X |
| White Oak | Quercus alba | X | X | | | X |

### Early Jefferson Era

From the earliest subfloor pit (feature 1546) at the North Hill Site, Raymer (2003) found a variety of cultivated grains: indigenous maize; European-introduced wheat, oats, and rye; and sorghum, a grain introduced from Africa that was typically associated with African slaves. The maize remains include kernels used for food and cob fragments (cupules) that were possibly used as fuel. Fruit remains include peach pits, which were probably cultivated in plantation orchards, and seeds from raspberry, elderberry, grapes, and sumac, which were probably gathered from forests, edge zones, or successional fields. Strawberry seeds were also recovered and may have come from slaves' personal gardens or from plants growing wild in the area. There were a number of seeds from plants that were probably consumed as greens (Raymer 1996) including amaranth, bedstraw, knotweed, and purslane. The small quantity of nutshells includes hickory and walnut. Seeds from possible medicinal plants include poppies, violets, and jimsonweed. Also recovered were seeds from weeds that were probably not deliberately used: copperleaf, nightshade, ragweed, and prickly mallow. These seeds probably represent accidentally charred seeds brought in from the local environment rather than seeds that were gathered intentionally. The charred wood recovered from flotation samples indicates a variety of hardwoods that were used as fuel, including oak, hickory, beech, basswood, elm, and sycamore.

## Later Jefferson Period

The later external pit from North Hill (feature 1476) contained fewer taxa. Raymer (2003) found cultigens such as beans and maize kernels and cupules. Gathered resources include acorns, hickory nutshells, and sunflower seeds. There were fewer types of fruits (persimmon), edible weedy plants, and weeds than in the earlier deposits, but there was a variety of types of charred wood. The smaller number of taxa in these features may relate to the function of the feature rather than to differences in plant use between the early and late deposits of this area.

The Quarter Site contained the remains of several slave dwellings. In a subfloor pit (feature 829), Raymer (1996) found the seeds of a variety of subsistence items: edible herbs, medicinal plants, and seeds from crops and weeds. Some edible taxa were crops, but others may have been garden weeds that were tolerated because they were useful as food, medicine, or other utilitarian products. Grains include maize, millet, and wheat, a mix of European-introduced cereals and Native American domesticates. Some cultigens may have come from slaves' gardens, but they may also have been planted in the plantation's fields.

Some of the seeds came from plants that probably were consumed as greens, including amaranth, bedstraw, goosefoot, purslane, and smartweed. These weedy plants were perhaps tolerated in gardens but certainly could have been found in disturbed areas around buildings, fences, and large plantings. Cultivated fruit include cherry, peach, and perhaps persimmon, while raspberry and huckleberry were probably gathered. Gathered wild foods include sunflower, goosefoot, smartweed, and a variety of nuts. Some plants were useful as medicine, and some seeds may relate to plant parts that had utilitarian uses—grass stems and leaves for matting, lining pits, and basketry. A small variety of wood including elm, some hickory, oak, and a relatively large amount of pine was recovered; oak was the predominant variety. Many plants in the assemblage may have served multiple uses. For example, maize kernels were used for food, but the cobs may have been burned for fuel; persimmons may have been planted both for their edible fruit and as ornamentals; and violets may have served as ornamentals but also could have been used for medicine or eaten.

## Hutter-Era Context

From the sixty-one analyzed light fractions from the subfloor pit a total of 2,316 seed remains, 455 plant remains, and 1,525 pieces of wood were collected and examined (Bowes and Trigg 2009). Botanicals recovered from the pit relate to food consumption, medicinal practices, domestic uses of plants, and fuel use. The range of plants includes edible fruit, field and garden crops, weeds, nutshells, and wood. The fruit seeds and pits identified are a combination of domestic and wild fruit that includes cherry, raspberry, peach, grape, watermelon, elderberry, and blueberry. Plantation crops include wheat and corn, but the slaves also grew corn[2] and possibly sorghum and millet in their own gardens (Leighton 1986, 203; Prance and Nesbitt 2005, 50, 57). Knotweed, purslane, mint, plantain, and jimsonweed are just some of the plants that represent various weedy plant species that may have been used for food or medicine. These plants can thrive in disturbed environments and waste areas and may have been tolerated in slaves' gardens. Acorns, walnuts, and hazelnuts were likely gathered from the local woods. In every sample analyzed, an unknown charred organic material was present. The material is amorphous and ranges in size from greater than 2 mm to less than 0.5 mm. There is a strong similarity between the unknown tissue in the sample and charred potatoes, although it cannot be definitively identified. The wood fragments examined were primarily hardwoods, mainly oak and chestnut, with only a small amount of pine and other unidentifiable softwoods.

These features span the period from Jefferson's years at Poplar Forest to the time when the Hutters owned the plantation. Thus, the period includes slave life from the final decades of the eighteenth century until the end of the Civil War. The features allow for an examination of changing slave subsistence practices and management strategies.

Slaves' Use of Plants and Habitats

The botanical remains recovered from the different periods make clear that a wide variety of plant taxa were used to sustain the slave community. Owners provided staple grains and perhaps some fruit, but slaves grew food in their own gardens. They also supplemented their diets and obtained medicine from wild plants growing in disturbed areas around the plantation core. Forests, forest margins and successional fields were sources for edible fruit, nuts, and especially fuel wood, a crucial part of food preparation.

While the botanical remains indicate that a variety of areas around the plantation provided subsistence items, we cannot use the quantities of a particular taxon as a direct indication of its importance because the recovery of botanical remains is strongly influenced by accidental preservation. For example, we cannot determine if slaves' garden crops contributed more to their diets than food from the plantation's fields. We can, however, examine changes in number of plant foods and the proportions of seeds coming from various areas around the plantation to explore changes in slaves' diets.

Table 8.3. Taxonomic richness of seeds and fruits recovered from various sites at Poplar Forest

| Site | Location | Type of Feature | Number of Species | Number of Genera | Number of Families | Total Richness |
|------|----------|-----------------|-------------------|------------------|--------------------|----------------|
| 1546 A-G | North Hill | Subfloor pit | 4 | 25 | 3 | 32 |
| 1476 B-D | North Hill | Exterior pit | 1 | 5 | 1 | 7 |
| 829 | Quarter Sit | Subfloor pit | 2 | 5 | 0 | 7 |
| 1206 | Quarter Site | Structure | 2 | 8 | 1 | 11 |
| 2352R-DD/4 | Site A (Hutter) | Subfloor pit | 6 | 25 | 6 | 37 |

Examining the number of different foods in the diet (diet breadth) is one way to investigate trends in slaves' subsistence practices. This method allows us to indentify suggestions of nutritional stress. For this analysis we use the taxonomic richness of the assemblages to estimate diet breadth. We compare the number of plant taxa recovered (richness) at various taxonomic levels (specific, generic, and family) in contexts dating to the various owner occupations: early and late Jefferson era and Hutter era.

The richness (table 8.3) of the slaves' diet is highest during Jefferson's early years and during Hutter's occupation and lowest when Jefferson was having the main house constructed and during the earliest years of his regular visits to the property. The species richness assessment was confirmed with a more rigorous ecological model, the Shannon-Wiener Diversity Index. Interpreting richness is difficult, especially in terms of its meaning for diet and subsistence. Increasing richness and increasing diet breadth is typically interpreted as an indication of increasing effort to obtain food (Nagaoka 2001). In plantation contexts, an increase in the variety of foods is usually taken to mean that slaves were supplementing their diets because the food provided by owners was insufficient (McKee 1999; Mrozowski, Franklin, and Hunt 2008). However, in the context of slavery, the foods consumed may be limited not only by the managers' decisions about the types and quantities of rations that were provided but also by restrictions on slaves' mobility and time and ultimately their ability to obtain or produce their own food. Thus, richness and diet breadth may not be a clear indication of the adequacy of slaves' diets or landowners' consideration for their needs.

To better understand the changes in the slaves' diet apparent in the differing taxa richness, we looked at the habitats the slaves were using. We grouped the plant food remains according to the area around the plantation where the plant could be found (table 8.4). Plantation crops are plants that were cultivated in the fields and orchards; garden plants are wild and domestic foods from slaves' gardens; and ruderals are gathered from highly disturbed areas around the plantation's fields and buildings. We assumed that forest margins, edge zones,

Table 8.4. Locations at Poplar Forest where seed and fruit taxa recovered from slave households are found

| Plantation Crops | Garden Plants | Ruderals | Forest Margin | Forest |
|---|---|---|---|---|
| Bean | Amaranth | Bedstraw | Elderberry | Acorn |
| Corn | Corn | Carpetweed | Hazelnut | Blueberry |
| Oats | Goosefoot | Cocklebur | Huckleberry | Grape |
| Peach | Ground cherry | Dock | Raspberry | Hickory |
| Persimmon | Jimsonweed | Knotweed | Sumac | Walnut |
| Rye | Millet | Plantain | | |
| Wheat | Mint | Sorrel | | |
| | Nightshade | Violet | | |
| | Poppy | | | |
| | Purslane | | | |
| | Sorghum | | | |
| | Strawberry | | | |
| | Sunflower | | | |
| | Vervain | | | |
| | Watermelon | | | |

and successional areas provided foods such as raspberry, elderberry, and sumac. Finally, the mature forest was the source of most types of nuts and grapes.

We compared the proportion of plants coming from each of the areas to look for changes over time (figure 8.1). The proportion of plants that came from the plantation core is highly variable, as is the proportion of plants from the mature forest. Some of this variability may relate to size of the assemblage because the number of seeds recovered is relatively small in feature 1476. However, the contexts that have a large number of seeds suggest that the use of ruderal plants from disturbed areas around the plantation remained constant throughout the Jefferson and Hutter occupations but that the use of forest plants was variable across all time periods. The proportion of crops from plantation fields and orchards appears to be stable during both the early and later Jefferson periods, but it decreased significantly during Hutter's occupation. This suggests that during the Jefferson era, provisioned rations played a greater role in the slaves' diets than they did later on. During Hutter's tenure, the increased proportion of plants coming from slaves' gardens and forest margins offset the reduced proportion of crops.

The increased use of forest margin plants during Hutter's occupation may be due to several factors, one of which is habitat change because of extensive exploitation of the land. Successional areas may have increased as croplands were worn out and abandoned. These lands may have provided habitats for the wild fruit, which would have made resources from these areas easier to obtain than in earlier years.

Because fuel is a critical resource, we also examined whether the amount of forested land had been compromised by years of altering which fields were

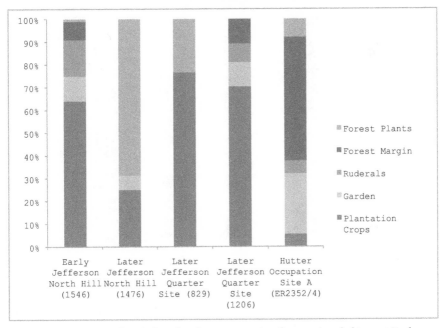

Figure 8.1. Proportion of seeds found at slave quarter sites from various habitats at Poplar Forest.

cultivated and the need for timber and firewood. During Hutter's tenure, forest plants, primarily nuts, comprise a smaller proportion of the assemblage, which may suggest that forests were smaller. To examine that possibility, we looked at the charred wood assemblage as an indication of the types of fuel the slaves were burning. A number of taxa were recovered from each feature; these included hardwood taxa such as oak, hickory, elm, and tulip poplar and softwoods, such as pine (table 8.2). We categorized the charred wood as excellent, good, or fair according to the heat value each wood generates (DeWald, Josiah, and Erdkamp 2005). Based on heat values, it appears that early Jefferson features are dominated by excellent fuel wood, but Quarter Site features from the later Jefferson period have a high proportion of fuel wood that is rated only fair in terms of the amount of heat it generates (figure 8.2). The Hutter-era assemblage is also dominated by wood with excellent heating properties. Thus it appears that even during Hutter's time, the slaves were able to obtain prime fuel woods.

The foods obtained from different areas on the plantation had a different cost and return on the investment of energy. Traveling to successional fields, forest edges, or mature forests or producing food in gardens may have required more of the slaves' effort than accepting rations provided by owners, but the use of these areas provides some indication of the slaves' control over their subsistence

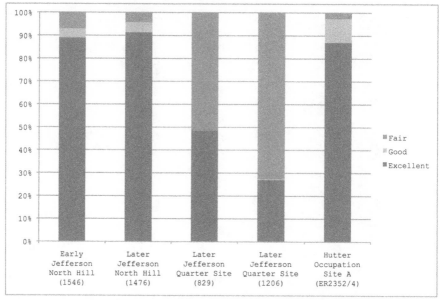

Figure 8.2. Proportion of wood with fair, good, and excellent heat value from samples found at Poplar Forest slave quarter sites.

activities and mobility. As other authors have noted (Heath 2001; Mrozowski, Franklin, and Hunt 2008), during leisure time slaves visited family members at other plantations. Traveling to and from their home plantation allowed them to learn about the location and extent of forest and forest margin resources. While slaves may have stolen food from plantation fields and orchards, they generally had little control over foods from these areas because such rations were controlled by the owner or overseer. However, the types and quantities of foods and medicine slaves grew in their gardens or gathered from disturbed areas in the plantation core were largely under their own control. The fact that wild resources were collected from forest margins, successional fields, and forests suggests that slaves had the ability or need to gather food in such places. While the analysis suggests that Hutter's slaves were not provisioned to the same degree as those under Jefferson, it may be that Hutter's slaves had a greater ability to travel, more time to do so and more latitude to make their own subsistence decisions.

The foods slaves gathered and grew in their gardens may also have provided a more balanced diet than would have been possible from rations alone. Rationing was highly variable among plantations. Each owner made decisions about what and how much to provide, but rations often included corn or corn meal, potatoes, and possibly occasional seasonal vegetables (Gibbs et al. 1980, 229). Jefferson's farm journal indicates that he regularly provided pork, corn, wheat, and salt, while his correspondence mentions his purchases of salted herring for slaves' consumption.[3] Starchy grains provide calories but typically lack critical vitamins and other nutrients. Weedy plants such as purslane and mint and fruit such as strawberries provide vitamin C, and nutmeats provide fats and fat-soluble nutrients such as vitamin A. While owners may have provided seasonal vegetables, gathered resources provided variety when crops were unavailable. Other plants may have helped season a bland diet of starchy grains (Trigg et al. 1994) or provided food security in times of seasonal shortages. Raymer (2003) suggests that the poppy seed she found might have served as a condiment and, like mint, may have provided both medicinal and culinary supplements to a nutritionally inadequate diet.

The different foods and fuels that indicate slaves' subsistence practices have implications for understanding differing management styles on the plantation. A decrease in taxonomic richness correlates with changes in plantation activity. This is attributed to either Jefferson's increased involvement as the main house was being built or a change Jefferson made in the overseers. His influence on the plantation, either by his physical presence or through his letters, may be a factor in the differences in botanical remains from the earlier North Hill Site seeds and the later North Hill and Quarter Site assemblages. It is possible that the slaves at Poplar Forest were provisioned differently under Jefferson's later ownership, which may correlate to the construction of the main house and his greater interest in the property. Jefferson meticulously recorded the daily plantation activities of his main home, Monticello, in his farm journal, and he recorded his ornamental plantings and experiments in his horticultural diary (Betts 1944), which also discusses activities at Poplar Forest but to a lesser degree than the farm journal. Jefferson's "legendary obsession for detail and control" (McDonald 2000, 177) certainly affected how he managed his slaves. Some plantation owners thought that gardening gave slaves too much autonomy, since it allowed them to earn money (Gibbs et al. 1980; Heath and Bennett 2000), and they did not allow slaves to produce their own food. However, Jefferson encouraged slaves to provide their own foods and even purchased eggs and seasonal produce from them (Heath 2001, 2004a). Even when they were adequately provisioned, slaves' diets typically lacked variety, which is one reason slaves stole food (Gibbs et al. 1980; Perdue, Barden, and Phillips 1976).

Hutter's management style was different from Thomas Jefferson's style (Heath et al. 2004), possibly because social perceptions of appropriate slave management changed. Hutter, like many of his contemporaries, leased, or hired out, his own slaves while occasionally hiring additional slaves himself. When Hutter hired out slaves to nearby plantations and businesses, he documented which slaves were leased, occasionally noting to whom they were hired. Unfortunately he did not note how long slaves were hired.[4] This practice may have given Hutter's slaves the opportunity to become familiar with new landscapes. Leased slaves who moved beyond the immediate plantation lands owned by Hutter were exposed to neighboring environments. Their knowledge of broader landscapes could have provided them with opportunities to exploit different habitats. Encouraging slaves to produce or gather their own foods from forests and successional lands no doubt eased Hutter's need to provide food, but it also enabled slaves to obtain a more balanced diet.

Conclusion

The plant remains recovered from eighteenth- and nineteenth-century slaves' dwellings allow us to understand some of the complexities of slaves' subsistence activities. The archaeobotanical assemblages from Poplar Forest describe a variety of activities in which the slaves were engaged in their daily lives: laboring in plantation fields, producing their own crops, gathering wild resources from areas within the curtilage, and gathering resources from old fields and forests for food, fuel, utilitarian items such as baskets and mats, and medicine. While these activities are apparent in plants recovered from the sites, slaves' subsistence practices from the early Jefferson period through Hutter's tenure reflect changes in plantation activities, in owners' and overseers' management styles and in control over slaves' lives.

Under Thomas Jefferson, slaves supplemented their diet more strongly while he was an absentee owner than when he had a stronger presence. Under Hutter, enslaved African Americans not only supplemented their diet much like the slaves had when Jefferson was an absentee owner but also appear to have exploited plants in the forest margin to a much greater degree. This may have been influenced by an increased familiarity with their local environment, a result of Hutter's practice of hiring out slaves.

Jefferson, either personally or through his overseer, may have provided slaves with proportionally more rations than Hutter did, and Hutter's slaves may have compensated for this by increasing their own production and gathering foods from forest margins. Provisioning does not necessarily translate into a nutritionally adequate diet, and some measures of dietary stress suggest that Jefferson's slaves, particularly during the later occupation, had the most adequate diet. Other analysis suggests that Hutter's slaves, who appear to have been responsible for more of their own foods, had a more nutritious diet. It is not our intention to suggest that slaves' lives or even their diets were better under Jefferson or Hutter, and indeed the botanical remains alone cannot tell us whether slaves were better treated or better fed by one owner or the other.

Other researchers have argued for the psychological value of self-sufficiency and control that came with a diet largely provided by the slaves themselves (Heath and Bennett 2000; Mrozowski, Franklin, and Hunt 2008). It may well be that there was a trade-off between self-determination and food security.

## Notes

1. Edward S. Hutter, Income and Expense Journal, July 1, 1856–January 1, 1862, The Corporation for Thomas Jefferson's Poplar Forest, Forest, Virginia.

2. Edward S. Hutter, Farm Journal, January 1, 1844–December 31, 1854," The Corporation for Thomas Jefferson's Poplar Forest, Forest, Virginia (hereafter Hutter Farm Journal).

3. Betts (1987, 185–187); Thomas Jefferson to Joseph Darmsdatt, May 27, 1810, July 30, 1813, June 9, 1816, and May 25, 1819, Coolidge Collection of Thomas Jefferson Manuscripts, Massachusetts Historical Society, Boston, Massachusetts; Joel Yancey to Thomas Jefferson, May 31, 1821, Coolidge Collection of Thomas Jefferson Manuscripts; Jefferson to Craven Peyton, June 5, 1821, Coolidge Collection of Thomas Jefferson Manuscripts.

4. Hutter Farm Journal.

# 9

## Consumerism, Social Relations, and Antebellum Slavery at Poplar Forest

LORI LEE

Enslaved people engaged in a significant informal economy of property owner-ship and trade throughout the South, particularly during the nineteenth cen-tury (Penningroth 2003). The ability of slaves to earn, own, and trade property augmented the formal economy of the plantation by shifting part of the bur-den of subsistence to the enslaved. The personal empowerment gained through consumer activities appealed to enslaved people. The benefit of the alleviation of subsistence expenses made these practices acceptable to many slave own-ers. By the late antebellum period, the consumer practices that enslaved people engaged in had become customary rights. These economic practices were sig-nificant because they provided enslaved people with the means to obtain mate-rial goods that they used to exercise a measure of control over their daily lives. This degree of control provided a sense of personal empowerment within the context of slavery.

Consumption is a useful framework for analyzing slavery in the antebellum period. Social and economic conditions were changing rapidly during this time because of external factors such as industrialization, changes in modes of trans-portation, and labor management practices. These factors increased the access of some enslaved laborers to the market economy, and the consumer behavior of these individuals transformed social and economic relationships between whites and African Americans and among African Americans. The conditions that shaped this process varied by context, which fluctuated according to re-gional differences, the form of labor enslaved individuals were engaged in, and the particular practices of slave owners (Penningroth 2003, 46).

Daniel Miller has developed a theory of consumption that emphasizes ob-jects and their meanings within social relations in modern cultures (Miller 1987). He emphasized how objects are recontextualized into "expressive environments and daily routines" (ibid., 8). Successful application of this framework in an archaeological context requires research to understand the historical context that shaped daily routines and ideologies in the past.

The historical context of antebellum daily life in central Virginia can be assessed through census data, family letters, newspapers, court records, merchant accounts, farm journals, plantation management literature, Works Progress Administration interviews, folklorists' interviews with former slaves, and secondary historical sources. While historic documents describe some aspects of daily plantation life, archaeological investigations provide insight into other dimensions of the lives of enslaved people that are missing from the historical record and sometimes challenge the veracity of the historical record.

Poplar Forest is an historic plantation in Bedford County, Virginia where Thomas Jefferson had a home built in 1806 on land inherited from his father-in-law (Chambers 1993, 4). Jefferson died in 1826 and left part of the estate to his grandson, Frances Eppes. Eppes inherited 1,075 acres that included the main house (ibid., 167). He sold Poplar Forest to William Cobbs in 1828.[1] William and Marian Cobbs's daughter, Emma, married Edward Sixtus Hutter in 1840, and Hutter took over management of the plantation in 1842 (Marmon 1991, part 2, 61).

Nineteenth-century communities in central Virginia were defined by the social and political context of the region as a slave society. Virginia was home to more slaves and slaveholders than any other state in 1860 (Link 2005, 3). By that year, four-fifths of the African American population in the state resided east of the Blue Ridge Mountains, while three-fifths of the white population resided to the west (ibid., 30). In 1860, 40 to 59 percent of white families owned slaves in the majority of western piedmont and tidewater counties (ibid., 40).

Population size and density grew quickly in the northern and mid-Atlantic states from 1820 to 1850, while Virginia's population remained relatively constant throughout these decades (Cressey 1999, 4). The population stasis in Virginia masks two significant, dynamic processes: emigration and the domestic slave trade. By 1850, nearly 400,000 native Virginians had emigrated to other states; many took their slaves with them (Majewski 2000, 20). These forced migrations tore apart many African American families. The rapid growth in transportation systems throughout the South facilitated these migrations.

Prior to 1840, Bedford County was relatively isolated. The Lynchburg and Salem Turnpike was the primary nonlocal road in the county (Daniel 1985, 99). The James River provided the other principle way for local residents to travel and to send and receive market goods. By 1860, the addition of the Kanawha Canal, three railroads, county roads, and several new turnpikes had supplemented local roads and constituted a broad transportation network that impacted the daily lives, fortunes, and misfortunes of free and enslaved Bedford County citizens (ibid.).

The enslaved community at Poplar Forest underwent a dramatic transformation when the property was sold to William Cobbs in 1828. When Eppes emigrated to Florida, most of the members of the enslaved community were dispersed throughout Virginia and beyond (Marmon 1991, part 3, 70–72). William and Marian Cobbs brought slaves of their own to work the land and serve their domestic needs. Slave census data, family letters, deeds, and a farm journal provide insight into the demography of the slave community and, in some cases, the kinship relations among the enslaved.

William Cobbs acquired several slaves upon the death of his father-in-law in 1822 (Marmon 1991, part 3, 80). Many of these people were the descendants of a woman named Mary.[2] Mary was about thirty-six years old when she, her twenty-year-old daughter Ellen, her eighteen-year-old daughter Lucy, her four-year-old daughter Matilda, her two-year-old son Smith, and her newborn son Sam were transferred to William Cobbs. Cobbs's father willed him eight slaves when he died.[3] Hutter descendants recalled that Cobbs purchased "Aunt Katie," from Francis Eppes. Katie was purported to be a former slave of Thomas Jefferson.[4] No other records suggest any continuity of the enslaved community in the transition from Eppes's ownership of Poplar Forest to the Cobbs's ownership of that property.

Edward Hutter kept a farm journal from 1844 to 1854. Although the daily entries are concise and rarely express reflection, they do describe the work routines of field laborers. Hutter documented that enslaved field workers were engaged in planting, tending, and preparing fields and harvesting crops on a regular basis. Their work included tilling fields, digging ditches, planting crops, and taking harvested crops to the market. Workers also frequently built and repaired their own houses and constructed plantation outbuildings.[5] Although Hutter's farm journal does not document how house servants spent their time or detail how enslaved people spent their leisure time, it does provide some clues about such matters.

In addition to producing agricultural crops for the Cobbs and Hutter families, enslaved laborers at Poplar Forest cultivated and stored their own crops. They worked on their "patches" on holidays, after regular labor hours, and during regular work hours as Hutter deemed appropriate, although this happened only rarely.[6] Enslaved laborers worked six days a week. They did not do work for the plantation on Sundays and could choose to cultivate garden patches on these days. The small plots of land provided food to supplement diet, and for at least some enslaved laborers, they also provided a way of producing goods to be bartered or sold to each other, to members of the Cobbs and Hutter families, and for market exchange. Such production of crops and crafts provided enslaved people with a degree of autonomy because they were not completely dependent upon the slave owner for all of their needs. Through this means of production, enslaved laborers were able to direct their labor toward their own goals.

Evidence of consumer activities of enslaved laborers in the antebellum period at Poplar Forest comes from the archaeological remains of a slave cabin that was occupied from around 1840 to 1860. This cabin was located on a manmade terrace southeast of the main house, immediately south of an extant brick slave cabin that was built about 1857 (Heath and Lee 2010). This area is known as Site A. The surviving features of the cabin that once stood here consist of a three-foot-square subfloor pit, a few postholes, and the remains of a stone chimney (map 9.1) (Heath et al. 2004; Lee 2008).

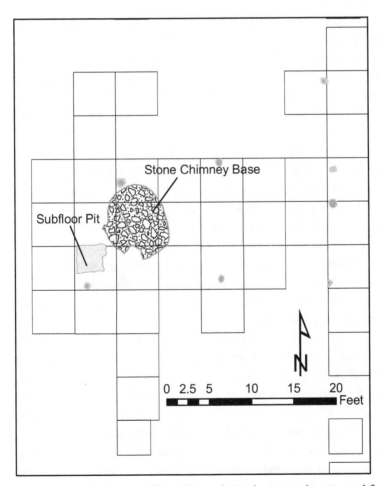

Map 9.1. Features of an antebellum cabin at the Poplar Forest plantation: subfloor pit, postholes, and stone chimney remains.

The artifacts recovered from this site provide evidence of production in the form of assemblages of work-related tools and other artifacts. Production is the first step in the process of consumption. Although Miller does not prioritize production in his approach to consumption, it is important to consider because it is relevant for understanding relationships among individuals, groups, and objects in the context of slavery (Heath 2004a, 19–38).

Sewing tools, files, and a folding knife indicate that work activities took place within the home. A count of complete pins and headed pin fragments yields a minimum of 277 brass pins found within the subfloor pit (Heath and Lee 2008). Three hundred forty-one buttons and partial buttons were recovered from Site A. The high number of buttons, the abundance of straight pins, the presence of needles and several thimbles, and the bone cap of a needle case suggest that a seamstress lived at Site A.

Hutter paid neighborhood white women to sew for his family and to make work clothes for enslaved laborers.[7] Enslaved women and girls also sewed for the Cobbs-Hutter family as well as for themselves and their families.[8] Sewing provided a potential means of acquiring money or bartering for services or goods with other community members. Hutter sometimes paid cash to a few enslaved men and possibly to some women instead of providing them with work clothes.[9] In these instances, the work clothes had probably already been made by women of the Poplar Forest slave community.

When Susan taught William Hutter the alphabet, Billy sold brooms to Edward Hutter, or George crafted shoes for the Hutter family, they each earned money from Edward Hutter.[10] In these and many similar ways, enslaved individuals at Poplar Forest sold services or crafts to the Cobbs-Hutter family and others. They used their earnings to participate in the informal and market economies. Social relations were entangled in these economic transactions. Sewing a shirt for a husband or brother reinforced family relationships. Repayment for this task, perhaps in the form of ribbons and beads purchased by men at the market, served the same purpose.

Documents suggest another way that some of Poplar Forest's enslaved laborers turned the critical resource of time into money through hard work. Some slaves were hired out to work in industrial environments (Morgan 1992, 65). The increasing frequency of this labor practice was one of the most significant changes in piedmont Virginia slavery in the nineteenth century. As labor-intensive tobacco-based plantation agriculture declined and mixed crops became more common, slaveholders had a surplus of laborers. They reacted by either selling slaves in the domestic trade or by hiring them out to other growing sectors of the economy such as manufacturing and transportation (Link 2005, 6). Industries that used the task system, such as ironworks, furnaces, tobacco factories, and lumbering sites, often offered incentives to hired enslaved laborers to encourage them to produce more (Morgan 1992, 65). The task system used predetermined work quotas. After the worker completed the daily work quota, his or her time was his or her own. Some slave owners and slave hirers offered incentives directly to slaves (not their owners) to do work beyond the work quota. These incentives were usually cash payments but they could also be in the form of extra time off from required tasks (ibid.).

Beginning in 1810, when salt production began in the area, Kanawha County, Virginia, was a racial frontier that was anomalous within the western part of the state because of its high slave population (Stealey 1993, 133–134). Salt furnaces operated there twenty-four hours a day, six days a week (ibid., 135). By the early 1820s, William Cobbs had hired out several enslaved men to salt furnaces and coal banks in Kanawha County, across the Blue Ridge Mountains and 205 miles away from Poplar Forest.[11] He continued this practice into the early 1840s.[12]

Ned and Tom, two enslaved men whom Cobbs leased to David Ruffner and Company in Kanawha County, borrowed a boat on one Thursday evening in 1827, allegedly to obtain some melons. Instead, they used the opportunity to run away. A letter to Cobbs notifying him that the men were missing stated: "Although they did not return on Sunday no suspicion was excited of their intention to run off, as it is very common for slaves to employ themselves about their little affairs—after performing their duties to their owners."[13] The fact that "no suspicion" was raised for three days suggests that Ned and Tom were working on a task system that rewarded them with time off, which they presumably needed to acquire melons.

Hiring out separated the members of enslaved families. While this separation created many problems, it also, ironically, extended social networks. The breadth of this network is suggested by the presence of an artifact at Site A that has been found in archaeological contexts only at antebellum African American sites in Virginia, Tennessee, and Maryland. (Fennell 2007b; McKee 1995; A. Russell 1997; Smith 1987; Yentsch 1994). The object, made of a stamped brass alloy, is known as a hand charm (A. Russell 1997, 66) (figure 9.1). It is a mass-produced clothing fastener that was likely modified to be worn as a pendant or charm. Through modification and use, the meaning of this industrially produced Victorian-inspired object was transformed.

Archaeologists have proposed various interpretations of the meaning of hand charms (Bartoy 2009; Fennell 2007b; McKee 1995, 40; A. Russell 1997, 67; Singleton 1991, 162; Smith 1987; Yentsch 1994, 33). Yentsch has documented that African Americans attributed hand charms, such as the one she recovered at the Calvert House in Annapolis, Maryland, with protective power over witches (Yentsch 1994, 33). Others suggest that hand charms may have been appealing because of their similarity to *figas* and Islamic Hand of Fatima symbols, both of which were used as protective charms in the Old and New Worlds (McKee 1995, 40; Singleton 1991, 162; Smith 1987). Fennell notes that the hand charms recovered at the Hermitage, Poplar Forest, and the Calvert House differ from *figas* and Hand of Fatima charms in form (Fennell 2007b, 22).

Fennell argues that hand charms were likely perceived in a more abstract sense wherein the hand itself is not the only significant element; the circle it is placed within and the horizontal crossbar that stabilizes the position of the hand within the circle were also likely seen as significant (see figure 9.1). He argues that meanings associated with each of these symbolic elements are found in the Bakongo belief system and notes that "these small hand ornaments would be of compelling interest to a person who subscribed to BaKongo cosmology" (ibid., 23–25, quote on 24).

Bartoy interprets the crossbar differently. He suggests that the crossbar is a shackle and argues that while other interpretations of the hand charms offered

Figure 9.1. Stamped brass alloy clothing fastener depicting a clenched right fist. Used by permission of Thomas Jefferson's Poplar Forest, Bedford County, Virginia.

by other archaeologists are plausible, none can be proven without additional evidence (Bartoy 2009). Instead of focusing primarily on the meanings associated with the charms, Bartoy looks at the context from which they came. Hand charms of the type shown in figure 9.1 have been found in archaeological contexts only in Tennessee, Virginia, and Maryland. Bartoy notes that it is significant that these states are all located in the Upper South, in the borderlands between slavery and freedom (ibid.). He suggests that hand charms were used as "active signaling devices . . . worn by the enslaved to communicate to like-minded people as to their beliefs in a resistance movement or abolitionist ideas" (ibid.).

Whether or not hand charms index resistance, the archaeological association of these objects with antebellum African American sites across three contiguous states suggests that African Americans assigned shared meanings to this polyvalent object. Their regional distribution suggests the widespread transmission of a shared cultural practice or an individual's participation in a similar social or cultural network. For hired slaves, these broad social networks were created at the expense of proximity to family members and shared resources, such as garden plots, on the home plantation. At the same time, hired slaves may have had greater access to money and markets than many family members and other members of the African American community who remained on the plantation.

Several of the enslaved workers at Poplar Forest plantation had access to money. At least some workers, including two women named Lucy and Matilda, also had access to the market.[14] However, access to money and markets was not equal, and disparities in access likely exacerbated class tensions within the enslaved community. Lucy and Matilda were part of a family group that William and Marian Cobbs inherited in the early 1820s from Marian's father, Samuel Scott; the group included the two sisters, their mother (Mary, mentioned above), siblings of the two girls, and other family members.[15] Marian clearly preferred to employ Mary's daughters as house servants, probably because she grew up with these women and trusted them.[16] One of Lucy and Matilda's tasks was to go to Lynchburg and purchase things for the Cobbs and Hutter families.[17] On these outings they were exposed to people who lived outside the plantation who could introduce them to ideas, objects, and people outside their everyday circle.

In 1841, Martha ran away from Poplar Forest.[18] Perhaps in response to this act of insubordination, she was hired out to various locations as far away as Buckingham County (a distance of forty-one miles) in the 1840s and early 1850s.[19] The regularity with which women were hired out was new to the nineteenth century. As urbanization created a demand for domestic help in towns, white families sought African American slaves and free blacks to meet the demand. White women shunned this type of work because of the racial stigma associated with domestic work and servitude in the South (Tripp 1997, 17).

Abroad marriages, or marriages between people who lived on two different plantations, are another way that social networks expanded. Martha was probably working off the plantation when she met her husband, Thomas, who was owned by Mr. Edwards. Martha and Thomas were married in 1853 (Patterson 1983, 208). In 1854 she returned to work at Poplar Forest, perhaps because the fact that she was married made it seem less likely that she would run away.[20] Martha's case illustrates how leasing provided a way for slaveholders to remove individuals from the plantation who they perceived as unmanageable, such as runaways, without selling them in the domestic trade. In the process Martha, like many hired slaves, broadened her circle of connections with other African Americans and whites who lived outside her home plantation.

Hiring out affected the enslaved community at Poplar Forest in several ways, both while people were gone and when they returned. In a letter written in 1835 to his hiring agent, Cobbs stated, "You wished me to inform you what to do with Peter and George. I think they would not like this country if they were to return."[21] Cobbs's insight into how Peter and George would perceive working at a Bedford County plantation after growing accustomed to different working conditions in Kanawha probably reflects less concern about the well-being of the two men than concerns about what sort of influence they might have within the slave community at Poplar Forest and whether or not they would run away.

After Peter became too feeble to maintain work productivity and Cobbs could no longer hire him out, he returned to Poplar Forest.[22] He probably had less autonomy there than he had experienced in Kanawha County. However, he was still allowed the right to refuse a hiring contract in 1842, even though the prospective hirer was Edward Hutter's brother.[23] George had returned by 1844, perhaps only for the Christmas holiday, but was sent away in mid-January of that year. Where he was sent is unclear.

Edward Hutter leased Poplar Forest slaves to local planters and businesses on a regular basis. The needs of the Cobbs and Hutter families, the market for hired labor, the gender and place in the life cycle of an enslaved individual, and seasonal crop requirements influenced how many slaves were expendable for leasing. Given the high number of individuals involved in hiring out, this labor practice certainly affected most of the enslaved families at Poplar Forest over time (table 9.1).

Hutter stopped keeping his farm journal at the end of 1854. From July 1856 through December 1861 he kept a journal of his domestic accounts instead. This Income and Expense Journal provides a good indication of what the Cobbs

Table 9.1. Partial list of slaves hired out from Poplar Forest, 1844–1861

| 1844 | Letia, Daniel, Catherine, Harriet, George, Martha, Harry, Rhoda |
|------|----------------------------------------------------------------|
| 1845 | Letia, Daniel, Catherine, Ned, Martha, Harry, Rhoda |
| 1846 | Doctor, Smith, Jack, Jacob, Catherine, Rhoda |
| 1847 | Martha |
| 1848 | Ned, Robert, Washington, William Armistead, Ada, Maria, Martha |
| 1849 | Doctor, Ned, Washington, William, Wm. Armistead, Robert, Ada, Martha |
| 1850 | Doctor, Washington, William, Martha, Ned, John, Maria, Louisa |
| 1851 | Ned, Martha, Doctor, Woodson, William, John, Louisa |
| 1852 | Ned, Doctor, Woodson, William, John, Martha, Louisa |
| 1853 | Ned, Doctor, Woodson, Washington, John Echols, Bartlett, Jesse, Martha, Susan & child, Louisa |
| 1854 | Jacob, Woodson, Wm. Armistead, Robert, Doctor, Ned, John Echols, Matilda & Margaret, Susan & Elizabeth & Coleman, Judy, Louisa |
| 1855 | Matilda, Susan, Washington |
| 1856 | Washington, Louisa |
| 1857 | Washington, Ned, Bob, Judy, Victorine, Louisa |
| 1858 | Washington, Dump, Judy, William Armistead, George, Louisa |
| 1859 | Washington, Victorine, Judy |
| 1860 | Washington, Louisa, Dump, Judy, Robert, William Armistead, George, Victorine |
| 1861 | Washington, Ellen, Victorine |

Source: Edward S. Hutter, Farm Journal, January 1, 1844–December 31, 1854, The Corporation for Thomas Jefferson's Poplar Forest, Forest, Virginia.

and Hutter families sold at market and what they purchased from Lynchburg businesses. In addition, the journal describes the complex social and economic relationships between Hutter and numerous enslaved workers ranging from starkly economic to economic under the guise of paternalism. Some of these social and economic relations were expressed in the forms of gifts and loans.

Hutter only documented one material gift given to an enslaved person. In 1860 he purchased a dress for one of Lydia Johnson's children.[24] The rarity of this act suggests that the dress was probably for an exceptional occasion, perhaps a baptism or a burial. In 1850, Lydia named her third child Ida Reeder, after Edward Hutter's niece.[25] Naming a child after a member of the slave owner's family was a means of strengthening social relations and reinforcing the fictive kin ties fabricated in the patriarchal system of antebellum slavery. The gift of a dress for an enslaved child and an enslaved mother's decision to bestow a Hutter family name on an enslaved daughter suggest that the Cobbs and Hutter family had a relationship with Lydia that entailed reciprocal obligations. The strength of this relationship is suggested by the longevity of the relationship. After emancipation, Mrs. Johnson continued to work for the Hutters until her death in 1919 (figure 9.2).[26] Whether she perceived her ties to the Cobbs and Hutter family as primarily emotional or economic (or both) is unknown.

Hutter fulfilled his obligations as patriarch when he provisioned enslaved workers with shoes and clothing or gave them small monetary or material

Figure 9.2. Mrs. Lydia Johnson, ca. 1910s. Used by permission of Thomas Jefferson's Poplar Forest, Bedford County, Virginia.

gifts.[27] Objects that were acquired through this method may have had less value for the enslaved workers than objects they chose for themselves through purchase or barter. Jean Howson (1995) has argued that articles that were provisioned retained an association with slave labor. Provisioned objects reinforced the master-slave relationship and the paternalism and dependency that relationship entailed (Lee 2008). Some transfer-printed ceramic patterns from Site A match the patterns, Amoy and Napier, on transfer-printed ceramics associated with the main house during the antebellum occupation (Heath et al. 2004, 33). A disdain for provisioned ceramics is suggested at Site A by the presence of a few complete and nearly complete Amoy and Napier vessels that appear to have been discarded while they were still functional.

The presence of unique ceramic types in the Site A assemblage suggests that residents might have acquired these objects for themselves. The owners of these objects likely invested more significance in self-acquired goods than those that they received from the slaveholder. Self-acquired objects may have also been used in different ways than provisioned objects: to express aesthetic preferences, to shape and reflect identity, and to create or maintain social relations (Galle 2006; Heath 1999b; Howson 1995; Lee 2008; Martin 2008, 173–193). The practices associated with earning and procuring items independently was also likely meaningful to the enslaved.

Instead of allowing some workers to engage in the market economy independently, Edward Hutter preferred to retain some control over the distribution process by sending the corn and oats some enslaved workers had raised to market for them and distributing the revenue brought by the crops.[28] Hutter assumed this intermediary position again when he facilitated market purchases for particular enslaved workers.[29] This mediator role reinforced the power of the master while at the same time the master yielded to the desires of the enslaved to gain access the market economy (Olwell 1994, 35).

Edward Hutter engaged in market relations with the enslaved when he bought crops, small animals, and craft products such as baskets, brooms, and mats from them. The individuals who sold these items were usually men. Hutter also paid some men and women for working on holidays.[30] Merchants' accounts indicate what kinds of purchases were being made with this money. Although no merchant account books documenting purchases made by antebellum slaves at Poplar Forest have been found, merchant account books for central Virginia demonstrate that cloth, sewing supplies, personal adornment items, alcohol, and sweeteners were the most common items slaves bought from 1780 to 1860 (Dew 1994; Heath 1997a, 1; Heath 2004a; Martin 2008). The archaeological record at Site A reveals the significance of sewing supplies and personal adornment items to the inhabitants of the cabin.

Objects of personal adornment were a significant means for slaves to express, negotiate, challenge, or maintain relations with owners. Material remains associated with households also provide a way to look at what it meant to be a slave from the inside perspective that is frequently lacking from historical documentation. The purchases of many enslaved workers documented in merchant account books were related to clothing or items of personal adornment (Dew 1994; Heath 2004a; Martin 2008). These objects were used to shape outward appearance, to reflect an individual's sense of him or herself, and to attract or signal information to others (Galle 2006; Heath 2004a). Through their roles in the practices of shaping identity, signaling information, and creating and maintaining social relations, mundane objects such as glass beads, ceramics, and stamped clothing fasteners became a means of experiencing personal empowerment within the context of slavery.

An abundance of personal adornment objects, including 24 wound-glass beads, 141 glass seed beads, 18 partial glass seed beads, 1 bone bead, 4 paste jewels, 3 copper-alloy earrings, and a carnelian brooch, were found at the Site A cabin (figure 9.3). Some of these objects were likely worn to enhance appearance and express personality. Other objects, such as glass beads, may have played additional roles in promoting health and well-being rather than solely serving as personal adornment items within the enslaved community (Lee 2008; A. Russell 1997, 68–71). Scholars have demonstrated that beads were used by African and African American peoples in the past and continue to be used in the present for medicinal and spiritual purposes (Caton 1997; Stine, Cabak, and Groover 1996). In the 1930s, former slaves told Works Progress Administration (WPA) interviewers that glass beads worn around the neck served the mundane purpose of easing teething for young children (Wilkie 1997, 86–87). WPA narratives also document that enslaved African Americans wore pierced coins for protection or well-being (Baker and Baker 1996, 235). A pierced Spanish real bearing teeth marks was recovered from the antebellum cabin site (figure 9.4). This find may indicate that the coin was worn by an infant for protection and (or instead) to ease teething pain. Mortality among the enslaved, particularly children, was high in the antebellum period. Directing resources toward well-being was one way enslaved people attempted to protect themselves from the harsh realities of daily life that included oppression, sickness, death, violence, and separation (Edwards-Ingram 2001, 2005).

The starkest of economic exchanges took place when Hutter sold enslaved laborers. Commodifying people and selling them away from their families was a brutal practice. These acts denied the rights of enslaved people to family life and all of the benefits it provides.

Figure 9.3. Personal adornment objects from Site A: black glass beads, black glass button, carnelian pendant, clear paste jewel in an alloy setting, stamped brass alloy earring. Used by permission of Thomas Jefferson's Poplar Forest, Bedford County, Virginia.

Figure 9.4. Pierced Spanish real with teeth marks. Used by permission of Thomas Jefferson's Poplar Forest, Bedford County, Virginia.

Historic records from Poplar Forest for the period 1840–1861 document white owners' suspicions that slaves were malingering, times when slaves ran away, and times when slaves were insubordinate. Harriett was whipped for insubordination in 1857.[31] She was sold a few years later when she continued to refuse to submit to Hutter's regulations.[32] This sale separated Harriett from her elderly mother and at least three of her five children. The ability of white owners to sell enslaved individuals is a powerful reminder of the differences in consumer choices available to those who were enslaved and those who owned African Americans and the power differential and social distance that existed between the two groups.

The value and meaning of objects owned by the Hutter family were recontextualized to some degree after emancipation. The value and meaning of the social relations that existed between the former master's family and the enslaved community were also recontextualized. These shifts in meaning were expressed at least once through the changed socioeconomic status of a person they had formerly owned. After plantation matriarch Marian Cobbs died in 1877, an estate sale was held at Poplar Forest. Washington Brown, who had once been a slave at Poplar Forest, purchased iron pots, bowls, saws, chairs, a cow, and a mule.[33] The meanings of these things to Mr. Brown thirteen years after emancipation were likely very different than the meanings of similar objects to him under slavery. This change in meaning was contingent upon a change in social and economic relations as well as a different historical situation. Mr. Brown had been hired out for several of the last fifteen years before emancipation.[34] This experience may have provided him with the economic resources, skills, and social networks that contributed to his ability to make these purchases.

The boundaries of the institution of slavery in Virginia became more fluid in the late antebellum era when slave hiring and industrial slavery became more common. These labor practices altered social and economic conditions, and master-slave relationships became increasingly complex. Combining knowledge from historical documents with material culture analysis increases our understanding of the processes of production, acquisition, use, and meaning that comprise consumption. Historical and archaeological analysis reveals that at least some of the enslaved people at Poplar Forest had increased access to material goods in the antebellum period. Although the access of enslaved people to a broader range of goods did not offer them control over their legal status as property, some of them used material culture in significant ways in their attempts to mediate the realities of life, gain varying degrees of control over their daily routines, and to create and maintain social relationships.

# Notes

1. Bedford County Deed Book 21, 184–185, Library of Virginia, Richmond, Virginia.

2. Bedford County Deed Book 29, 177–178, Library of Virginia, Richmond, Virginia.

3. Campbell County Will Book 6, 1827–1831, 418, Library of Virginia, Richmond, Virginia.

4. Christian Hutter, Notes, 1909, The Corporation for Thomas Jefferson's Poplar Forest, Historical Collections, Forest, Virginia; Nora Carter, "Survey Report, Poplar Forest—Home of Thomas Jefferson, 1937 June 7," unpublished manuscript, Library of Virginia, Richmond, Virginia.

5. Edward S. Hutter, Farm Journal, January 1, 1844–December 31, 1854, The Corporation for Thomas Jefferson's Poplar Forest, Forest, Virginia (hereafter Hutter Farm Journal).

6. Ibid.

7. For examples, see entries for August 26, 1856, December 12, 1856, December 24, 1856, December 26, 1856, and May 21, 1857, Edward S. Hutter, Income and Expense Journal, July 1, 1856–January 1, 1862, The Corporation for Thomas Jefferson's Poplar Forest, Forest, Virginia (hereafter Hutter Income and Expense Journal).

8. Entries for January 14, 1850, and January 21–23, 1852, Hutter Farm Journal; Marian Scott Cobbs to Emma Williams Cobbs Hutter, April 18, 1854, Hutter Family Manuscripts, The Corporation for Thomas Jefferson's Poplar Forest, Forest, Virginia (hereafter Hutter Family Manuscripts).

9. Entries for April 19, 1857, and May 1, 1858, Hutter Income and Expense Journal.

10. Edward Sixtus Hutter to Emma Williams Cobbs Hutter, June 27, 1844, Hutter Family Manuscripts; Christian Jacob Hutter to Edward Sixtus Hutter, June 18, 1844, Hutter Family Manuscripts; entries for March 4, 1859, and December 9, 1861, Hutter Income and Expense Journal.

11. *William Cobbs v. Thomas Law and David Ruffner*, 1822; *William Cobbs v. John D. Shrewsbury Sr. and John D. Shrewsbury Jr.*, 1826; and *William Cobbs v. John Shrewsbury Sr. and Samuel Shrewsbury Sr.*, 1826, all in West Virginia University Library, Morgantown, West Virginia.

12. Edward Hutter to Emma Williams Cobbs Hutter, May 11, 1841, Hutter Family Manuscripts.

13. Richard E. Putney to William Cobbs August 15, 1827, William Cobbs Letters 1827–1841, Library of Virginia, Richmond, Virginia (hereafter William Cobbs Letters).

14. Emma Williams Cobbs Hutter to Edward Sixtus Hutter, July 21, 1857, Hutter Family Manuscripts.

15. Bedford County Deed Book 29, 177–178.

16. Hutter Farm Journal, January 1st entry, 1844–1854.

17. Emma Williams Cobbs Hutter to Edward Sixtus Hutter, July 21, 1857, Hutter Family Manuscripts.

18. Emma Williams Cobbs Hutter to Edward Sixtus Hutter, September 8, 1841, Hutter Family Manuscripts.

19. Entries for October 19, 1847, January 1, 1848, January 16, 1849, December 25–28, 1849, January 1, 1851, January 1, 1852, and January 1, 1853, Hutter Farm Journal.

20. Entry for January 1, 1854, Hutter Farm Journal.

21. William Cobbs to William R. Cox, December 31, 1835, William Cobbs Letters.

22. William R. Cox to William Cobbs, January 6, 1833, William Cobbs Letters.

23. Christian J. Hutter to Edward S. Hutter, December 31, 1842, Hutter Family Manuscripts.

24. Entry for July 21, 1861, Hutter Income and Expense Journal.

25. Entry for June 30, 1850, Hutter Farm Journal.

26. *The News* (Lynchburg, Virginia), October 22, 1919, Jones Memorial Library, Lynchburg.

27. Hutter Farm Journal, December 7, 1844. Hutter Income and Expense Journal: May 26, June 1, June 27, July 6, September 21, October 3, and December 22, 1857; January 12, March 24, April 5, May 1, June 12, August 2, August 30, and November 12, 1858; June 6, November 9, December 24, and December 27, 1859; March 7, June 23, October 9, and December 20, 1860; and January 1 and April 1, 1861.

28. For example, see entries for October 18, 1856, November 19, 1856, December 16, 1856, December 24–25, 1856, January 1, 1857, and January 10, 1857, Hutter Income and Expense Journal.

29. For example, see entries for August 3, 1856, October 19, 1856, May 6, 1857, May 30, 1857, February 20, 1858, and September 22, 1858, Hutter Income and Expense Journal.

30. Hutter Income and Expense Journal, April 24, 1858, April 17, 1860, and April 21, 1860.

31. Entry for September 19, 1859, Hutter Income and Expense Journal.

32. Charles McKersham to Col. E. Whittlesey, June 15, 1866, Records of the Bureau of Refugees, Freedmen, and Abandoned Lands, Record Group 105, NARA.

33. Bedford County Will Book 24, 1877–1880, 389, Library of Virginia, Richmond, Virginia.

34. Hutter Income and Expense Journal.

# IO

## Founding Families

### Reflections on the Archaeology of Poplar Forest

STEPHEN A. MROZOWSKI

## Introduction

In the pantheon of American cultural heroes, few stand as tall as Thomas Jefferson. Founding father, author of the Declaration of Independence, president, and gentleman farmer—Jefferson was all of these and more. Yet like any man, he was not solely responsible for everything he accomplished. Jefferson, a learned, worldly, inventive, and enterprising man, represented a distinctly American personality whose love of country and beauty was reflected in the spaces he created at his homes at Monticello and Poplar Forest. The time he spent in Europe and England is evident in the architecture and landscapes of both of his homes. The space he created as both retreat and social center at Poplar Forest is also imbued with his sensibilities and his love of classical history. When he shared this space with his friends and family, especially his grandchildren, his aspirations for the world they would know were visible in the landscapes he created. These aspirations were also visible in the interior spaces of his home and took shape at his dinner table.

Jefferson was a man of his time. In many respects he was ahead of his time, but his world, that which he knew as farmer, president, ambassador, academic, and farmer again, was one riven by hierarchies and inequalities. Yet there were contexts where these divisions were played out in spatial arenas that were both shared and contested. At Poplar Forest, for example—Jefferson's social circle, which included his children, his friends, and local acquaintances, moved through a space also used by the many enslaved African Americans he owned.

As the work in the preceding chapters attests, all of these individuals contributed in some way to the history that unfolded at Poplar Forest.

In framing the work at Poplar Forest, it is difficult to find a concept that encompasses all of the elements that contributed to its landscape and its roles as a commercial enterprise, a center of cultural expression, and a canvas across which history was layered. For me the concept of space is perhaps the best way to envision what was created at Poplar Forest. The model I would like to use envisions space as a multidimensional reality that contains elements of numerous cultural traditions and histories (Mrozowski 2010a; Mrozowski, Hayes, and Hancock 2007). This conceptualization of space draws heavily on the work of Henri Lefebvre (1991), Edward Soja (1989, 2000, 2010), David Harvey (1982, 1989, 2000), Susan Zukin (1991), and James Delle (1998). It remains a work in progress and should be viewed as such, yet I believe it helps frame what we do as archaeologists. Dimensions of time and space have interacted to create the landscapes we investigate and interpret. In some instances the differences that characterized the lives of those who inhabited these spaces are difficult if not impossible to discern archaeologically. In this sense it is as if the space we investigate is a seamless reality that belies the divisions that characterized life in the past.

Because our interpretations are contemporary observations, our own space is part of the intellectual landscape. Woven through this space are traces of those who have come before us, not just the Jeffersons or Hutters or the enslaved Africans and their descendants who toiled at Poplar Forest but also the historians, the architectural historians, and the archaeologists whom Barbara Heath eloquently describes as setting the stage for the kind of archaeology discussed in this book. These individuals have also contributed to the intellectual space that is historical archaeology and its particular focus on the recent past. The interdisciplinary character of the historical archaeology that Barbara Heath and Jack Gary and their colleagues have employed at Poplar Forest has its own intellectual history. Some of the paradigms of that history have been maintained, and others have been forgotten (Mrozowski 2010b).

## Multidimensional Space

Virtually every introductory textbook contains a discussion of time and space as the central dimensions of archaeological research. The researchers at Poplar Forest have been confronted by a variety of spaces that exist simultaneously. There is the archaeological space that is comprised of the deposits they have uncovered and the many elements and features that constitute this record. This archaeological space is what archaeologists excavate, record, analyze, and interpret, and it includes all of the material culture and biological specimens collected as part of their work. The people who created this space moved through their own social spaces, which belonged to the landscape in which they lived. In some instances this landscape was a unique blend of nature shaped by human action; the garden is perhaps the most common example of this blend. The social space of Poplar Forest was shaped by the social relations of production that characterized a particular form of political economy: that of plantation slavery and the hierarchies of power it engendered. The landscapes of work yards, the various quarters of the enslaved workers, the fields, the gullies, the nurseries, as well as the architectural traditions that shaped the built environment formed a space that served as the context for the daily interaction of those who lived and worked at Poplar Forest. This social space also extended to the interiors of the buildings and the material culture within them. For example, the plates and bowls that were used to prepare and serve food each day helped craft social spaces.

Together these various elements formed the material world at Poplar Forest, where an amalgam of cultural traditions existed. These various traditions were part of the different histories that individuals brought to Poplar Forest. As a plantation, Poplar Forest was, as Barbara Heath notes, a complex operation that involved agriculture and commerce and a work regime built around slavery. Although its connection to an individual as illustrious as Thomas Jefferson obviously makes its place in history noteworthy, as a plantation Poplar Forest was not that different from many similar places in the South. It was established during the eighteenth century, a period that saw an assortment of plantation types created in colonial settings across the earth (Chatterjee, Gupta, and Rath 2010; Singleton 2005). These plantations differed in their purpose, in their commercial makeup, and in what they produced, yet they shared a common thread: a reliance on some form of slavery or servitude. The various populations of these plantations created cultural identities that were reproduced in myriad ways through spatial practices, foodways, and materiality.

The varied approaches used in this volume to analyze the households at Poplar Forest reveal a complex and detailed picture of daily life on the plantation and the management of the plantation over time. Indeed, one of the most interesting facets of the portrait presented by the authors is just how visible change was on the landscape, in the demographic profile of the various households, in the agriculture being practiced at Poplar Forest, and in the cultural practices of its inhabitants. The world outside the plantation was also evident at Poplar Forest. This broader world, that of the eighteenth and nineteenth centuries, was also a space—a cultural space—comprised of traditions and histories that helped in shaping the landscape of a plantation such as Poplar Forest as well as the behavior of its inhabitants. Jefferson presents one of the best documented examples of a person whose experiences influenced the way he shaped his material world, but all who lived and worked at Poplar Forest brought something of the larger world they knew to this smaller stage. For example, there is evidence that African influences shaped the cultural practices of some of the enslaved workers on the plantation. This larger world often appears in the form of material culture, landscape designs, agricultural practices, and cultural practices.

The many layers the researchers at Poplar Forest have revealed present a picture that is both multiscalar and multidimensional. It is also a picture that reveals changes over time that were linked to cultural and economic changes at the local, regional, and global levels. From this perspective the deep contextualization of the work at Poplar Forest, from the role the plantation played in the economic history of Bedford County to the role of recent investigations in the growth of plantation archaeology, represents an ideal model of how such research should be carried out.

In an effort to place the work at Poplar Forest in a broader perspective I would like to focus on several points where the lines of evidence convergence thematically. Among these the most obvious is landscape, but there are others, including household archaeology, changes in farming practices, and the differences between how Jefferson and Hutter managed Poplar Forest. In framing these points of convergence I will focus on how change is reflected spatially in the archaeological, social, and cultural-historical spaces that comprised Poplar Forest. I will conclude by arguing that the model employed at Poplar Forest represents a productive avenue for others to follow.

Landscape at Poplar Forest

The landscape at Poplar Forest represents a patchwork of agricultural and gardening practices that changed over time. Archaeological, documentary, and botanical analysis show that some of the changes visible on the landscape were brought about by a combination of factors. Among the most profound was erosion caused by tobacco farming. The history of Poplar Forest and of virtually all of Bedford County was tied directly to the growing of tobacco. Although the piedmont of Virginia was settled much later than the Chesapeake region, it underwent a rapid transformation driven by tobacco farming. The growth of Lynchburg as a hub of tobacco processing and shipping is the most obvious example of this trajectory, but at Poplar Forest tobacco cultivation shaped both the landscape and the work regime of enslaved workers. One of the more interesting examples of how these forces converged was the way erosion problems resulted in new uses for what had formerly been arable land. The most obvious example of this is the decision to relocate African quarters to land that was so eroded that it could no longer be used for cultivation. Erosion problems also led Jefferson to begin using an area that had formerly been under cultivation as a nursery.

The problems of erosion and soil exhaustion tied to tobacco cultivation were well documented at Poplar Forest, perhaps best captured in comments made by Francis and Mary Elizabeth Eppes about how tobacco had left the soil exhausted and had created a landscape punctuated by gullies and worn-out fields.

As Poplar Forest matured as a landscape, it must have presented a set of contrasts. The traces of weeds and other ruderal plants in the botanical record discussed by Bowes and Trigg point to the processes of ecological succession that would have been set in motion by the periodic abandonment of fields. This picture of a mosaic in which some fields were under cultivation and some were exhausted and eroding contrasts with the more genteel elements of a landscape shaped by influences from England and Europe. Tim Trussell notes Jefferson's love of European, especially English, gardens and describes how these served as inspiration for his landscape treatments at both Monticello and Poplar Forest. Although oval-shaped planting beds and botanical evidence of weeds may evoke very different images of the landscape, they are part of the same reality, the same social space. The landscape is, after all, a blend of biological and cultural processes.

Virginia farmers were able to draw upon a growing literature of scientific farming in their efforts to maintain tobacco as a cash crop, and eventually the influence of scientific farming appears to have provided some relief from erosion. Despite the impact of tobacco cultivation on the fertility and stability of piedmont soils, it remained the mainstay of the local economy, and it seems that Edward Hutter briefly attempted to continue to grow it. Using new fertilizers and a variety of trenching and harrowing techniques, Hutter appears to have succeeded where Jefferson did not.

Barbara Heath points to other changes at Poplar Forest, such as the demographic profile of the enslaved work force and the housing for this community. The various quarters on the plantation and the housing and yards that comprised them were just as much a part of the landscape of Poplar Forest as Jefferson's classically inspired dwelling. In her discussion of quarter housing Heath notes how important it is to consider demographic and life-cycle changes when looking at household-level interpretations, She notes, for example, that by 1783 most of enslaved households at Poplar forest included individuals related to one another and that by 1819 the community was made up of households comprised almost entirely of individuals who were related by birth or marriage. These kind of demographic changes do not seem to have resulted in changes in the archaeological record of subterranean pits for example. Heath says that the use of pits and their numbers seems to remain fairly consistent between the eighteenth and nineteenth centuries.

Archaeological evidence of change is also discussed in the chapter presented by Bowes and Trigg who argue that Edward Hutter allowed his slaves to collect and grow some of their own food. Bowes and Trigg use botanical information to determine whether the habitats slaves exploited for food changed over time. Their results seem to show that the forested margins of the plantation were more widely exploited after Jefferson's tenure at Poplar Forest. Their work points to the usefulness of botanical information in reconstructing habitat exploitation patterns. Lori Lee notes that under Hutter's stewardship, skilled enslaved workers worked on other plantations or even in industrial settings. These types of changes in food production patterns and in work regimes may have brought other changes that were visible archaeologically at the household level.

## Household Archaeology at Poplar Forest

Few would think of Poplar Forest without thinking first of Thomas Jefferson, but his was only one of the households that contributed to the history of the plantation. Jefferson was preceded as owner by his father-in-law, John Wayles, and Jefferson bequeathed it to his own descendents. When his grandson and his wife received Poplar Forest, it seemed to be a plantation that was exhausted. With the help of innovation, Edward Hutter, a later owner, revived the plantation by changing to grains as the main cash crops. Each of these households, including the women and children that populated them, left their mark on Poplar Forest. Heath notes that one of the advantages of household archaeology, is its focus on the role of gender relations. Another advantage of household-level archaeology is that documentary sources often provide us with information about the individuals who made up those households. In instances where figures such as Jefferson and Hutter are involved, it is possible to fill in our portraits of the past with some sense of the cultural-historical space in which they lived. These contexts were shaped by intellectual and economic trends that can sometimes be detected archaeologically. Certainly this is the case at Poplar Forest.

Beyond the obvious connections between landscape treatments and their European or English influences or the improvements made by Hutter and their possible links to the growing literature of scientific farming, other evidence is linked more directly to the lives that were lived in the social space that comprised the plantation. The changes that shaped the history of that space are touched upon in each of the chapters, from Proebsting's discussion of how the Virginia piedmont was rich in the resources needed to sustain Native American society to Lee's concluding discussion of how choices made by Edward Hutter ushered in a new agricultural regime at Poplar Forest. In that new regime, his enslaved workers supplied more of their own food, engaged in more work off of the plantation, and ultimately built identities that appear to be different from those suggested by the archaeology of Jefferson's period of ownership.

This social space also involved changes in the composition of the households of the enslaved people on the plantation. It was also visible in the way interior space was apportioned and used. Jack Gary's discussion of the transfer-printed ware Jefferson used suggests that the same influences that affected his landscape choices extended to the way his dinner table was set. Gary notes that Jefferson's experiences as a foreign ambassador and as president often involved the use of social settings for diplomacy and business. In this sense it comes as little surprise that one of Jefferson's guests was Archibald Robertson, the local merchant who provided many of the goods used to outfit the main house at Poplar Forest. When Jefferson died in 1826, his debt to Robertson was close to $6,000, a figure that reflects Jefferson's tastes as well as his need to supply his plantation operation. Ultimately, Jefferson was unable to support either of these things.

What makes Gary's discussion of the ceramics Jefferson used at Poplar Forest so interesting is their connection to England's preeminent educational institutions, Oxford and Cambridge universities. At the time J & W Ridgway was producing the Oxford and Cambridge College ceramic series, their plates, bowls, and teacups were replete with classical images that evoked a bond between modern England and the world of antiquity. These classical elements were also visible in the architecture of the buildings and landscape at Poplar Forest, as they were at Monticello. Like the designers of English ceramics who sought to reinforce a link between an emerging British empire and the classical states of Greece and Rome, Jefferson sought to establish a similar lineage for himself and the United States as a whole. Jefferson's choices reflected his desire to imbue his surroundings with material goods that expressed his self-image as an educated, modern leader. Gary notes that Jefferson sought to pass on this appreciation for classical beauty to his grandchildren. Beyond what this suggests about Jefferson's own sensibilities, it also serves as a reminder that over time the role of the women and children in the various households at Poplar Forest contributed to the construction of the site's materiality and identity. Jefferson's self-image extended to his commercial dealings and his oversight of the operation at Poplar Forest. But as the evidence attests, his lack of success in these areas resulted in a household mired in debt.

The management style of Edward Hutter presents something of a contrast to that of Jefferson. Like Jefferson, however, Hutter brought an intellectual approach to his stewardship of Poplar Forest. In her discussion of the agricultural regime Hutter employed, Lee notes that his decisions were shaped in good measure by a shifting economy. Although tobacco remained the mainstay of the broader piedmont agricultural economy, Hutter experimented with wheat cultivation and new field management techniques at Poplar Forest. His reliance on new approaches was not limited to his work with crop rotation and fertilizers. With the drop in tobacco prices that Lee discusses in her chapter, farmers turned to mixed crops that in turn resulted in a surplus of laborers. As a result farmers sought to hire out their enslaved workers to other farmers and to southern industrialists. Hutter seems to have embraced this approach.

Another facet of household archaeology that was revealed by the archaeology at Poplar Forest is evidence of pipe manufacturing. Lee's discussion of local pipe production at the plantation suggests that the designs were inspired by a combination of English, African, and Native American influences. Her research also suggests that while pipe-making was not a major enterprise, it may have provided a commodity that the enslaved African Americans of the plantation could trade for food or other goods.

Archaeological evidence of small-scale manufacturing is not restricted to the production of smoking pipes. There is also strong evidence of sewing that can be linked to the production of clothing for exchange either with other households on the plantation or markets outside of Poplar Forest. The manufacture of pipes and clothing by members of the enslaved households at Poplar Forest was tied to the other developments during the time when Edward Hutter owned and operated the plantation.

During this same period it seems that the cultural identity of the enslaved population may have been undergoing a transformation. Although Heath and Lee analyze different classes of material culture, they both suggest that a greater sense of social cohesion may have characterized the households of the enslaved African Americans. I have already mentioned the small numbers of subfloor pits that Heath describes and the possibility that they indicate more sharing of resources and closer affinal ties between the households at Poplar Forest. Lee points to the presence of glass beads and possible charms that may reflect the influence of Igbo members of the plantation's African-descended population. She goes on to argue that items of personal adornment that may have been obtained by the enslaved populations through exchange may have helped in shaping identities and providing some form of personal empowerment. Lee contrasts these items with others, such as some ceramics, that may have been tainted by their association with the owners of the plantations. If Lee is correct, then it may be possible to extend this argument to the results presented by Bowes and Trigg suggesting that supplying some of their own food may have also contributed to self-identity and feelings of empowerment.

## Founding Families and Plantation Archaeology

In their introduction to this volume, Barbara Heath and Jack Gary place their research and that of their colleagues at Poplar Forest in a broader context that includes the history of the property, the role of the property as a plantation owned and operated by one of the most venerable figures in American history, and the ways the property is an example of plantation archaeology. In seeking to place their work in this broader context Heath and Gary present an inclusive story of Poplar Forest and those who shaped its destiny. Many of those who worked at Poplar Forest will remain forever nameless (see Connerton 1989, 2008; Mills and Walker 2008; Trouillot 1995; Van Dyke and Alcock 2003), while others such as Thomas Jefferson or Edward Hutter will continue to be the focus of historical inquiry. Yet the volume that Heath and Gary have produced stands as a prime example of the power of historical archaeology to end historical silence. In this sense, the volume's greatest success is that it breathes new life into the households of people who labored at Poplar Forest. Through a richly textured interdisciplinary approach, the authors in this volume have painstakingly pieced together some of the details of lives long silenced, but lives that continue to have a story worth telling and reading. What makes it exciting is the way seemingly small features of daily life—the use of glass beads, the presence of African-inspired charms, the classical elements visible in the buildings, gardens, and tableware of Jefferson's time—are all linked to a wider world. The various spaces in which these elements existed were linked to form a world in which lives were played out and fortunes were made and lost.

What perhaps stands out most about the work at Poplar Forest is the way the lives of those less illustrious than Jefferson continue to provide evidence of a shared history. But although these histories were shared, they were starkly different. The enslaved workers of Jefferson's time would not share his glory or his sensibilities, yet they were instrumental in maintaining a world he sought to pass on to his grandchildren. Whether one could argue that the life Edward Hutter provided for his enslaved workers was materially or spiritually better or worse than that furnished by Jefferson is difficult to say without knowing how it felt to be those individuals or hearing testimony from them. Perhaps the presence of glass beads or charms provides some level of answer if we choose to interpret them as media of self-expression. What does seem clear is that the combined evidence paints a picture in which tobacco, plantation slavery, commercial development, ecological transformation, and the growth of scientific farming all converge to shape the destiny of this single, albeit important, farm in Bedford County, Virginia. It was home to one of the most celebrated and cherished figures in early American history, a founding father if there ever was one. But Jefferson was not the only person to contribute to the history of Poplar Forest; he was not its only founding father. All who worked on the plantation—tilling the soil, planting crops, shaping the landscape, sewing and washing clothes, and cooking meals—were members of a group of families who are just as responsible for the United States we see today as was Jefferson. This is the humbling reality of archaeology; the story it unearths is seldom the one certain people wanted to create. In this instance the narrative that emerges in the writings of Heath and Gary and their colleagues is a much richer story than would have been possible if the written word was their only source of information. Through analysis of the material remnants of life at Poplar Forest, these archaeologists have been able to contribute to the continuing work of those interested in the history of slavery to end historical silences that until recently sought to reserve its spotlight for the likes of Thomas Jefferson. While he undoubtedly deserves the attention, he was far from alone in shaping the history of Poplar Forest.

# Bibliography

## Manuscript Collections

AMERICAN PHILOSOPHICAL SOCIETY, PHILADELPHIA, PENNSYLVANIA

Thomas Jefferson Papers, 1775–1825

THE COLLEGE OF WILLIAM AND MARY, SPECIAL COLLECTIONS RESEARCH
    CENTER, EARL GREGG SWEM LIBRARY, WILLIAMSBURG, VIRGINIA

Tucker-Coleman Papers

THE CORPORATION FOR THOMAS JEFFERSON'S POPLAR FOREST, FOREST,
    VIRGINIA

Francis Eppes, Memorandum, 1826
Christian Hutter, Notes, 1909
Edward S. Hutter, Farm Journal, January 1, 1844–December 31, 1854. Estate of Mrs. Edwin C.
    Hutter, Princeton, New Jersey, on loan.
Edward S. Hutter, Income and Expense Journal, July 1, 1856–January 1, 1862. Estate of Mrs.
    Edwin C. Hutter, Princeton, New Jersey, on loan.
Hutter Family Manuscripts, Estate of Mrs. Edwin C. Hutter, Princeton, New Jersey. Copies
    on file.
Thomas Jefferson, "1809 Plat of the Tomahawk Quarter Farm at Poplar Forest." Estate of Mrs.
    Edwin C. Hutter, Princeton, New Jersey, on loan.

DAVID LIBRARY OF THE AMERICAN REVOLUTION, WASHINGTON CROSSING,
    PENNSYLVANIA

Sol Feinstone Collection of the American Revolution

GILDER LEHRMAN INSTITUTE OF AMERICAN HISTORY, NEW YORK, NEW YORK

LIBRARY OF CONGRESS, WASHINGTON, D.C.

Thomas Jefferson Papers, 1606–1827
Joshua Frye and Peter Jefferson, *Map of the Inhabited Part of Virginia Containing the Whole
    Province of Maryland*, 1751.

## LIBRARY OF VIRGINIA, RICHMOND, VIRGINIA

Albemarle County Surveyor's Book 1, part 1, 1744–1750

Albemarle County Will Book 9, 1826–1829

Bedford County Deed Book 21, 1828–1829

Bedford County Deed Book 29, 1841–1842

Bedford County Will Book 24, 1877–1880

Campbell County Will Book 6, 1827–1831

Nora Carter, "Survey Report, Poplar Forest—Home of Thomas Jefferson, 1937 June 7," unpublished manuscript.

William Cobbs Letters, 1827–1841

Henrico County Deeds and Wills, 1725–1737, Number 1, Part 2

Henrico County Deed Book, ca. 1744–1748


## MASSACHUSETTS HISTORICAL SOCIETY, BOSTON, MASSACHUSETTS

Coolidge Collection of Thomas Jefferson Manuscripts


## NATIONAL ARCHIVES AND RECORDS ADMINISTRATION, WASHINGTON, D.C.

Records of the Bureau of Refugees, Freedmen, and Abandoned Lands, Record Group 105

U.S. Manuscript Census, Eighth Census of the United States, 1860, Microfilm M653, Records of the Bureau of the Census, 1790–2007, Record Group 29


## ROSENBACH MUSEUM AND LIBRARY, PHILADELPHIA, PENNSYLVANIA

Jefferson Papers


## SOUTHERN HISTORICAL COLLECTION, LOUIS ROUND WILSON SPECIAL COLLECTIONS LIBRARY, UNIVERSITY OF NORTH CAROLINA, CHAPEL HILL, NORTH CAROLINA

Nicholas Philip Trist Papers


## ALBERT AND SHIRLEY SMALL SPECIAL COLLECTIONS LIBRARY, UNIVERSITY OF VIRGINIA, CHARLOTTESVILLE, VIRGINIA

Edgehill-Randolph Family Papers

Thomas Jefferson Papers

Ledgers of Spring Tobacco Warehouse, 2 vols., 1793–1796 and 1805–1806

Nicholas Lewis Account Book


## WEST VIRGINIA UNIVERSITY LIBRARY, MORGANTOWN, WEST VIRGINIA

West Virginia and Regional History Special Collections, Circuit Superior Court, Mason County Court Records

*William Cobbs v. Thomas Law and David Ruffner,* 1822

*William Cobbs v. David Ruffner, Lewis Ruffner, Daniel Ruffner, and Richard E. Putney, Doing Business as David Ruffner and Company,* 1828.

*William Cobbs v. John D. Shrewsbury Sr. and John D. Shrewsbury Jr.,* 1826

*William Cobbs v. John Shrewsbury Sr. and Samuel Shrewsbury Sr.,* 1826

## Published Sources

Adams, Keith. 1996. "Final Report: Phase I Intensive Archaeological Survey Jefferson's Poplar Forest." Manuscript on file, Thomas Jefferson's Poplar Forest, Forest, Va.

———. 1997. "Poplar Forest Land Use Research Project, Final Report." Manuscript on file, Thomas Jefferson's Poplar Forest, Forest, Va.

———. 2008. "A Summary of Prehistoric Archaeology at Poplar Forest." *Quarterly Bulletin of the Archeological Society of Virginia* 63(3): 115–123.

Adams, William Howard. 1976. *The Eye of Thomas Jefferson.* Charlottesville: University of Virginia Press.

———. 1997. *The Paris Years of Thomas Jefferson.* New Haven, Conn.: Yale University Press.

Agbe-Davies, Anna. 2003. "Richneck Quarter: Background." Digital Archaeology Archive of Comparative Slavery, Thomas Jefferson Foundation, Charlottesville. http://www.daacs.org/resources/sites/background/35/, accessed March 5, 2010.

Altshuler, Nathan, Edward Ayers, Norman Barka, and Arthur Barnes. 1979. "Interpretation of Flowerdew Hundred Virginia." Manuscript on file, Southside Historical Sites, Inc., Williamsburg, Va.

Ambers, Rebecca K. R., Daniel L. Druckenbrod, and Clifford P. Ambers. 2006. "Geomorphic Response to Historical Agriculture at Monument Hill in the Blue Ridge Foothills of Central Virginia." *Catena* 65: 49–60.

Anderson, Anna C. B. 2002. "A Study in Transition Plantation Economy: George Washington's Whiskey Distillery, 1799." MA thesis, College of William and Mary, Williamsburg.

Anderson, Scott, and R. Brunner-Jass. 2000. "Pollen Analysis of Historic Features at Thomas Jefferson's Poplar Forest Estate Bedford County, Virginia." Manuscript on file, Thomas Jefferson's Poplar Forest, Forest, Va.

Anderson, Virginia DeJohn. 2002. "Animals into the Wilderness: The Development of Livestock Husbandry in the Seventeenth-Century Chesapeake." *William and Mary Quarterly* 3d Series, 59(2):377–408.

Andrews, Susan T. 1993. "Faunal Analysis of Slave Quarter Site at Poplar Forest." Manuscript on file, Thomas Jefferson's Poplar Forest, Forest, Va.

———. 1994 "Inside Archaeology: The Archaeology Lab and How to Make Bones Talk." *Notes on the State of Poplar Forest* 2: 25–30.

———. 1999. "Faunal Analysis of North Hill Features, Poplar Forest." Manuscript on file, Thomas Jefferson's Poplar Forest, Forest, Va.

Anonymous. 1929. "Some Notes on 'Green Spring.'" *Virginia Magazine of History and Biography* 37(4): 289–300.

Archer, Steve. 2004. "Poplar Forest Phytolith Analysis Report." Manuscript on file, Thomas Jefferson's Poplar Forest, Forest, Va.

Arrom, José Juan, and Manuel García Arevalo. 1986. *Cimarrón.* Santo Domingo: Fundación García-Arevalo.

Ashmore, Wendy, and Richard R. Wilk. 1988. "Household and Community in the Mesoamerican Past." In *Household and Community in the Mesoamerican Past,* edited by Richard R. Wilk and Wendy Ashmore, 1–27. Albuquerque: University of New Mexico Press.

Baker, T. Lindsay, and Julie Baker (editors). 1996. *The WPA Oklahoma Slave Narratives.* Norman: University of Oklahoma Press.

Balée, William. 1998. "Historical Ecology: Premises and Postulates." In *Advances in Historical Ecology,* edited by William Balée, 13–29. New York: Columbia University Press.

———. 2006. "The Research Program of Historical Ecology." *Annual Review of Anthropology* 35: 75–98.

Balée, William, and Clark L. Erickson. 2006. "Time, Complexity, and Historical Ecology." In *Time and Complexity in Historical Ecology: Studies in the Neotropical Lowlands,* edited by William Balée and Clark L. Erickson, 1–17. New York: Columbia University Press.

Barber, Michael. 1976. "The Vertebrate Fauna from a Late Eighteenth Century Well: The Bray Plantation, Kingsmill, Virginia." *Historical Archaeology* 10: 68–72.

Barile, Kerri S., and Jamie C. Brandon (editors). 2004. *Household Chores and Household Choices: Theorizing the Domestic Sphere in Historical Archaeology.* Tuscaloosa: University of Alabama Press.

Barka, Norman F. 1978. "Archaeology of George Washington Birthplace, Virginia." Manuscript on file, Southside Historical Sites, Inc., and Department of Anthropology, College of William and Mary, Williamsburg, Va.

———. 1996. "The Historical Archaeology of Virginia's Golden Age: An Overview." In *The Archaeology of 18th-Century Virginia,* edited by Theodore R. Reinhart, 1–46. Special Publication No. 35 of the Archeological Society of Virginia. Richmond: Dietz Press.

Barka, Norman F., and Nathan Altshuler. 1976. "Archaeological, Historical and Cultural Study of Flowerdew Hundred Plantation, Virginia." Manuscript on file, Southside Historical Sites, Inc., and Department of Anthropology, College of William and Mary, Williamsburg, Va.

Barka, Norman F., and Douglas Sanford. 1976. "The Archaeology of Highland (Ash Lawn), Albemarle, Virginia." Manuscript on file, Southside Historical Sites, Inc., and Department of Anthropology, College of William and Mary, Williamsburg, Va.

Bartoy, Kevin. 2009. "The Other Hermitage: The Enslaved at the Andrew Jackson Plantation." www.blackpast.org/?q=perspectives/other-hermitage-enslaved-andrew-jackson-plantation, accessed July 8, 2011.

Beaman, Thomas E. 2000. "Fables of the Reconstruction: Morley Jeffers Williams and the Excavation of Tryon Palace, 1952–1962." *North Carolina Archaeology* 49: 1–22.

Bear, James A., Jr., and Lucia Stanton (editors). 1997. *Jefferson's Memorandum Books: Accounts, with Legal Records and Miscellany, 1767–1826.* 2 vols. The Papers of Thomas Jefferson, 2nd ser. Princeton, N.J.: Princeton University Press.

Beaudry, Mary C. 1996. "Reinventing Historical Archaeology." In *Historical Archaeology and the Study of American Culture,* edited by Lu Ann De Cunzo and Bernard L. Herman, 473–497. Knoxville: University of Tennessee Press.

———. 1999. "House and Household: The Archaeology of Domestic Life in Early America." In *Old and New Worlds,* edited by Geoff Egan and R. L. Michael, 117–126. Oxford: Oxbow Books.

Bedini, Silvio A. 1990. *Thomas Jefferson: Statesman of Science.* New York: Macmillan.

Beiswanger, William L. 1984. "The Temple in the Garden: Thomas Jefferson's Vision of the Monticello Landscape." In *British and American Gardens in the Eighteenth Century: Eighteen Illustrated Essays on Garden History,* edited by Robert P. Maccubbin and Peter Martin, 170–188. Williamsburg: The Colonial Williamsburg Foundation.

———. 1993. "Jefferson's Sources from Antiquity in the Design of Monticello." *Antiques Magazine* 144(1): 58–69.

———. 2000. "Thomas Jefferson and the Art of Living Out of Doors." *Antiques Magazine* 225(1): 594–605.

Bell, Alison K., Kerri Barile, Douglas W. Sanford, and Michael Smith. 1998. "Archaeology at Stratford: The Old Orchard Field, the 1998 Field School Season." Manuscript on file, Center for Historic Preservation, Mary Washington College, Fredericksburg, Va.

Bender, Donald R. 1967. "A Refinement of the Concept of Household: Families, Co-Residence, and Domestic Functions." *American Anthropologist* 69(5): 493–504.

Bessey, S. Fiona, and Dennis J. Pogue. 2006. "Blacksmithing at George Washington's Mount Vernon." *Quarterly Bulletin of the Archeological Society of Virginia* 61(4): 176–185.

Betts, Edwin Morris (editor). 1944. *Thomas Jefferson's Garden Book, 1766–1824: With Relevant Extracts from His Other Writings.* Philadelphia, Pa.: The American Philosophical Society.

———. 1987. *Thomas Jefferson's Farm Book with Commentary and Relevant Extracts from Other Writings.* Charlottesville: University Press of Virginia.

Binford, Lewis. 1962. "Archaeology as Anthropology." *American Antiquity* 28: 217–225.

———. 1965. "Archaeological Systematics and the Study of Cultural Processes." *American Antiquity* 31: 203–210.

Blanton, Dennis B., and Julia A. King (editors). 2004. *Indian and European Contact in Context: The Mid-Atlantic Region.* Gainesville: University Press of Florida.

Bon-Harper, Sara. 2009. "Spatial Variation and Activity Areas at Monticello's Site 8." Poster presented at the 42nd Annual Conference on Historical and Underwater Archaeology, Toronto, Canada.

———. 2010. "Contrasting Worlds: Plantation Landscapes at Monticello." Paper presented at the 43rd Annual Conference on Historical and Underwater Archaeology, Amelia Island, Fla.

Bon-Harper, Sara, Jennifer Aultman, Derek Wheeler, and Nick Bon-Harper. 2004. "Methods in the Analysis of Slave-Occupied Plowzone Sites at Monticello." Poster presented at the 75th Annual Conference of the Society for American Archaeology, St. Louis, Mo.

Bowen, Joanne. 1996. "Foodways in the 18th-Century Chesapeake." In *The Archaeology of 18th-Century Virginia*, edited by Theodore R. Reinhart, 87–130. Special Publication No. 35 of the Archeological Society of Virginia. Richmond, Va.: Dietz Press.

———. 1999. "The Chesapeake Landscape and the Ecology of Animal Husbandry." In *Old and New Worlds*, edited by Geoff Egan and R. L. Michael, 358–367. Oxford: Oxbow Books.

———. 2010. "Transformation of the Chesapeake Landscape." Paper presented at the 43rd Conference on Historical and Underwater Archaeology, Amelia Island, Fla.

Bowes, Jessica. 2009. "Provisioned, Produced, Procured: Slave Subsistence Strategies as Indicators of Plantation Social Relations at Thomas Jefferson's Poplar Forest." MA thesis, University of Massachusetts Boston.

Bowes, Jessica, and Heather Trigg. 2009. "Macrobotanical Analysis of Feature ER2352/4, A Subfloor Pit Associated with a 19th-Century Slave Cabin from Thomas Jefferson's Poplar Forest." Andrew Fiske Memorial Center for Archaeological Research Culture Resource Management Study No. 29. Report submitted to Thomas Jefferson's Poplar Forest. Forest, Va.

Boyd, Julian P. (editor). 1954. *The Papers of Thomas Jefferson.* Vol. 9, *1 November 1785 to 22 June 1786.* Princeton, N.J.: Princeton University Press.

———. 1955. *The Papers of Thomas Jefferson.* Vol. 12, *7 August 1787 to 21 March 1788.* Princeton, N.J.: Princeton University Press.

———. 1956. *The Papers of Thomas Jefferson.* Vol. 13, *[March 1788] to 7 October 1788.* Princeton, N.J.: Princeton University Press.

———. 1958. *The Papers of Thomas Jefferson.* Vol. 15, *27 March 1789 to 30 November 1789.* Princeton, N.J.: Princeton University Press.

————. 1961. *The Papers of Thomas Jefferson.* Vol. 16, *30 November 1789 to 4 July 1790.* Princeton, N.J.: Princeton University Press.

Bradley, Charles. 2000. "Smoking Pipes for the Archaeologist." In *Studies in Material Culture Research,* edited by Karlis Karklins, 104–133. Uniontown, Pa.: Society for Historical Archaeology.

Breckenridge, Curt. 2009. "Recent Investigations of George Washington's Upper Garden, Mount Vernon, VA." Paper presented at the 39th annual meeting of the Middle Atlantic Archaeological Conference, Ocean City, Maryland.

Breen, Eleanor E. 2004. "Whose Trash Is It, Anyway? A Stratigraphic and Ceramic Analysis of the South Grove Midden (44FX762/17), Mount Vernon, Virginia." *Northeast Historical Archaeology* 33: 111–130.

Breen, Eleanor, and Barbara Heath. 2010. "Subfloor Pit Sampling Protocols from Wingos Quarter, Bedford County, Virginia." Manuscript on file, University of Tennessee, Knoxville.

Breen, Eleanor E., and Esther C. White. 2006. "'A pretty considerable distillery': Excavating George Washington's Whiskey Distillery." *Quarterly Bulletin of the Archeological Society of Virginia* 61(4): 209–220.

Breen, T. H. [1985] 2001. *Tobacco Culture: The Mentality of the Great Tidewater Planters on the Eve of the Revolution.* 2nd ed. Princeton, N.J.: Princeton University Press.

Briceland, Alan V. 1987. *Westward from Virginia: The Exploration of the Virginia-Carolina Frontier, 1650–1710.* Charlottesville: University Press of Virginia.

Brooks, Alasdair. 1994. "A Summary of Recent Wing Site Ceramic Analysis at Poplar Forest." Manuscript on file, Thomas Jefferson's Poplar Forest, Forest, Va.

————. 2000. "The Comparative Analysis of Late 18th- and 19th-Century Ceramics: A Trans-Atlantic Perspective." PhD dissertation, University of York, York, United Kingdom.

Brooks, Alasdair M., and Dana B. Heck. 1995. "On a Wing and a Square: Comparative Problems in 19th Century Ceramic Analysis." Paper presented at the 28th Annual Conference of the Society for Historical and Underwater Archaeology, Washington, D.C.

Brown, Allan C. 1990. "Thomas Jefferson's Poplar Forest: The Mathematics of an Ideal Villa." *Journal of Garden History* 10(2): 117–139.

Brown, David A. 2006. "Fairfield Quarter: Background." Digital Archaeology Archive of Comparative Slavery, Thomas Jefferson Foundation, Charlottesville. http://www.daacs.org/resources/sites/background/13/, accessed March 5, 2010.

Brown, David A., and Thane Harpole. 2007. "The Changing Landscape of Fairfield Plantation." *Quarterly Bulletin of the Archeological Society of Virginia* 62(3): 164–170.

Bruce, Kathleen. 1932. "Virginian Agricultural Decline to 1860: A Fallacy." *Agricultural History* 6(1): 3–13.

Buchanan, William T., Jr., and Edward F. Heite. 1971. "The Hallowes Site: A Seventeenth-Century Yeoman's Cottage in Virginia." *Historical Archaeology* 5: 38–48.

Bureau of Land Management. 2010. *Historic Glass Bottle Identification & Information Website.* Bureau of Land Management and the Society for Historical Archaeology. www.sha.org/bottle/, accessed March 1, 2010.

Cabell, Mrs. Clifford. 1879. "Reminiscences of a Poet and of a Statesman." *Arthur's Illustrated Home Magazine* 47(2): 74–75.

Canel, Hannah. 1996. "Poplar Forest's Schist Smoking Pipes." Paper presented at the conference African Impact on the Material Culture of the Americas, Museum of Early Southern Decorative Arts, Winston-Salem, N.C.

Carson, Cary, Norman F. Barka, William M. Kelso, Garry Wheeler Stone, and Dell Upton. 1981. "Impermanent Architecture in the Southern American Colonies." *Winterthur Portfolio* 16(2–3): 135–196.

Carson, Cary, Joanne Bowen, Willie Graham, Martha McCartney, and Lorena Walsh. 2008. "New World, Real World: Improvising English Culture in Seventeenth-Century Virginia." *The Journal of Southern History* 74(1): 31–88.

Caton, Alex Suzanne. 1997. "Beads and Bodies: Embodying Change in Bead Practices in Banda, Ghana." MA thesis, Binghamton University, Binghamton, New York.

Caywood, Louis R. 1955. "Excavations at Green Spring Plantation." In *Pots, Pipes and Trash Pits,* edited by Edward Bottoms and Cynthia S. Hansen, 108–115. Vol. 1 of the Jamestown 2007 Trilogy. Richmond, Va.: Archeological Society of Virginia.

———. 1957. "Green Spring Plantation." *Virginia Magazine of History and Biography* 65(1): 67–83.

Chambers, Douglas. 1996. *"He Gwine Sing He Country": Africans, Afro-Virginians, and the Development of Slave Culture in Virginia 1690–1810.* PhD dissertation, University of Virginia. Ann Arbor, Mich.: University Microfilms International.

———. 1997. "'My own nation': Igbo Exiles in the Diaspora." In *Routes to Slavery: Direction, Ethnicity and Mortality in the Atlantic Slave Trade,* edited by David Eltis and David Richardson, 72–97. London: Frank Cass.

———. 1999. "The Transatlantic Slave Trade to Virginia in Comparative Historical Perspective, 1698–1778." In *Afro-Virginian History and Culture,* edited by John Saillant, 3–28. New York: Garland.

———. 2000. "Tracing Igbo into the African Diaspora." In *Identifying Enslaved Africans: The "Nigerian" Hinterland and the African Diaspora,* edited by Paul Lovejoy, 55–71. London: Continuum.

———. 2005. *Murder at Montpelier: Igbo Africans in Virginia.* Jackson: University Press of Mississippi.

Chambers, S. Allen, Jr. 1981. *Lynchburg: An Architectural History.* Charlottesville: University Press of Virginia.

———. 1993. *Poplar Forest and Thomas Jefferson.* Forest, Va.: The Corporation for Jefferson's Poplar Forest.

Chatterjee, Piya, Monisha Das Gupta, and Richard Cullen Rath. 2010. "Imperial Plantations: Past, Present and Future Directions." *Journal of Historical Sociology* 23(1): 446–461.

Chew, Elizabeth V. 2005. "Carrying the Keys: Women and Housekeeping at Monticello." In *Dining at Monticello: In Good Taste and Abundance,* edited by Damon Lee Fowler, 29–35. Charlottesville: Thomas Jefferson Foundation.

Chew, Elizabeth V., and Sara Bon-Harper. 2007. "Assessing the Habits of the Table: Archaeology and Interpretation at Monticello." Paper presented at the annual conference of the Omohundro Institute of Early American History and Society of Early Americanists, Williamsburg, Va.

Christian, W. Asbury. 1900. *Lynchburg and Its People.* Lynchburg, Va.: J. P. Bell.

Christie's New York. 2004. *Printed and Manuscript Americana including the Civil War.* Sales catalogue. 9 June.

Clayton, John. 1912. "John Clayton's Transcript of the Journal of Robert Fallam." In *The First Explorations of the Trans-Allegheny Region by the Virginians,* edited by Clarence W. Alvord and Lee Bidgood, 183–195. Cleveland, Ohio: Arthur H. Clark.

Clites, Elizabeth, and Lynsey Bates. 2008. "Whose Trash Is This? Unraveling Ethnostratigraphy on Monticello Mountain." Poster presented at the 73rd Annual Conference of the Society for American Archaeology, Vancouver, B.C.

Coleman, Jon T. 2004. *Vicious: Wolves and Men in America.* New Haven, Conn.: Yale University Press.

Connerton, Paul. 1989. *How Societies Remember.* Cambridge: Cambridge University Press.

———. 2008. "Seven Types of Forgetting." *Memory Studies* 1(1): 59–71.

Cotter, John L. 1994. *Archaeological Excavations at Jamestown, Virginia.* Second Edition with a New Introduction and Background Material. Special Publication No. 32. Richmond: Archeological Society of Virginia.

Coysh, A. W., and R. K. Henrywood. 1982. *The Dictionary of Blue and White Printed Pottery, 1780–1880.* Woodbridge, Suffolk: The Antique Collectors' Club.

Crader, Diana C. 1984. "The Zooarchaeology of the Storehouse and the Dry Well at Monticello." *American Antiquity* 49: 542–558.

———. 1990. "Slave Diet at Monticello." *American Antiquity* 55: 690–717.

Craven, Avery O. 1926. *Soil Exhaustion as a Factor in the Agricultural History of Virginia and Maryland, 1606–1860.* Urbana: University of Illinois.

Cressey, Pamela. 1999. "Setting the Scene: Virginia in the 19th Century." In *The Archaeology of 19th-Century Virginia,* edited by John H. Sprinkle and Theodore. R. Reinhart, 1–10. Special Publication No. 36 of the Archeological Society of Virginia. Richmond, Va.: Spectrum Press.

Cronon, William. 1983. *Changes in the Land: Indians, Colonists, and the Ecology of New England.* New York: Hill and Wang.

Crosby, Alfred W. 1972. *The Columbian Exchange: Biological and Cultural Consequences of 1492.* Westport, Conn.: Greenwood.

———. 1986. *Ecological Imperialism: The Biological Expansion of Europe, 900–1900.* Cambridge: Cambridge University Press.

———. 1994. *Germs, Seeds, and Animals: Studies in Historical Ecology.* Armonk, N.Y.: M. E. Sharp.

Crumley, Carole. 1994. "Historical Ecology: A Multidimensional Ecological Orientation." In *Historical Ecology: Cultural Knowledge and Changing Landscapes,* edited by Carole Crumley, 1–16. Santa Fe, N.M.: School of American Research Press.

———. 1998. "Foreword." In *Advances in Historical Ecology,* edited by William Balée, ix–xiv. New York: Columbia University Press.

Cummings, Linda Scott. 1995. "Phytolith Analysis of a Probable Dung Repository at Mount Vernon, VA, August 1995." Paleo Research Labs, Technical Report 95–33, Golden, Colorado.

———. 2008. "Pollen and Phytolith Analysis of Four Soil Samples from Flower Gardens Associated with George Washington's Plantation at Mount Vernon, VA, March 2008." Paleo Research Labs, Technical Report 07–110, Golden, Colorado.

Cusick, James G. 1998a. "Introduction." In *Studies in Culture Contact: Interaction, Culture Change, and Archaeology,* edited by James G. Cusick, 1–20. Occasional Paper No. 25, Center for Archaeological Investigations. Carbondale, Ill.: Southern Illinois University.

———. 1998b. "Historiography of Acculturation: An Evaluation of Concepts and Their Application in Archaeology." In *Studies in Culture Contact: Interaction, Culture Change, and Archaeology,* edited by James G. Cusick, 126–145. Occasional Paper No. 25, Center for Archaeological Investigations. Carbondale: Southern Illinois University.

DAACS. 2004. *The Digital Archaeological Archive of Comparative Slavery*. Charlottesville, Va., The Thomas Jefferson Foundation. www.daacs.org, accessed March 1, 2010.

Daniel, William H. 1985. *Bedford County, Virginia, 1840–1860: The History of An Upper Piedmont County in the Late Antebellum Era*. Bedford, Va.: The Print Shop.

Dawdy, Shannon Lee. 2000. "Understanding Cultural Change through the Vernacular." *Historical Archaeology* 34(3): 107–123.

De Cunzo, Lu Ann. 1996. "Introduction: People, Material Culture, Context, and Culture in Historical Archaeology." In *Historical Archaeology and the Study of American Culture*, edited by Lu Ann De Cunzo and Bernard L. Herman, 1–31. Knoxville: University of Tennessee Press.

Deagan, Kathleen. 1996. "Avenues of Inquiry in Historical Archaeology." In *Images of the Recent Past: Readings in Historical Archaeology*, edited by Charles Orser, 26–41. Walnut Creek, Calif.: Altamira Press.

Deagan, Kathleen, and Darcie Macmahon. 1995. *Fort Mose: Colonial America's Black Fortress of Freedom*. Gainesville: University of Florida Press.

DeCorse, Christopher. 2001. *An Archaeology of Elmina: Africans and Europeans on the Gold Coast*. Washington, D.C.: Smithsonian Institution Press.

Deetz, James. 1977. *In Small Things Forgotten: The Archaeology of Early American Life*. New York: Anchor Books.

———. 1988. "American Historical Archaeology: Methods and Results." *Science* 239(4838): 362–367.

———. 1990. "Prologue: Landscapes as Cultural Statements." In *Earth Patterns: Essays in Landscape Archaeology*, edited by William M. Kelso and Rachel Most, 1–4. Charlottesville: University Press of Virginia.

———. 1995. *Flowerdew Hundred: The Archaeology of a Virginia Plantation, 1619–1864*. Charlottesville: University Press of Virginia.

———. 1996. *In Small Things Forgotten: An Archaeology of Early American Life*. 2nd ed. New York: Anchor Books.

Delcourt, Hazel, and Paul Delcourt. 1997. "Pre-Columbian Native American Use of Fire on Southern Appalachian Landscapes." *Conservation Biology* 11: 1010–1014.

Delle, James A. 1998. *An Archaeology of Social Space: Analyzing Coffee Plantations in Jamaica's Blue Mountains*. New York: Plenum Press.

Dew, Charles. 1994. *Bond of Iron: Master and Slave at Buffalo Forge*. New York: W. W. Norton.

DeWald, Scott, Scott Josiah, and Becky Erdkamp. 2005. *Heating with Wood: Producing, Harvesting and Processing Firewood*. NebGuide, no. G1554. Lincoln: University of Nebraska-Lincoln Extension and Institute of Agriculture and Natural Resources.

Dimmick, Jesse. 1929. "Green Spring." *William and Mary Quarterly* 9(2): 129–130.

Druckenbrod, Daniel L., and Herman H. Shugart. 2004. "Forest History of James Madison's Montpelier Plantation." *Journal of Torrey Botanical Society* 131: 204–219.

Duchesne, Nicholas. 1775. *Traité de la formation des jardins*. Paris: Dorez.

Dunn, Richard S. 1972. *Sugar and Slaves: The Rise of the Planter Class in the English West Indies, 1624–1713*. Chapel Hill: University of North Carolina Press.

Earle, Carville. 1988. "The Myth of the Southern Soil Miner: Macrohistory, Agricultural Innovation, and Environmental Change." In *The Ends of the Earth: Perspectives on Modern Environmental History*, edited by Donald Worster, 175–210. Cambridge: Cambridge University Press.

Earle, Carville, and Ronald Hoffman. 2001. "Genteel Erosion: The Ecological Consequences of Agrarian Reform in the Chesapeake, 1730–1840." In *Discovering the Chesapeake: The History of an Ecosystem,* edited by Philip D. Curtin, Grace S. Brush, and George W. Fisher, pp. 279–303. Baltimore, Md.: Johns Hopkins University Press.

Edwards-Ingram, Ywone. 1998. "An Interdisciplinary Approach to African American Medicinal and Health Practices in Colonial America." *Watermark* 20(3): 67–73.

———. 2001. "African American Medicine and the Social Relations of Slavery." In *Race and the Archaeology of Identity,* edited by Charles Orser Jr., 34–53. Salt Lake City: University of Utah Press.

———. 2005. "Medicating Slavery: Motherhood, Health Care, and Cultural Practices in the African Diaspora." PhD dissertation, College of William and Mary, Williamsburg, Va.

Egan, Dave, and Evelyn A. Howell (editors). 2001. *The Historical Ecology Handbook: A Restorationist's Guide to Reference Ecosystems.* Washington, D.C.: Island Press.

Egloff, Keith, and Deborah Woodward. 2000. *First People: The Early Indians of Virginia.* Charlottesville: University Press of Virginia.

Ellis, Joseph J. 1997. *American Sphinx: The Character of Thomas Jefferson.* New York: Alfred A. Knopf.

Emerson, Matthew. 1988. *Decorated Clay Tobacco Pipes from the Chesapeake.* PhD dissertation, University of California at Berkeley. Ann Arbor, Mich.: University Microfilms International.

———. 1994. "Decorated Clay Tobacco Pipes from the Chesapeake: An African Connection." In *Historical Archaeology of the Chesapeake,* edited by Paul Shackel and Barbara Little, 35–49. Washington, D.C: Smithsonian Institution Press.

Epperson, Terence W. 1990. "Race and the Disciplines of the Plantation." *Historical Archaeology* 24(4): 29–36.

———. 1999. "Constructing Difference; the Social and Spatial Order of the Chesapeake Plantation." In *I, Too, Am America: Archaeological Studies of African-American Life,* edited by Theresa A. Singleton, 159–172. Charlottesville: University Press of Virginia.

———. 2000. "Panoptic Plantations: The Garden Sights of Thomas Jefferson and George Mason." In *Lines That Divide: Historical Archaeologies of Race, Class, and Gender,* edited by James A. Delle, Stephen A. Mrozowski, and Robert Paynter, 58–77. Knoxville: University of Tennessee Press.

———. 2001. "'A Separate House for the Christian Slaves, One for the Negro Slaves': The Archaeology of Race and Identity in Late Seventeenth-Century Virginia." In *Race and the Archaeology of Identity,* edited by Charles E. Orser Jr., 54–70. Salt Lake City: University of Utah Press.

Farber, Joseph C., and Henry Hope Reed. 1980. *Palladio's Architecture and Its Influence.* London: Dover.

The Farmers' Register. 1837. "Remarks on the Agriculture of Nelson and Amherst—No. 1." *Farmer's Register: A Monthly Publication* 5: 651.

Fennell, Christopher C. 2007a. *Crossroads and Cosmologies: Diasporas and Ethnogenesis in the New World.* Gainesville: University Press of Florida.

———. 2007b. "Multivalent Figures of an Enclosing Hand." *African Diaspora Archaeology Newsletter* (December). www.diaspora.uiuc.edu/news1207/news1207-2.pdf, accessed March 10, 2008.

Ferguson, Leland. 1992. *Uncommon Ground: Archaeology and Early African America, 1650–1800.* Washington, D.C.: Smithsonian Institution Press.

Fesler, Garrett R. 2003. "44JC298: Background." Digital Archaeology Archive of Comparative

Slavery, Thomas Jefferson Foundation, Charlottesville. http://www.daacs.org/resources/sites/background/14/, accessed March 5, 2010.

———. 2004a. "Living Arrangements among Enslaved Women and Men at an Early-Eighteenth-Century Virginia Quartering Site." In *Engendering African American Archaeology, A Southern Perspective,* edited by Jillian E. Galle and Amy L. Young, 177–236. Knoxville: University of Tennessee Press.

———. 2004b. *Houses to Homes: An Archaeological Case Study of Household Formation at the Utopia Slave Quarter, ca. 1675 to 1775.* PhD dissertation, University of Virginia. Ann Arbor, Mich.: University Microfilms International.

———. 2010. "Excavating the Spaces and Interpreting the Places of Enslaved Africans and their Descendants." In *Cabin, Quarter, Plantation: Architecture and Landscapes of North American Slavery,* edited by Clifton Ellis and Rebecca Ginsburg, 27–49. New Haven, Conn.: Yale University Press.

Fischer, David Hackett, and James C. Kelly. 2000. *Bound Away: Virginia and the Westward Movement.* Charlottesville: University Press of Virginia.

Fischer, Lisa. 1993. "Report on the Chemical Analysis at the Poplar Forest Quarter Site." Manuscript on file, Thomas Jefferson's Poplar Forest, Forest, Va.

———. 2001. "Recovering Elements in Historical Archaeology: The Use of Soil Chemical Analysis for Overcoming the Effects of Post-Depositional Plowing." MA thesis, The College of William and Mary, Williamsburg, Va.

Flannery, Kent (editor). 1976. *The Early Mesoamerican Village.* New York: Academic Press.

Ford, Benjamin. 2008. "Phase III Data Recovery Investigations: The Foster Site 44AB525." VDHR File No. 2004–0046. Report on file at the Virginia Department of Historic Resources, Richmond.

Franklin, Maria. 1997. *Out of Site, Out of Mind: The Archaeology of an Enslaved Virginian Household, ca. 1740–1778.* PhD dissertation, University of California, Berkeley. Ann Arbor, Mich.: University Microfilms International.

———. 2001. "The Archaeological Dimensions of Soul Food: Interpreting Race, Culture, and Afro-Virginian Identity." In *Race and the Archaeology of Identity,* edited by Charles E. Orser Jr., 88–107. Salt Lake City: University of Utah Press.

———. 2004. *An Archaeological Study of the Rich Neck Slave Quarter and Enslaved Domestic Life.* Colonial Williamsburg Research Publications. Richmond: Dietz Press.

———. 2007. "The Palace Lands Site: Background." Digital Archaeology Archive of Comparative Slavery, Thomas Jefferson Foundation, Charlottesville, Va. http://www.daacs.org/resources/sites/background/34/, accessed March 5, 2010.

Freeman, Mark A. 2010. "Game On—Using Interactivity and Gaming to Further Archaeology Learning." Paper presented at the 43rd Annual Conference on Historical and Underwater Archaeology, Amelia Island, Fla.

Freeman, Mark A., and Barbara J. Heath. 2008. "People, Place, Perspective, and Period: A Phenomenological Approach to Interpretation on the Web." Paper presented at the 41st Annual Conference on Historical and Underwater Archaeology, Albuquerque, N.M.

Galle, Jillian. 2004. "Designing Women: Measuring Acquisition and Access at the Hermitage Plantation." In *Engendering African American Archaeology, A Southern Perspective,* edited by Jillian E. Galle and Amy L. Young, 39–72. Knoxville: University of Tennessee Press.

———. 2006. *Strategic Consumption: Archaeological Evidence for Costly Signaling among Enslaved Men and Women in the Eighteenth-Century Chesapeake.* PhD dissertation, University of Virginia. Ann Arbor, Mich.: University Microfilms International.

———. 2010. "Costly Signaling and Gendered Social Strategies among Slaves in the Eighteenth-Century Chesapeake: An Archaeological Perspective." *American Antiquity* 75(1): 19–43.

Gallivan, Martin. 2004. "Reconnecting the Contact Period and Late Prehistory: Household and Community Dynamics in the James River Basin." In *Indian and European Contact in Context: The Mid-Atlantic Region*, edited by Dennis B. Blanton and Julia A. King, 22–46. Gainesville: University Press of Florida.

Gary, Jack. 2008. "Jefferson's Curtilage Landscape: Preliminary Interpretations of Site B." *Quarterly Bulletin of the Archeological Society of Virginia* 63(3): 137–151.

Gary, Jack, and Elizabeth Paull. 2008. "A Minimum Vessel Count for Site B." *Quarterly Bulletin of the Archeological Society of Virginia* 63(3): 152–164.

Gary, Jack, and Eric Proebsting. 2010. "Finding the Middle Ground: Uncovering the Curtilage Landscape at Thomas Jefferson's Poplar Forest." Paper presented at the 43rd Annual Conference on Historical and Underwater Archaeology, Amelia Island, Fla.

Gary, Jack, Eric Proebsting, and Lori Lee. 2010. "'Culture of the Earth': The Archaeology of the Ornamental Plant Nursery and an Antebellum Slave Quarter at Thomas Jefferson's Poplar Forest." Manuscript on file, Thomas Jefferson's Poplar Forest, Forest, Va.

Gemborys, Stanley R. 1974. "The Structure of Hardwood Forest Ecosystems of Prince Edward County, Virginia." *Ecology* 55(3): 614–621.

Gibb, James G., and Julia A. King. 1991. "Gender, Activity Areas, and Homelots in the 17th-Century Chesapeake Region." *Historical Archaeology* 25(4): 109–131.

Gibbs, Tyson, Kathleen Cargill, Leslie Sue Lieberman, and Elizabeth Reitz. 1980. "Nutrition in a Slave Population: An Anthropological Examination." *Medical Anthropology* 4(1980): 233–262.

Giese, Ronald L. 2003. "Tobacco Cultivation in Virginia, 1610–1863, and Patterns of Thought and Management Related to Thomas Jefferson." Monograph 2. Manuscript on file, Thomas Jefferson's Poplar Forest, Forest, Va.

———. 2007. "Early Virginia Grain Cultivation and Thomas Jefferson." Monograph 4. Manuscript on file, Thomas Jefferson's Poplar Forest, Forest, Va.

Gijanto, Liza. 2010. "Change and the Era of the Atlantic Trade: Commerce and Interaction in the Niumi Commercial Center (The Gambia)." PhD dissertation, Syracuse University, Syracuse, N.Y.

Girardin, René L. 1783. *An Essay on Landscape: Or, on the Means of Improving and Embellishing the Country Round Our Habitations*. Translated by de Lille. London: J. Dodsley. Originally published as *De la composition des paysages*. Paris, 1777.

Girouard, Mark. 1978. *Life in the English Country House: A Social and Architectural History*. New Haven, Conn.: Yale University Press.

Goode, June. 1998. "Forest." In *Bedford Villages—Lost and Found*, vol. 2, 83–96. Bedford, Va.: Peaks of Otter Chapter, Daughters of the American Revolution.

Graham, Willie, Carter L. Hudgins, Carl R. Lounsbury, Fraser D. Neiman, and James P. Whittenburg. 2007. "Adaptation and Innovation: Archaeological and Architectural Perspectives on the Seventeenth-Century Chesapeake." *William and Mary Quarterly*, 3rd ser., 66(3): 451–522.

Grayson, Donald K. 1973. "On the Methodology of Faunal Analysis." *American Antiquity* 38(4): 432–439.

Gremillion, Kristen J. 1993. "Paleoethnobotany." In *The Development of Southeastern Archaeology*, edited by Jay K. Johnson, 132–159. Tuscaloosa: University of Alabama Press.

Grigg, Milton L. 1939. "Restoration of Thomas Jefferson's Gardens at Monticello." *Commonwealth* 6: 11–12.

Groover, Mark D. 2003. *An Archaeological Study of Rural Capitalism and Material Life: The Gibbs Farmstead in Southern Appalachia.* New York: Springer.

———. 2004. "Household Succession as a Catalyst of Landscape Change." *Historical Archaeology* 38(4): 25–42.

Gruber, Anna. 1990. "The Archaeology of Mr. Jefferson's Slaves." MA thesis, University of Delaware, Newark, Del.

———. 1991. "The Archaeology of Slave Life at Thomas Jefferson's Monticello: Mulberry Row Slave Quarters 'r, s, t.'" *Quarterly Bulletin of the Archeological Society of Virginia* 46(1): 2–9.

Hafertepe, Kenneth. 2000. "An Inquiry into Thomas Jefferson's Ideas of Beauty." *Journal of the Society of Architectural Historians* 59(2): 216–231.

Handler, Jerome. 2008. "Aspects of the Atlantic Slave Trade: Smoking Pipes, Tobacco, and the Middle Passage." *African Diaspora Archaeology Newsletter.* www.diaspora.uiuc.edu/news0608/news0608.html#5, accessed August 18, 2010.

Handler, Jerome, and Frederick Lange. 1978. *Plantation Slavery in Barbados.* Cambridge, Mass: Harvard University Press.

Handler, Jerome, and Neil Norman. 2007. "From West Africa to Barbados: A Rare Pipe from a Plantation Slave Cemetery." *African Diaspora Archaeology Newsletter.* www.diaspora.uiuc.edu/news0907/news0907-2.pdf, accessed March 10, 2010.

Hantman, Jeffrey L. 1990. "Between Powhatan and Quirank: Reconstructing Monacan Culture and History in the Context of Jamestown." *American Anthropologist* 92(3): 676–690.

———. 1992. "Monacan Archaeology and History." *Lynch's Ferry: A Journal of Local History* 5(1): 6–11.

———. 2001. "Monacan Archaeology of the Virginia Interior, A.D. 1400–1700." In *Societies in Eclipse: Archaeology of the Eastern Woodlands Indians, A.D. 1400–1700,* edited by David S. Brose, C. Wesley Cowan, and Robert C. Mainfort, 107–124. Washington D.C.: Smithsonian Institution Press.

Hardin, Garrett. 1968. "The Tragedy of the Commons." *Science* 162(3859):1243–1248.

Harpole, Thane, and David A. Brown. 2007a. "Fairfield Plantation: Uncovering a Forgotten Virginia Landmark." *Quarterly Bulletin of the Archeological Society of Virginia* 62(3): 121–122.

———. 2007b. "The Architecture of the Fairfield Manor House: The Convergence of Wealth, Style and Practicality." *Quarterly Bulletin of the Archeological Society of Virginia* 62(3): 136–148.

Harrington, Jean C. 1994. "From Architraves to Artifacts, A Metamorphosis." In *Pioneers in Historical Archaeology, Breaking New Ground,* edited by Stanley South, 1–14. New York: Plenum Press.

Harvey, David. 1982. *The Limits of Capital.* Chicago: University of Chicago Press.

———. 1989. *The Condition of Postmodernity.* Oxford: Oxford University Press.

———. 2000. *Spaces of Hope.* Berkeley: University of California Press.

Hatch, D. Brad. 2009. "Bottomless Pits: The Decline of Subfloor Pits and the Rise of African American Consumerism in Virginia." MA thesis, The College of William and Mary, Williamsburg, Va.

Hatch, Peter J. 1992. *The Gardens of Thomas Jefferson's Monticello.* Charlottesville: Thomas Jefferson Foundation.

Heath, Barbara J. 1991a. "Artisan Housing at Monticello: The Stewart/Watkins Site." *Quarterly Bulletin of the Archeological Society of Virginia* 46(1): 10–16.

———. 1991b. "A Report on the Archaeological Excavations at Monticello, Charlottesville, VA, The Stewart/Watkins House 1989–1990." Manuscript on file, Department of Archaeology, Thomas Jefferson Foundation, Charlottesville.

———. 1993a. "Report on the Archaeological Testing for the Proposed Tree Screen, March–April 1993." Manuscript on file, Thomas Jefferson's Poplar Forest, Forest, Va.

———. 1993b. "A Report on the 1992–1993 Excavations: The Perimeter of the House and Excavations Related to the Restoration Drainage/Foundation Work at Poplar Forest, Virginia." Manuscript on file, Thomas Jefferson's Poplar Forest, Forest, Va.

———. 1994. "An Interim Report on the 1993 Excavations: The Quarter Site at Poplar Forest, Forest, Virginia." Manuscript on file, Thomas Jefferson's Poplar Forest, Forest, Va.

———. 1995. "Excavations at 44CP20: Point of Honor Stable, Lynchburg, Virginia." Manuscript on file, Lynchburg Museum, Lynchburg, Va.

———. 1996. "Temper, Temper: Recent Scholarship on Colonoware in Eighteenth-Century Virginia." In *The Archaeology of Eighteenth-Century Virginia*, edited by Theodore R. Reinhart, 149–175. Special Publication No. 35 of the Archeological Society of Virginia. Richmond: Dietz Press.

———. 1997a. "Slavery and Consumerism: A Case Study from Central Virginia." *African American Archaeology: Newsletter of the African-American Archaeology Network* 19: 1–7.

———. 1997b. "Archaeology and Interpretation at Thomas Jefferson's Monticello and Poplar Forest." In *Presenting Archaeology to the Public: Digging for Truths*, edited by John H. Jameson, 177–192. Walnut Creek, Calif.: Altamira Press.

———. 1999a. "Buttons, Beads and Buckles: Self-Definition within the Bounds of Slavery." In *Historical Archaeology, Identity Formation and the Interpretation of Ethnicity*, edited by Maria Franklin and Garrett R. Fesler, 47–69. Colonial Williamsburg Research Publications. Richmond: Dietz Press.

———. 1999b. *Hidden Lives: The Archaeology of Slave Life at Thomas Jefferson's Poplar Forest*. Charlottesville: University Press of Virginia.

———. 1999c. "'Your Humble Servant': Free Artisans in the Monticello Community." In *"I, Too, Am America": Archaeological Studies of African-American Life*, edited by Theresa A. Singleton, 193–217. Charlottesville: University Press of Virginia.

———. 2001. "Bounded Yards and Fluid Borders: Landscapes of Slavery at Poplar Forest." In *Places of Cultural Memory, African Reflections on the American Landscape: Conference Proceedings, May 9–12, 2001, Atlanta, Georgia*, 69–81. U.S. Washington, D.C.: Department of the Interior, National Park Service. www.cr.nps.gov/crdi/conferences/AFR_69-82_Heath.pdf, accessed March 5, 2010.

———. 2003. "Interpreting Slavery at Thomas Jefferson's Poplar Forest: Challenges and Opportunities." Paper presented at the Fifth World Archaeological Congress, Washington, D.C.

———. 2004a. "Engendering Choice: Slavery and Consumerism in Central Virginia." In *Engendering African American Archaeology*, edited by Jillian Galle and Amy Young, 19–38. Knoxville: University of Tennessee Press.

———. 2004b. "North Hill: Background." Digital Archaeology Archive of Comparative Slavery, Thomas Jefferson Foundation, Charlottesville. http://www.daacs.org/resources/sites/background/25/, accessed March 5, 2010.

———. 2004c. "Quarter Site: Background." Digital Archaeology Archive of Comparative Slavery, Thomas Jefferson Foundation, Charlottesville. www.daacs.org/resources/sites/background/26/, accessed March 5, 2010.

———. 2006. "Exploring African American Kinship Ties in Central Virginia." Paper presented at the Middle Atlantic Archaeological Conference, Virginia Beach, Va.

———. 2007. "Thomas Jefferson's Landscape of Retirement." In *Estate Landscapes: Design, Im-*

*provement, and Power in the Post-Medieval Landscape,* edited by Jonathan Finch and Kate Giles, 129–147. Rochester, N.Y.: Boydell and Brewer.

———. 2008a. "Introduction." *Quarterly Bulletin of the Archeological Society of Virginia* 63(3): 109–114.

———. 2008b. "Rediscovering Thomas Jefferson's Poplar Forest." *Quarterly Bulletin of the Archeological Society of Virginia* 63(3): 124–136.

———. 2010a. "Dynamic Landscapes: The Emergence of Formal Spaces in the Chesapeake." Paper presented at the 43rd Annual Conference on Historical and Underwater Archaeology, Amelia Island, Fla.

———. 2010b. "Space and Place within Plantation Quarters in Virginia, 1700–1825." In *Cabin, Quarter, Plantation: Architecture and Landscapes of North American Slavery,* edited by Clifton Ellis and Rebecca Ginsburg, 156–176. New Haven, Conn.: Yale University Press.

Heath, Barbara J., and Amber Bennett. 2000. "'The Little Spots Allow'd Them': The Archaeological Study of African-American Yards." *Historical Archaeology* 34(2): 38–55.

Heath, Barbara J., and Eleanor Breen. 2012. "Assessing Variability among Quartering Sites in Virginia." *Northeast Historical Archaeology* 38: 1–28.

Heath, Barbara J., Eleanor E. Breen, Dustin S. Lawson, and Daniel W. H. Brock, with contributions by Jonathan Baker and Kandace Hollenbach. 2009. "Archaeological Reassessment of Newman's Neck (44NB180)." Report to the Virginia Department of Historic Resources, Richmond, from the Department of Anthropology, University of Tennessee, Knoxville.

Heath, Barbara, and Lori Lee. 2008. "The Smallest Things Forgotten: Comparative Analyses of Three Subfloor Pit Assemblages at Poplar Forest." Paper presented at the 41st Annual Conference on Historical and Underwater Archaeology, Albuquerque, N.M.

———. 2010. "Memory, Race and Place: African American Landscapes at Poplar Forest." *History Compass* 8(12): 1352–1368.

Heath, Barbara J., Randy Lichtenberger, Keith Adams, and Elizabeth Paull. 2004. "Poplar Forest Archaeology: Studies in African American Life, Excavations and Analysis of Site A, Southeast Terrace and Site B, Southeast Curtilage June 2003–June 2004." Report to the Public Welfare Foundation. Manuscript on file, Thomas Jefferson's Poplar Forest, Forest, Va.

———. 2005. "Poplar Forest Archaeology: Studies in Plantation Life and Landscape, Excavations and Analysis of Site B, Southeast Curtilage, June 2004–August 2005." Report to the Public Welfare Foundation. Manuscript on file, Thomas Jefferson's Poplar Forest, Forest, Va.

Heikkenen, Herman J. 1997. "Final Report, The Last Year of Tree Growth for Selected Timbers within the West Barn of Poplar Forest as Derived from Key-Year Dendrochronology." Manuscript on file, Department of Architectural Restoration, Thomas Jefferson's Poplar Forest, Forest, Va.

Heite, Edward F. 1967. "Historic Archaeology in Virginia, 1858." *Quarterly Bulletin of the Archeological Society of Virginia* 21(3): 94.

Hendon, Julia A. 1996. "Archaeological Approaches to the Organization of Domestic Labor: Household Practice and Domestic Relations." *Annual Review of Anthropology* 25: 45–61.

Higgins, Thomas F., Benjamin Ford, Charles M. Downing, Veronica L. Deitrick, Stevan C. Pullins, and Dennis B. Blanton. 2000. "Wilton Speaks: Archaeology at an Eighteenth- and Nineteenth-Century Plantation, Data Recovery at Site 44HE493, Associated with the Proposed Route 895 Project, Henrico County, Virginia." Report to the Virginia Department of Transportation, Richmond, from the William and Mary Center for Archaeological Research, Williamsburg.

Hicks, Dan, and Mary C. Beaudry. 2006. "Introduction: The Place of Historical Archaeology." In *The Cambridge Companion to Historical Archaeology*, edited by Dan Hicks and Mary C. Beaudry, 1–9. Cambridge: Cambridge University Press.

Hill, Martha. 2003. "Building *s*: Background." Digital Archaeology Archive of Comparative Slavery, Thomas Jefferson Foundation, Charlottesville. http://www.daacs.org/resources/sites/background/6/, accessed December 12, 2010.

Hodges, Charles T. 1990. "Excavations at 44NB180 and 44NB174: An Early, English Colonial Plantation and Prehistoric Shell Midden in Northumberland County, Virginia." Manuscript on file, the Virginia Department of Historic Resources, Richmond.

———. 1993. "Private Fortifications in 17th-Century Virginia: A Study of Six Representative Works." In *The Archaeology of Seventeenth-Century Virginia*, edited by Theodore R. Reinhart and Dennis J. Pogue, 183–221. Special Publication No. 30 of The Archeological Society of Virginia. Richmond: Dietz Press.

———. 2009. *Forts of the Chieftains: A Study of Vernacular, Classical and Renaissance Influence on Defensible Town and Villa Plans in 17th-Century Virginia*. Volumes in Historical Archaeology, XLVII. Columbia: South Carolina Institute of Archaeology and Anthropology.

Hosmer, Charles B., Jr. 1965. *Presence of the Past: A History of the Preservation Movement in the United States before Williamsburg*. New York: Putnam.

———. 1981. *Preservation Comes of Age, From Williamsburg to the National Trust, 1926–1949*. 2 vols. Charlottesville: University Press of Virginia.

———. 1985. "The Colonial Revival in the Public Eye: Williamsburg and Early Garden Restoration." In *The Colonial Revival in America*, edited by Alan Axelrod, 52–70. New York: W. W. Norton.

Howson, Jean. 1995. *Colonial Goods and the Plantation Village: Consumption and the Internal Economy in Montserrat from Slavery to Freedom*. PhD dissertation, New York University, New York. Ann Arbor, Mich.: University Microfilms International.

Hudgins, Carter, L. 1977. "Historical Archaeology and Salvage Archaeological Excavations at College Landing, An Interim Report." Manuscript on file, The Virginia Department of Historic Resources, Richmond.

———. 1985. "The 'King's' Realm: An Archaeological and Historical Analysis of Robert Carter's Corotoman." Manuscript on file, the Virginia Department of Historic Resources, Richmond.

———. 1996. "The Archaeology of Plantation Life in 18th-Century Virginia." In *The Archaeology of 18th-Century Virginia*, edited by Theodore R. Reinhart, 47–56. Special Publication No. 35 of the Archeological Society of Virginia. Richmond: Dietz Press.

Hunt, John Dixon. 1991. "'Ut Pictura Poesis': The Garden and the Picturesque in England (1710–1750)." In *The Architecture of Western Gardens*, edited by Monique Mosser and Georges Teyssot, 231–242. Cambridge, Mass.: MIT Press.

Hunt, John Dixon, and Peter Willis (editors). 1990. *The Genius of the Place: The English Landscape Garden 1620–1820*. Cambridge, Mass.: MIT Press.

Irwin, James R. 1988. "Exploring the Affinity of Wheat and Slavery in the Virginia Piedmont." *Explorations in Economic History* 25(3): 295–322.

Jacobucci, Susan. 2009a. *An Analysis of Pollen from Eighteen Soil Samples Recovered from the Upper Garden Area (44FX762/43) at George Washington's Mount Vernon, VA*. Andrew Fiske Memorial Center for Archaeological Research, University of Massachusetts Boston, Cultural Resources Management Study No. 30, Boston.

———. 2009b. "A Pollen Analysis of the South Profile of a Gully from Site B from Thomas Jefferson's Poplar Forest." Manuscript on file, Thomas Jefferson's Poplar Forest, Forest, Va.

Jefferson, Thomas. [1787] 1954. *Notes on the State of Virginia.* Edited by William Peden. Chapel Hill: University of North Carolina Press.

Johns, Anne Page. 1935. "The Rolfe Property Warren House at 'Smith's Fort Plantation,' 1652–1935." *Virginia Magazine of History and Biography* 43(3): 200–208.

Johnson, Matthew. 2007. *Ideas of Landscape.* Malden Mass.: Blackwell.

Jones, John G. 2001. "Analysis of Pollen from Poplar Forest, Virginia." Manuscript on file, Thomas Jefferson's Poplar Forest, Forest, Va.

———. 2002. "Analysis of Pollen from Poplar Forest, Virginia." Manuscript on file, Thomas Jefferson's Poplar Forest, Forest, Va.

Jordan, Weymouth T. 1950. "The Peruvian Guano Gospel in the Old South." *Agricultural History* 24(4): 211–221.

Kealofer, Lisa. 1997. "Poplar Forest Phytolith Analysis." Manuscript on file, Thomas Jefferson's Poplar Forest, Forest, Va.

———. 1999. "The South Lawn at Poplar Forest, Phytolith Analysis." Manuscript on file, Thomas Jefferson's Poplar Forest, Forest, Va.

Kelly, Kenneth G. 2001. "Change and Continuity in Coastal Bénin." In *West Africa during the Atlantic Slave Trade,* edited by Christopher DeCorse, 81–100. London: Leicester University Press.

Kelso, William M. 1971. "A Report on Exploratory Excavations at Carter's Grove Plantation, James City County, Virginia (June 1970–September 1971)." Edited by Neil Frank. Colonial Williamsburg Foundation Research Report No. 111, Williamsburg.

———. 1982. "A Report on the Archaeological Excavations at Monticello, Charlottesville, Virginia 1979–1981." Manuscript on file, Department of Archaeology, Thomas Jefferson Memorial Foundation, Charlottesville.

———. 1984a. *Kingsmill Plantations, 1619–1800: Archaeology of Country Life in Colonial Virginia.* Orlando Fla.: Academic Press.

———. 1984b. "Landscape Archaeology: A Key to Virginia's Cultivated Past." In *British and American Gardens in the Eighteenth Century: Eighteen Illustrated Essays on Garden History,* edited by Robert P. Maccubbin and Peter Martin, 159–169. Williamsburg: Colonial Williamsburg Foundation.

———. 1986. "The Archaeology of Slave Life at Monticello: A Wolf by the Ears." *Journal of New World Archaeology* 6(4): 5–20.

———. 1990. "Landscape Archaeology at Thomas Jefferson's Monticello." In *Earth Patterns: Essays in Landscape Archaeology,* edited by William M. Kelso and Rachel Most, 7–22. Charlottesville: University Press of Virginia.

———. 1992. "Big Things Remembered: Anglo-Virginian Houses, Armorial Devices, and the Impact of Common Sense." In *The Art and Mystery of Historical Archaeology: Essays in Honor of James Deetz,* edited by Anne Elizabeth Yentsch and Mary C. Beaudry, 127–145. Boca Raton, Fla.: CRC Press.

———. 1997. *Archaeology at Monticello: Artifacts of Everyday Life in the Plantation Community.* Charlottesville: Thomas Jefferson Memorial Foundation.

Kelso, William M., Douglas W. Sanford, Anna Gruber, Diana Crader Johnson, and Ann Morgan Smart. 1985. "Monticello Black History/Craft Life Archaeological Project 1984–1985

Progress Report." Manuscript on file, Department of Archaeology, Thomas Jefferson Memorial Foundation, Charlottesville.

Kelso, William M., and Douglas W. Sanford, with Dinah [Diana] Crader Johnson, Sondy Sanford, and Anna Gruber. 1984. "A Report on the Archaeological Excavations at Monticello, Charlottesville, Virginia 1982–1983." Manuscript on file, Department of Archaeology, Thomas Jefferson Memorial Foundation, Charlottesville.

Kelso, William M., M. Drake Patten, and Michael A. Strutt. 1991. "Poplar Forest Archaeology Research Report for NEH Grant 1990–1991." Manuscript on file, Thomas Jefferson's Poplar Forest, Forest, Va.

Kern, Susan A. 1999. "Where did the Indians Sleep? An Archaeological and Ethnohistorical Study of Mid-Eighteenth-Century Piedmont Virginia." In *Historical Archaeology, Identity Formation, and the Interpretation of Ethnicity,* edited by Maria Franklin and Garrett Fesler,31–46. Colonial Williamsburg Research Publications. Dietz Press: Richmond.

———. 2005a. *The Jeffersons at Shadwell: The Social and Material World of a Virginia Family.* PhD dissertation, The College of William and Mary. Ann Arbor, Mich.: University Microfilms International.

———. 2005b. "The Material World of the Jeffersons at Shadwell." *William and Mary Quarterly,* 3rd ser., 62(2): 213–242.

———. 2010. *The Jeffersons at Shadwell.* New Haven, Conn.: Yale University Press.

Kimball, Fiske. 1943. "In Search of Jefferson's Birthplace." *Virginia Magazine of History and Biography* 51(4): 313–325.

———. 1968. *Thomas Jefferson, Architect: Original Designs in the Coolidge Collection of the Massachusetts Historical Society.* New York: Da Capo Press.

King, Julia A. 1988. "Comparative Midden Analysis of a Household and Inn in St. Mary's City, Maryland." *Historical Archaeology* 22(2): 17–39.

———. 1990. *An Intrasite Spatial Analysis of the van Sweringen Site, St. Mary's City, Maryland.* PhD dissertation, University of Pennsylvania. Ann Arbor, Mich.: University Microfilms International.

———. 2006. "Household Archaeology, Identities, and Biographies." In *The Cambridge Companion to Historical Archaeology,* edited by Dan Hicks and Mary C. Beaudry, 293–313. Cambridge: Cambridge University Press.

King, Julia A., and Henry M. Miller. 1987. "View from the Midden: An Analysis of Midden Distribution and Composition at the Van Sweringen Site, St. Mary's City, Maryland." *Historical Archaeology* 21(2): 37–59.

King, Thomas F. 1998. *Cultural Resource Laws & Practice, An Introductory Guide.* Walnut Creek, Calif.: Altamira Press.

Klein, Herbert S., and Ben Vinson III. 2007. *African Slavery in Latin America and the Caribbean.* 2nd ed. New York: Oxford University Press.

Klingelhofer, Eric. 1987. "Aspects of Early Afro-American Material Culture: Artifacts from the Slave Quarters at Garrison Plantation, Maryland." *Historical Archaeology* 21(2): 112–119.

Klippel, Walter E., Jennifer A. Synstelien, and Barbara J. Heath. 2011. Taphonomy and Fish Bones from an Enslaved African American Context at Poplar Forest, Virginia, USA. *Archaeofauna* 20(October):27–45.

Knight, Anthony P., and Richard G. Walter. 2001. *A Guide to Plant Poisoning of Animals in North America.* Jackson, Wyo.: Teton New Media.

Koch, Adrienne. 1963. "The Versatile George Tucker." *Journal of Southern History* 29(4): 502–512.

Kolchin, Peter. 1993. *American Slavery, 1619–1877.* New York: Hill and Wang.

Kulikoff, Allan. 1986. *Tobacco and Slaves: The Development of Southern Cultures in the Chesapeake, 1680–1800.* Chapel Hill: University of North Carolina Press.

Laird, Mark. 1991. "Approaches to Planting in the Late Eighteenth Century: Some Imperfect Ideas on the Origins of the American Garden." *Journal of Garden History* 11(3): 154–172.

———. 1999. *The Flowering of the Landscape Garden: English Pleasure Grounds, 1720–1800.* Philadelphia: University of Pennsylvania Press.

Lee, Lori. 2008. "Late Antebellum Slavery at Poplar Forest (1828–1862)." *Quarterly Bulletin of the Archeological Society of Virginia* 63(3): 165–177.

———. 2010. "Someone's in the Kitchen: Interpreting Slavery at Thomas Jefferson's Poplar Forest." Paper presented at the conference Many Voices, One Story? Public History Narratives of Native American and African American Histories, North Carolina State University, Raleigh, N.C.

Lefebvre, Henri. 1991. *The Production of Space.* Oxford: Blackwell.

Leighton, Ann. 1986. *American Gardens in the Eighteenth Century: "For Use or for Delight."* Boston: Houghton Mifflin.

Lembo, Lois. 2001. "Fifty Years of Gunston Hall Archaeology." Manuscript on file, Gunston Hall Plantation, Gunston Hall, Va.

Leone, Mark P. 1984. "Interpreting Ideology in Historical Archaeology: Using the Rules of Perspective in the William Paca Garden in Annapolis, Maryland." In *Ideology, Power, and Prehistory,* edited by Daniel Miller and Christopher Tilley, 25–36. Cambridge: Cambridge University Press.

Lichtenberger, Randy, Barbara Heath, Keith Adams, Michael Jennings, Heather Olson, Lori Lee, Bree Detamore, and Tim Trussell. 2006. "Archaeological Mitigation of the Proposed Pump House Site at Thomas Jefferson's Poplar Forest, Forest, Virginia." Manuscript on file, Thomas Jefferson's Poplar Forest, Forest, Va.

Linebaugh, Donald W. 1994. "'All the Annoyances and Inconveniences of the Country': Environmental Factors in the Development of Outbuildings in the Colonial Chesapeake." *Winterthur Portfolio* 29(1): 1–18.

———. 1996. *"The Road to Ruins and Restoration": Roland W. Robbins and the Professionalization of Historical Archaeology.* PhD dissertation, The College of William and Mary. Ann Arbor, Mich.: University Microfilms International.

Link, William. 2005. *Roots of Secession: Slavery and Politics in Antebellum Virginia.* Chapel Hill: University of North Carolina Press.

Linzey, Donald W. 1998. *The Mammals of Virginia.* Blacksburg, Va.: McDonald & Woodward Publishing.

Little, Barbara J., 1996. "People with History: An Update on Historical Archaeology in the United States." In *Images of the Recent Past: Readings in Historical Archaeology,* edited by Charles Orser, 42–78. Walnut Creek, Calif.: Altamira Press.

Luccketti, Nicholas. 1989. "Preliminary Archaeological Report on Arlington." Manuscript on file, James River Institute for Archaeology, Jamestown, Va.

———. 1990. "Archaeological Excavations at Bacon's Castle, Surry County, Virginia." In *Earth Patterns: Essays in Landscape Archaeology,* edited by William M. Kelso and Rachel Most, 23–42. Charlottesville: University Press of Virginia.

———. 2010. "Nansemond Fort, Suffolk, Virginia." Paper presented at the 43rd Annual Conference on Historical and Underwater Archaeology, Amelia Island, Fla.

MacCord, Howard, Sr. 1996. "The Fout Site, Frederick County, Virginia." *Quarterly Bulletin of the Archeological Society of Virginia* 51(1): 1–41.

Maccubbin, Robert, and Peter Martin. 1984. *British and America Gardens in the Eighteenth Century: Eighteen Illustrated Essays on Garden History.* Williamsburg: Colonial Williamsburg Foundation.

Mahoney, Meredith A. 2007. "Space and Perspective in Four Burwell Gardens." *Quarterly Bulletin of the Archeological Society of Virginia* 62(3): 153–157.

Majewski, John. 2000. *A House Dividing: Economic Development in Pennsylvania and Virginia before the Civil War.* Cambridge: Cambridge University Press.

Malone, Dumas. 1948. *Jefferson and His Time.* Vol. 1, *Jefferson the Virginian.* Boston: Little, Brown and Company.

———. 1981. *Jefferson and His Time.* Vol. 6, *The Sage of Monticello.* Boston: Little, Brown and Company.

Maloy, Mark. 2007. "Searching for the Seventeenth-Century Fairfield." *Quarterly Bulletin of the Archeological Society of Virginia* 62(3): 130–135.

Mapp, Amber, and Lynn Wojcik. 2004. "Historical Note." In *Finding Aids to Personal Papers and Special Collections in the Smithsonian Institution Archives, Record Unit 7322, C. Malcolm Watkins Papers, 1935–1979 and Undated.* Washington, D.C.: Smithsonian Institution Archives. siarchives.si.edu/findingaids/faru7322.htm, accessed February 3, 2010.

Markotic, Vladimir. 1958. "Archaeological Excavation at Monticello." Manuscript on file, Thomas Jefferson Foundation, Charlottesville.

Marmon, Lee. 1991. "Poplar Forest Research Report, Revised Edition." Manuscript on file, Thomas Jefferson's Poplar Forest, Forest, Va.

Martin, Ann Smart. 1993. *Buying into the World of Goods: Eighteenth-Century Consumerism and the Retail Trade from London to the Virginia Frontier.* PhD dissertation, The College of William and Mary. Ann Arbor, Mich.: University Microfilms International.

———. 2008. *Buying into the World of Goods: Early Consumers in Backcountry Virginia.* Studies in Early American Economy and Society from the Library Company of Philadelphia. Baltimore, Md.: Johns Hopkins University Press.

Martin, Peter. 1991. *The Pleasure Gardens of Virginia: From Jamestown to Jefferson.* Princeton, N.J.: Princeton University Press.

Maryland Archaeological Conservation Lab. 2002. *Diagnostic Artifacts of Maryland.* Jefferson Patterson Park and Museum, St. Leonard. www.jefpat.org/diagnostic/index.htm, accessed March 1, 2010.

———. 2005–2007. *A Comparative Archaeological Study of Colonial Chesapeake Culture.* Jefferson Patterson Park and Museum, St. Leonard. www.chesapeakearchaeology.org, accessed March 1, 2010.

McDaniel, John, Kurt Russ, and Parker Potter. 1979. "A Description and Analysis of Tobacco Pipes Excavated at Liberty Hall." *Quarterly Bulletin of the Archeological Society of Virginia* 34(2): 83–92.

McDonald, Travis C. 1994. "Poplar Forest: Synthesis of a Lifetime." In *Notes on the State of Poplar Forest,* vol. 2, 1–7. Forest, Va.: The Corporation for Jefferson's Poplar Forest.

———. 2000. "Constructing Optimism: Thomas Jefferson's Poplar Forest." *Perspectives in Vernacular Architecture* 8: 176–200.

———. 2006–2007. "The Fundamental Practice of Fieldwork at Colonial Williamsburg." *Perspectives in Vernacular Architecture* 13(2): 36–53.

McEwan, Barbara. 1991. *Thomas Jefferson: Farmer*. Jefferson, N.C.: McFarland.

McKee, Larry W. 1987. "Delineating Ethnicity from the Garbage of Early Virginians: Faunal Remains from the Kingsmill Plantation Slave Quarter." *American Archaeology* 6(1): 31–39.

———. 1989. *Plantation Food Supply in Nineteenth-Century Tidewater Virginia*. PhD dissertation, University of California, Berkeley. Ann Arbor, Mich.: University Microfilms International.

———. 1992. "The Ideals and Realities behind the Design and Use of 19th Century Virginia Slave Cabins." In *The Art and Mystery of Historical Archaeology, Essays in Honor of James Deetz*, edited by Anne Elizabeth Yentsch and Mary C. Beaudry, 195–213. Boca Raton, Fla.: CRC Press.

———. 1995. "The Earth Is Their Witness." *The Sciences* (March/April): 36–41.

———. 1999. "Food Supply and Plantation Social Order." In *"I, Too, Am America": Archaeological Studies of African-American Life*, edited by Theresa A. Singleton, 218–239. Charlottesville: University Press of Virginia.

McKnight, Justine Woodard. 1999. "Appendix C: Botanical Analysis." In *Traces of Historic Kecoughtan: Archaeology at a Seventeenth-Century Plantation*, by Thomas F. Higgins III, Charles Downing, and Donald Linebaugh. Report to the Virginia Department of Transportation from the William and Mary Center for Archaeological Research, Williamsburg.

———. 2000. "Appendix G: Analysis of Flotation-Recovered Plant Remains from the Wilton Site (44HE493), Henrico County, Virginia." In "Wilton Speaks: Archaeology at an Eighteenth- and Nineteenth-Century Plantation, Data Recovery at Site 44R493, Associated with the Proposed Route 895 Project, Henrico County, Virginia," by Thomas F. Higgins, Benjamin Ford, Charles M. Downing, Veronica L. Deitrick, Stevan C. Pullins, and Dennis B. Blanton. Report to the Virginia Department of Transportation, Richmond, from the William and Mary Center for Archaeological Research, Williamsburg.

———. 2003. "Appendix E: Botanical Analysis." In "Southall's Quarter: Archaeology at an 18th-Century Slave Quarter in James City County, Data Recovery at Site 44JC969 Associated with the Proposed Route 199 Project, James City County, Virginia," by Stevan C. Pullins, Joe B. Jones, John R. Underwood, Kimberly A. Ettinger, David W. Lewes, with contributions from Justine W. McKnight and Gregory J. Brown. Report to the Virginia Department of Transportation, Richmond from the William and Mary Center for Archaeological Research, Williamsburg. web.wm.edu/wmcar/tr32Apps.pdf, accessed March 5, 2010.

———. 2004a. "George Washington's Distillery (44FX2262) Wood Identification, Batch One (Eight Samples), March 8, 2004." Manuscript on file, Archaeology Department, Mount Vernon Ladies' Association, Mount Vernon.

———. 2004b. "George Washington's Distillery (44FX2262) Wood Identification, Batch Two (Three Samples), July 9, 2004." Manuscript on file, Archaeology Department, Mount Vernon Ladies' Association, Mount Vernon.

———. 2006. "Wood Remains Identified from the Washington's Distillery Well, (44FX2262/837R) (Seven Samples), July 28, 2006." Manuscript on file, Archaeology Department, Mount Vernon Ladies' Association, Mount Vernon.

McLaughlin, Jack. 1988. *Jefferson and Monticello: The Biography of a Builder*. New York: Henry Holt.

McLearen, Douglas C., and L. Daniel Mouer. 1994. "Jordan's Journey III: A Preliminary Report on the 1992–93 Excavations at Archaeological Site 44PG307." Richmond: Virginia Commonwealth University Archaeological Research Center.

McMahon, Bernard. 1806. *The American Gardener's Calendar; Adapted to the Climates and Seasons of the United States.* Philadelphia: B. Graves.

Middleton, Robin. 1992. "Introduction." In *The Genius of Architecture,* by Nicholas Le Camus De Mézières, 16–64. Translated by David Britt. Santa Monica, Calif.: The Getty Center for the History of Art and the Humanities.

Miller, Daniel. 1987. *Material Culture and Mass Consumption.* New York: Basil Blackwell.

Miller, George L. 1991. "A Revised Set of CC Index Values for English Ceramics." *Historical Archaeology* 25(1): 1–25.

Miller, George L., Ann Smart Martin, and Nancy S. Dickinson. 1994. "Changing Consumption Patterns: English Ceramics and the American Market from 1770 to 1840." In *Everyday Life in the Early Republic,* edited by C. E. Hutchins, 219–248. Winterthur, Del.: Henry Francis du Pont Winterthur Museum.

Miller, George L., with Patricia Samford, Ellen Schlasko, and Andrew Madsen. 2000. "Telling Time for Archaeologists." *Northeast Historical Archaeology* 29: 1–22.

Miller, Naomi F. 1989. "What Mean These Seeds: A Comparative Approach to Archaeological Seed Analysis." *Historical Archaeology* 23(2): 50–59.

Mills, Barbara J., and William H. Walker (editors). 2008. *Memory Work: Archaeologies of Material Practices.* Santa Fe, N.M.: School for Advanced Research Press.

Mintz, Sydney W. 1985. *Sweetness and Power: The Place of Sugar in Modern History.* New York: Penguin Books.

Mintz, Sidney W., and Richard Price. 1976. *An Anthropological Approach to the Afro American Past: A Caribbean Perspective.* Occasional Papers in Social Change No. 2. Philadelphia: Institute of the Study for Human Issues.

Monticello Archaeology. 2011. "Current Research, Site 6." www.monticello.org/site/research-and-collections/site-6, accessed April 26, 2011.

Monticello Plantation Database. 2008. Monticello Plantation Database. plantationdb.monticello.org/nMonticello.html, accessed May 12, 2010.

Morel, Jean-Marie. 1776. *Théorie des jardins.* Paris: Pissot.

Morgan, Lynda. 1992. *Emancipation in Virginia's Tobacco Belt, 1850–1870.* Athens: University of Georgia Press.

Morgan, Philip D. 1998. *Slave Counterpoint: Black Culture in the Eighteenth-Century Chesapeake & Lowcountry.* Chapel Hill: University of North Carolina Press.

Morgan, Philip D., and Michael L. Nicholls. 1989. "Slaves in Piedmont Virginia, 1720–1790." *William and Mary Quarterly,* 3rd ser., 46(2): 212–251.

Mouer, L. Daniel. 1993. "Chesapeake Creoles: The Creation of Folk Culture in Colonial Virginia." In *The Archaeology of 17th-Century Virginia,* edited by Theodore R. Reinhart and Dennis J. Pogue, 105–166. Special Publication No. 30 of the Archeological Society of Virginia. Richmond: Dietz Press.

Mouer, L. Daniel, Mary Ellen N. Hodges, Stephen R. Potter, Susan L. Henry Renaud, Ivor Noël Hume, Dennis J. Pogue, Martha M. McCartney, and Thomas E. Davidson. 1999. "Colonoware Pottery, Chesapeake Pipes and 'Uncritical Assumptions,'" in *I, Too, Am America: Archaeological Studies of African-American Life,* edited by Theresa Singleton, 83–115. Charlottesville: University Press of Virginia.

Mouer, L. Daniel, Douglas C. McLearen, R. Taft Kiser, Chistopher P. Egghart, Beverly J. Binns, and Dane T. Magoon. 1992. "Jordan's Journey: A Preliminary Report on Archaeology at Site 44PG302, Prince George County, Virginia 1990–1991." Report to the Virginia Department of Historic Resources and the National Geographic Society from the Virginia Commonwealth University Archaeological Research Center, Richmond.

Mrozowski, Stephen. 1996. "Nature, Society, and Culture: Theoretical Considerations in Historical Archeology." In *Historical Archaeology and the Study of American Culture*, edited by Lu Ann De Cunzo and Bernard L. Herman, 447–472. Knoxville: University of Tennessee Press.

———. 1999. "Colonization and the Commodification of Nature." *International Journal of Historical Archaeology* 3(3): 153–166.

———. 2006. "Environments of History: Biological Dimensions of Historical Archaeology." In *Historical Archaeology*, edited by Martin Hall and Stephen W. Silliman, 23–41. Oxford: Blackwell.

———. 2010a. "Creole Materialities: Archaeological Explorations of Hybridized Realities on a North American Plantation." *Journal of Historical Sociology* 23(1): 462–484.

———. 2010b. "New and Forgotten Paradigms: The Environment and Economics in Historical Archaeology." *Historical Archaeology* 44(3): 117–127.

Mrozowski, Stephen A., Maria Franklin, and Leslie Hunt. 2008. "Archaeobotanical Analysis and Interpretations of Enslaved Virginian Plant Use at Rich Neck Plantation." *American Antiquity* 73(4): 699–728.

Mrozowski, Stephen A., Katherine Howlett Hayes, and Anne Hancock. 2007. "The Archaeology of Sylvester Manor." *Northeast Historical Archaeology* 36: 1–16.

Mullins, Paul R. 2001. "Racializing the Parlor: Race and Victorian Bric-a-Brac Consumption." In *Race and the Archaeology of Identity*, edited by Charles Orser Jr., 158–176. Salt Lake City: University of Utah Press.

Muraca, David, Philip Levy, and Leslie McFaden. 2003. *The Archaeology of Rich Neck Plantation (44WB52): Description of the Features*. Williamsburg: Department of Archaeological Research, Colonial Williamsburg Foundation. research.history.org/Files/Archaeo/Major Studies/Rich%20Neck%20Technical%20Interim.pdf, accessed March 5, 2010.

Museum of London. 2010. *Clay Tobacco Pipe Makers' Marks from London*. Museum of London Collections, Museum of London, London, UK. www.museumoflondon.org.uk/claypipes/index.asp, accessed March 1, 2010.

Nagaoka, Lisa. 2001. "Using Diversity Indices to Measure Changes in Prey Choice at the Shag River Mouth Site, Southern New Zealand." *International Journal of Osteoarchaeology* 11: 101–111.

Neiman, Fraser. 1978. "Domestic Architecture at the Clifts Plantation: The Social Context of Early Virginia Building." *Northern Neck of Virginia Historical Magazine* 28(1): 3096–3128.

———. 1980a. "Field Archaeology of the Clifts Plantation Site." Manuscript on file, Robert E. Lee Memorial Association, Stratford, Va.

———. 1980b. *The "Manner House" before Stratford: Discovering the Clifts Plantation*. Stratford, Va.: Robert E. Lee Memorial Association.

———. 1997. "Sub-Floor Pits and Slavery in 18th and Early 19th-Century Virginia." Paper presented at the 30th Conference on Historical and Underwater Archaeology, Corpus Christi, Tex.

———. 2008. "The Lost World of Monticello: An Evolutionary Perspective." *Journal of Anthropological Research* 64(2): 161–193.

Neiman, Fraser D., Sara Bon-Harper, John Jones, Julie K. Stein, and Derek Wheeler. 2003. "Landscape Dynamics at Monticello: A Geo-Archaeological Perspective." Poster presented at 68th Annual Conference of the Society for American Archaeology, Milwaukee, Wis.

Neiman, Fraser D., Leslie McFaden, and Derek Wheeler. 2000. "Archaeological Investigation of the Elizabeth Hemings Site (44AB438)." Monticello Department of Archaeology Technical Report Series No. 2. Charlottesville, Va.: Thomas Jefferson Foundation.

Nelson, Lee H. 1968. "Nail Chronology as an Aid to Dating Old Buildings." American Association for State and Local History Technical Leaflet 48. *History News* 24(11).

Nelson, Lynn A. 1998. *The Agroecologies of a Southern Community: The Tye River Valley of Virginia, 1730–1860.* PhD dissertation, College of William and Mary. Ann Arbor, Mich.: University Microfilms International.

———. 2007. *Pharsalia: An Environmental Biography of a Southern Plantation, 1780–1880.* Athens: University of Georgia Press.

Nichols, Frederick D. 1984a. *Thomas Jefferson's Architectural Drawings Compiled and with Commentary and a Check List.* Charlottesville: University Press of Virginia.

———. 1984b. "Thomas Jefferson's Poplar Forest." In *Historical Sketches from the Iron Worker,* edited by William R. Dunn and T. Gibson Hobbs Jr., 26–37. Lynchburg, Va.: Lynchburg Historical Foundation.

Noël Hume, Ivor. 1962a. *Excavations at Rosewell, Gloucester County, Virginia 1957–1959.* Contributions from the Museum of History and Technology, Paper 18, United States National Museum Bulletin 225. Washington, D.C.: Smithsonian Institution Press.

———. 1962b. "An Indian Ware of the Colonial Period." *Quarterly Bulletin of the Archeological Society of Virginia* 17: 2–14.

———. 1966a. *Excavations at Clay Bank in Gloucester County, Virginia 1962–1963.* Contributions from the Museum of History and Technology, Paper 52, United States National Museum Bulletin 249. Washington, D.C.: Smithsonian Institution Press.

———. 1966b. *Excavations at Tutter's Neck in James City County, Virginia, 1960–61.* Contributions from the Museum of History and Technology, Paper 53. United States. National Museum Bulletin, 249. Washington, D.C.: Smithsonian Institution Press.

———. 1969. *Historical Archaeology.* New York: Alfred A. Knopf.

———. 1980. *A Guide to the Artifacts of Colonial America.* New York: Alfred A. Knopf.

———. 1982. *Martin's Hundred: The Discovery of a Lost Colonial Virginia Settlement.* New York: Delta Publishing.

Oberg, Barbara (editor). 2001. *1 March 1796–31 December 1797.* Vol. 29 of *The Papers of Thomas Jefferson.* Princeton, N.J.: Princeton University Press.

O'Brien, Michael J., and Dennis E. Lewarch (editors). 1981. *Plowzone Archaeology: Contributions to Theory and Technique.* Publications in Anthropology No. 27. Nashville: Vanderbilt University.

Olsen, Bjørnar. 2003. "Material Culture after Text: Re-Membering Things." *Norwegian Archaeological Review* 36(2): 87–104.

Olwell, Robert. 1994. "'A Reckoning of Account': Patriarchy, Market Relations, and Control on Henry Lauren's Lowcountry Plantations, 1762–1785." In *Working Toward Freedom: Slave Society and Domestic Economy in the American South,* edited by Larry Hudson Jr., 33–52. Rochester, N.Y.: University of Rochester Press.

Orwig, David A., and Marc D. Abrams. 1994. "Land-Use History (1720–1992), Composition, and Dynamics of Oak-Pine Forests within the Piedmont and Coastal Plain of Northern Virginia." *Canadian Journal of Forest Research* 24: 1216–1225.

Outlaw, Alain Charles. 1974. "Excavations at Wilton." Manuscript on file, William and Mary Center for Archaeological Research, Williamsburg.

———. 1990. *Governor's Land: Archaeology of Early Seventeenth-Century Virginia Settlements.* Charlottesville: University Press of Virginia.

Ozanne, Paul. 1962. "Notes on the Early Historic Archaeology of Accra." *Transactions of the Historical Society of Ghana* 6: 51–70.

———. 1976. "Tobacco-Pipes of Accra and Shai." Manuscript on file, University of Ghana Department of Archaeology, Legon.

Painter, Floyd E. 1958. "The Helmet Site." In *Pots, Pipes, and Trash Pits,* edited by Edward Bottoms and Cynthia S. Hansen, 67–78. Vol. 1 of the Jamestown 2007 Trilogy. Richmond, Va.: Archeological Society of Virginia.

———. 1959. "The Chesopean Site." In *Pots, Pipes, and Trash Pits,* edited by Edward Bottoms and Cynthia S. Hansen, 79–83. Vol. 1 of the Jamestown 2007 Trilogy. Richmond, Va.: Archeological Society of Virginia.

Palladio, Andrea. 1965. *The Four Books of Architecture.* Edited by Adolf Placzec. New York: Dover.

Parent, Anthony S., Jr. 2003. *Foul Means: The Formation of a Slave Society in Virginia, 1660–1740.* Chapel Hill: University of North Carolina Press.

Parker, Kathleen, and Jacqueline Hernigle. 1990. "Portici: Portrait of a Middling Plantation in Piedmont Virginia." Regional Archaeology Program, National Capital Region, National Park Service, Occasional Report, No. 3. Washington, D.C.

Parker, Scott K., Lynne G. Lewis, Larry D. Dermody, and Ann L. Miller. 1996. "Crafty Businessmen: A New Perspective on 18th-century Plantation Economics." In *The Archaeology of 18th-Century Virginia,* edited by Theodore R. Reinhart, 183–207. Printed for the Archeological Society of Virginia. Richmond: Dietz Press.

Patten, M. Drake. 1992. "Mankala and Minkisi: Possible Evidence of African-American Folk Beliefs and Practices." *African American Archaeology: Newsletter of the African-American Archaeology Network* 6: 5–7.

Patterson, Helen S. 1983. *St. Stephen's Episcopal Church of Bedford County.* Forest, Va.: The Historical Records Committee of St. Stephens Episcopal Church.

Pecoraro, Luke J. 2010. "'Of chusing and takinge some place of Advantage, and there to make some Pallisadoes': Atlantic Connections at the Nansemond Fort, Virginia." MA thesis, Boston University, Boston, Mass.

Penningroth, Dylan. 2003. *The Claims of Kinfolk: African-American Property and Community in the Nineteenth-Century South.* Chapel Hill: University of North Carolina Press.

Perdue, Charles L., Jr., Thomas E. Barden, and Robert K. Phillips (editors). 1976. *Weevils in the Wheat: Interviews with Virginia Ex-Slaves.* Charlottesville: University Press of Virginia.

Philadelphia Museum of Art. 1946. *Seventieth Annual Report of the Philadelphia Museum of Art for the Year Ended May 31, 1946, with the List of Members.* Philadelphia: Philadelphia Museum of Art. www.archive.org/details/annualreportofph13phil, accessed February 4, 2010.

Philips, John. 1983. "African Smoking and Pipes." *The Journal of African History* 24(3): 303–319.

Pi-Sunyer, Oriol. 1963. "Excavations at Mulberry Row, Monticello." *Explorer* 5(4): 20–25.

Pi-Sunyer, Oriol, and James A. Bear. 1957. "Archaeological Excavation at Monticello along Mulberry Row." Manuscript on file, Thomas Jefferson Foundation, Charlottesville.

Pogue, Dennis J. 1988a. "Archaeology at George Washington's Mount Vernon: 1931–1987." Archaeology Department, Mount Vernon Ladies Association, File Report No. 1, Mount Vernon, Va.

———. 1988b. "Spatial Analysis of the King's Reach Plantation Homelot, ca. 1690–1715." *Historical Archaeology* 22(2): 40–56.

———. 1992. "Archaeological Investigations at the "Vineyard Inclosure" (44FX763/4) Mount Vernon Plantation, Mount Vernon, Virginia." Archaeology Department, Mount Vernon Ladies Association, File Report No. 3, Mount Vernon, Va.

———. 1996. "Giant in the Earth: George Washington, Landscape Designer." In *Landscape*

*Archaeology: Reading and Interpreting the American Historical Record,* edited by Rebecca Yamin and Karen B. Metheny, 52–69. Knoxville: University of Tennessee Press.

———. 2001a. "Slave Lifeways at Mount Vernon: An Archaeological Perspective." In *Slavery at the Home of George Washington,* edited by Philip J. Schwartz, 110–135. Mount Vernon, Va.: Mount Vernon Ladies Association.

———. 2001b. "The Transformation of America: Georgian Sensibility, Capitalist Conspiracy, or Consumer Revolution?" *Historical Archaeology* 35(2): 41–57.

———. 2002. "The Domestic Architecture of Slavery at George Washington's Mount Vernon." *Winterthur Portfolio* 37(1): 3–22.

———. 2006. "Archaeology at George Washington's Mount Vernon, 1931–2006." *Quarterly Bulletin of the Archeological Society of Virginia* 61(1): 165–175.

Pogue, Dennis J., and Esther C. White. 1991. "Summary Report on the 'House for Families' Slave Quarter Site (44FX762/40-47), Mount Vernon Plantation, Mount Vernon, Virginia." *Quarterly Bulletin of the Archeological Society of Virginia* 46(4): 189–206.

———. 1994. "Reanalysis of Features and Artifacts Excavated at George Washington's Birthplace, Virginia." *Quarterly Bulletin of the Archeological Society of Virginia* 49(1): 32–45.

Polk, Harding, II. 1991. "Archaeological Investigations at the Dairy at Sully Plantation, Fairfax County, Virginia." Paper presented at the 24th Annual Conference on Historical and Underwater Archaeology, Richmond, Va.

Prance, Sir Ghillean, and Mark Nesbitt. 2005. *The Cultural History of Plants.* New York: Routledge.

Proebsting, Eric, Jack Gary, and Lori Lee. 2010. "Presenting Historical Archaeology with Digital Technologies at Thomas Jefferson's Poplar Forest." Poster presented at the 75th Annual Conference of the Society for American Archaeology, St. Louis, Mo.

Ptacek, Crystal. 2009. "Excavating the 18th-Century Garden: A Synthesis of Garden Books and Archaeological Findings." Paper presented at the Mid Atlantic Archaeological Conference, Ocean City, Md.

Pullins, Stevan C., Joe B. Jones, John R. Underwood, Kimberly A. Ettinger, David W. Lewes, Justine McKnight, and Gregory J. Brown. 2003. "Southall's Quarter: Archaeology at an Eighteenth-Century Slave Quarter in James City County, Data Recovery at Site 44JC969 Associated with the Proposed Route 199 Project, James City County, Virginia." Williamsburg, Va.: William and Mary Center for Archaeological Research. web.wm.edu/wmcar/tr32.pdf?svr=www, accessed March 5, 2010.

Quinby, Lee. 1982. "Thomas Jefferson: The Virtue of Aesthetics and the Aesthetics of Virtue." *American Historical Review* 87(2): 337–56.

Ragland, H. S. 1930. "Transit Book 365A: Notes of the Excavations of the Site of the Colonial Governor's Palace Williamsburg Virginia Archaeological Report Block 20, Building 3; Excavation of Site of Colonial Governor's Palace." Colonial Williamsburg Foundation Library Research Report Series 1420. Williamsburg, Va.: Colonial Williamsburg Foundation Library. research.history.org/DigitalLibrary/View/index.cfm?doc=ResearchReports\RR0122.xml, accessed February 3, 2010.

Randall, Henry S. [1857] 1970. *The Life of Thomas Jefferson.* Vol. 3. Freeport, N.Y.: Books for Libraries Press.

Randolph, Sarah Nicholas. [1871] 1978. *The Domestic Life of Thomas Jefferson.* Charlottesville: University Press of Virginia.

Raymer, Leslie E. 1996. "Macroplant Remains from the Jefferson's Poplar Forest Slave Quarter:

A Study in African American Subsistence Practices." New South Associates Technical Report #402, Stone Mountain, Ga.

———. 2003. "Archaeobotanical Analysis from Data Recovery Excavations at the North Hill and Quarter Sites, Jefferson's Poplar Forest: A Study of Enslaved African-American Subsistence Patterns." New South Associates Technical Report #781. Stone Mountain, Georgia.

Reeves, Matthew. 2010. "The Landscape of Slavery at Montpelier." Paper presented at the 43rd Annual Conference on Historical and Underwater Archaeology, Amelia Island, Fla.

Reinhart, Theodore R. (editor). 1984. *The Archaeology of Shirley Plantation*. Charlottesville: University Press of Virginia.

Renaud, Susan L. Henry. 1996. "Material Culture and the Creolization of 18th-Century Virginia: Some Thoughts on Sanford and Heath." In *The Archaeology of 18th-Century Virginia*, edited by Theodore R. Reinhart, 177–182. Special Publication No. 35 of the Archeological Society of Virginia. Richmond: Dietz Press.

Rice, Howard Crosby. 1976. *Thomas Jefferson's Paris*. Princeton, N.J.: Princeton University Press.

Riordan, Timothy. 1988. "Interpretation of 17th Century Sites through Plow Zone Surface Collections: Examples from St. Mary's City, Maryland." *Historical Archaeology* 22(2): 2–16.

Robert, Joseph C. [1938] 1965. *The Tobacco Kingdom: Plantation, Market, and Factory in Virginia and North Carolina, 1800–1860*. Gloucester, Mass: Peter Smith.

Rockwell, Timothy O. 1974. "Belle Grove Excavations, Middletown, Virginia, 1972–1973." Report prepared for the National Trust for Historic Preservation, Washington, D.C.

Russell, Aaron. 1997. "Material Culture and African-American Spirituality at the Hermitage." *Historical Archaeology* 31(2): 63–80.

Russell, Emily W. B. 1997. *People and the Land through Time: Linking Ecology and History*. New Haven, Conn.: Yale University Press.

Rust, William F., III. 1985. "An Archaeological Investigation of Sully Plantation." Manuscript on file, Virginia Department of Historic Resources, Richmond, Va.

Safina, Carl. 1997. *Songs for the Blue Ocean: Encounters along the World's Coasts and Beneath the Seas*. New York: Henry Holt.

Samford, Patricia M. 1991. "Archaeological Investigations of a Probable Slave Quarter at Richneck Plantation." Manuscript on file, Department of Archaeological Research, Colonial Williamsburg Foundation, Williamsburg, Va.

———. 1996. "The Archaeology of African-American Slavery and Material Culture." *William and Mary Quarterly*, 3rd ser., 53(1): 87–114.

———. 1999. "'Strong is the Bond of Kinship': West African-Style Ancestor Shrines and Subfloor Pits on African American Quarters." In *Historical Archaeology, Identity Formation, and the Interpretation of Ethnicity*, edited by Maria Franklin and Garrett Fesler, 71–91. Colonial Williamsburg Research Publications. Richmond: Dietz Press.

———. 2000. *Power Runs in Many Channels: Subfloor Pits and West African-Based Spiritual Traditions in Colonial Virginia*. Ph.D. diss., University of North Carolina, Chapel Hill. Ann Arbor, Mich.: University Microfilms International.

———. 2004. "Engendering Enslaved Communities on Virginia's and North Carolina's Eighteenth- and Nineteenth-Century Plantations." In *Engendering African American Archaeology, A Southern Perspective*, edited by Jillian E. Galle and Amy L. Young, 151–175. Knoxville: University of Tennessee Press.

———. 2007. *Subfloor Pits and the Archaeology of Slavery in Colonial Virginia*. Tuscaloosa: University of Alabama Press.

Sanford, Douglas. 1984. "The Nailery Addition 'J.'" In "A Report on the Archaeological Exca-
vations at Monticello, Charlottesville, Virginia 1982–1983," edited by William Kelso and
Douglas W. Sanford, 26–61. Unpublished manuscript, Department of Archaeology, Thomas
Jefferson Memorial Foundation, Charlottesville.

———. 1990. "The Gardens at Germanna, Virginia." In *Earth Patterns: Essays in Landscape Archaeology*, edited by William M. Kelso and Rachel Most, 43–57. Charlottesville: University
Press of Virginia.

———. 1994. "The Archaeology of Plantation Slavery in Piedmont Virginia: Context and Process." In *Historical Archaeology of the Chesapeake*, edited by Paul A. Shackel and Barbara J.
Little, 115–130. Washington, D.C.: Smithsonian Institution Press.

———. 1995. *The Archaeology of Plantation Slavery at Thomas Jefferson's Monticello: Context and
Process in an American Slave Society*. PhD dissertation, University of Virginia. Ann Arbor,
Mich.: University Microfilms International.

———. 1996. "Searching and Re-Searching for the African Americans of 18th-Century Virginia." In *The Archaeology of 18th-Century Virginia*, edited by Theodore R. Reinhart, 131–148.
Special Publication No. 35 of the Archeological Society of Virginia. Richmond: Dietz Press.

———. 1999a. "Landscape, Change, and Community at Stratford Hall Plantation: An Archeological and Cultural Perspective." *Quarterly Bulletin of the Archeological Society of Virginia*
54(1): 2–19.

———. 1999b. "Archaeology at Stratford: The Old Orchard Field (2nd Season)—The 1999 Field
School Season." Manuscript on file, Center for Historic Preservation, Mary Washington
College, Fredericksburg, Va.

———. 2000. "Archaeology at Stratford: The Old Orchard Field (3rd Season), The 2000 Field
School Season." Manuscript on file, Center for Historic Preservation, Mary Washington
College, Fredericksburg, Va.

———. 2003. "ST116: Background." Digital Archaeology Archive of Comparative Slavery,
Thomas Jefferson Foundation, Charlottesville. http://www.daacs.org/resources/sites/back
ground/27/, accessed March 5, 2010.

Savitt, Todd L. 1978. *Medicine and Slavery: The Diseases and Health Care of Blacks in Antebellum Virginia*. Urbana: University of Illinois Press.

Sawyer, Elizabeth, and Karen Smith. 2011. "Building MRS 2: Background." Manuscript on file,
Department of Archaeology, Thomas Jefferson Foundation, Charlottesville.

Schroedl, Gerald F. (editor). 1986. "Overhill Cherokee Archaeology at Chota-Tanasee." Report
of Investigations 38, Tennessee Valley Authority., Knoxville Tenn.: University of Tennessee
Department of Anthropology.

Schlereth, Thomas J. 1982. *Material Culture Studies in America*. Nashville: American Association for State and Local History.

Scofield, Merry Ellen. 2006. "The Fatigues of His Table: The Politics of Presidential Dining
during the Jefferson Administration." *Journal of the Early Republic* 26(3): 449–469.

Scruggs, Philip Lightfoot. 1978. *The History of Lynchburg, Virginia 1786–1946*. Lynchburg, Va.:
J. P. Bell Co.

Shackelford, George Green. 1995. *Thomas Jefferson's Travels in Europe, 1784–1789*. Baltimore,
Md.: Johns Hopkins University Press.

Shaw, Thurstan. 1960. "Early Smoking Pipes: In Africa, Europe, and America." *Journal of the
Royal Anthropological Institute for Great Britain and Ireland* 90(2): 272–305.

Sheridan, Richard B. 1960. "The British Credit Crisis of 1772 and the American Colonies." *The Journal of Economic History* 20(2): 161–186.

Shick, Laura. 2005. "An Analysis of Archaeobotanical Evidence from the House for Families Slave Quarter, Mount Vernon Plantation, Virginia." MA thesis, American University. Ann Arbor, Mich.: University Microfilms International.

Shott, George C., Jr. 1978. "US Army Engineer Museum, Archaeological Investigations of Belvoir Historic Site, Ft. Belvoir, Virginia." Manuscript on file, U.S. Army Engineer Center and Fort Belvoir, Fort Belvoir, Va.

Silver, Timothy. 1990. *A New Face on the Countryside: Indians, Colonists, and Slaves in South Atlantic Forests, 1500–1800*. Cambridge: Cambridge University Press.

———. 2001. "A Useful Arcadia: European Colonists as Biotic Factors in Chesapeake Forests." In *Discovering the Chesapeake: The History of an Ecosystem*, edited by Philip D. Curtin, Grace S. Brush, and George W. Fisher, pp. 149–166. Baltimore, Md.: Johns Hopkins University Press.

Singleton, Theresa. 1990. "The Archaeology of the Plantation South: A Review of Approaches and Goals." *Historical Archaeology* 24(4): 70–77.

———. 1991. "The Archaeology of Slave Life." In *Before Freedom Came: African-American Life in the Antebellum South*, edited by Edward Campbell and Kym Rice, 155–175. Charlottesville: The Museum of the Confederacy and University Press of Virginia.

———. 1995. "The Archaeology of Slavery in North America." *Annual Review of Anthropology* 24: 119–140.

———. 1998. "Cultural Interaction and African American Identity." In *Studies in Culture Contact: Interaction, Culture Change, and Archaeology*, edited by James G. Cusick, 172–188. Center for Archaeological Investigations Research Paper No. 25. Carbondale, Ill.: Southern Illinois University.

———. 2005. "Before the Revolution: Archaeology and the African Diaspora on the Atlantic Seaboard." In *North American Archaeology*, edited by Timothy R. Pauketat and Diana DiPaolo Loren, 319–336. London: Blackwell.

Skaggs, Jimmy. 1994. *The Great Guano Rush: Entrepreneurs and American Overseas Expansion*. New York: St. Martins.

Sloan, Herbert E. 1995. *Principle and Interest: Thomas Jefferson and the Problem of Debt*. Charlottesville: University Press of Virginia.

Smith, Monica L. 2007. "Inconspicuous Consumption: Non-Display Goods and Identity Formation." *Journal of Archaeological Method and Theory* 14(4): 412–438.

Smith, Samuel. 1987. "Archaeology of Slavery: Some Tennessee Examples." Paper presented at the Afro-American Local History Sixth Annual Conference, Nashville, Tenn.

Sobel, Mechal. 1987. *The World They Made Together: Black and White Values in Eighteenth-Century Virginia*. Princeton, N.J.: Princeton University Press.

Soja, Edward. 1989. *Postmodern Geographies: The Reassertion of Space in Critical Social Theory*. London: Verso.

———. 2000. *Postmetropolis: Critical Studies of Cities and Regions*. London: Blackwell.

———. 2010. *Seeking Spatial Justice: Globalization and Community*. Minneapolis: University of Minnesota Press.

South, Stanley. 1977. *Method and Theory in Historical Archaeology*. New York: Academic Press.

Spencer-Wood, Suzanne M. 1987. "Miller's Indices and Consumer Choice Profiles: Status-Related Behaviors and White Ceramics." In *Consumer Choice in Historical Archaeology,* edited by Suzanne M. Spencer-Wood, 321–358. New York: Plenum Press.

Sprinkle, John H. 1991. "The Contents of Charles Cox's Mill House Chest." *Historical Archaeology* 25(3): 91–93.

Squibb, Robert. [1787] 1980. *The Gardener's Calendar for South-Carolina, Georgia, and North-Carolina.* Athens: University of Georgia Press.

Stahl, Ann. 2001. "Historical Process and the Impact of the Atlantic Trade on Banda, Ghana, c. 1800–1920." In *West Africa during the Atlantic Slave Trade,* edited by Christopher DeCorse, 38–58. London: Leicester University Press.

Stanton, Lucia C. 1993. "'Those Who Labor for My Happiness': Thomas Jefferson and His Slaves." In *Jeffersonian Legacies,* edited by Peter S. Onuf, 147–180. Charlottesville: University Press of Virginia.

———. 2000. *Free Some Day, The African-American Families of Monticello.* Charlottesville, Va.: The Thomas Jefferson Foundation.

Stealey, William, III. 1993. *The Salt Furnaces of the Kanawha Valley 1797–1868.* Lexington: University Press of Kentucky.

Stein, Susan. 1993. *The Worlds of Thomas Jefferson at Monticello.* New York: Harry N. Abrams.

Stephenson, Christie, Kaylyn Hipps, April Oettinger, and Gina Haney. 2010. "Fiske Kimball, Master of the Diverse Arts: An Exhibition Celebrating the 25th Anniversary of the Fiske Kimball Fine Arts Library, University of Virginia, Charlottesville, Virginia, September 1995–July 1996." University of Virginia Library, Charlottesville. www2.lib.virginia.edu/finearts/exhibits/fiske/index.html, accessed February 4, 2010.

Stine, Linda, Melanie Cabak, and Mark Groover. 1996. "Blue Beads as African-American Cultural Symbols." *Historical Archaeology* 30(3): 49–75.

Stoll, Steven. 2002. *Larding the Lean Earth: Soil and Society in Nineteenth-Century America.* New York: Hill and Wang.

Straube, Beverly A. 1995. "The Colonial Potters of Tidewater Virginia." *Journal of Early Southern Decorative Arts* 21(2): 1–39.

Strutt, Michael. 1998a. "A Report on Excavations at the West Barn at Thomas Jefferson's Poplar Forest." Manuscript on file, edited by Timothy Trussell. Thomas Jefferson's Poplar Forest, Forest, Va.

———. 1998b. "Remote Sensing Survey of a Historic Brick Kiln in Forest Virginia." Manuscript on file, edited by Timothy Trussell. Thomas Jefferson's Poplar Forest, Forest, Va.

———. 1999. "The Solitude of a Hermit: Thomas Jefferson and His Landscape at Poplar Forest." In *The Archaeology of 19th-Century Virginia,* edited by John H. Sprinkle Jr. and Theodore R. Reinhart, 111–139. Archeological Society of Virginia Special Publication No. 36. Richmond, Va.: Spectrum Press.

Swanson, Drew Addison. 2009. "Fighting over Fencing: Agricultural Reform and Antebellum Efforts to Close the Virginia Open Range." *Virginia Magazine of History and Biography* 117(2): 104–139.

Terrell, Bruce G. 1992. "The James River Bateau: Tobacco Transport in Upland Virginia, 1745–1840." East Carolina University Research Report 7. Program in Maritime History and Underwater Research, East Carolina University, Greenville, North Carolina.

Thompson, Stephen. 2010. "The Archaeology of Bowles' Lot: Phase III Data Recovery Excavations at 44AB374, a Late Eighteenth to Nineteenth Century Free African American Rural Domestic Site in Albemarle County, Virginia." VDHR File #2006-0394. Report on file at Virginia Department of Historic Resources, Richmond.

Thornton, John. 1998. *Africa and Africans in the Making of the Atlantic World, 1400–1800.* 2nd ed. Cambridge: Cambridge University Press.

T. L. C. Genealogy. 2000. *Bedford County Virginia Order Book 1, 1754–1761.* Miami Beach, Fla.: T. L. C. Genealogy.

Trickett, Mark. 2010. "Excavations at Montpelier's South Yard." Paper presented at the 43rd Annual Conference on Historical and Underwater Archaeology, Amelia Island, Fla.

Trigg, Heather B., Richard I. Ford, John G. Moore, and Louise D. Jessop. 1994. "Coprolite Evidence for Prehistoric Foodstuffs, Condiments, and Medicines." In *Eating on the Wild Side: The Pharmacologic, Ecologic, and Social Implications of Using Noncultigens,* edited by Nina Etkin, 210–223. Tucson: University of Arizona Press.

Trigger, Bruce. 2006. *A History of Archaeological Thought.* Cambridge: Cambridge University Press.

Tripp, Steven. 1997. *Yankee Town, Southern City: Race and Class Relations in Civil War Lynchburg.* New York: New York University Press.

Trouillot, Michel-Rolph. 1995. *Silencing the Past: Power and the Production of History.* Boston: Beacon Press.

Trussell, Timothy D. 1999. "The 'Peter's Field' Tobacco Barn: Excavation Report for Thomas Jefferson's Poplar Forest." Manuscript on file, Thomas Jefferson's Poplar Forest, Forest, Va.

———. 2000. "Jefferson's Villa in the Garden: A Report on the Landscape Archaeology Project at Thomas Jefferson's Poplar Forest, 1998–1999." Manuscript on file, Thomas Jefferson's Poplar Forest, Forest, Va.

———. 2004. "The Utility of High Pollen Counts: A Case Study from Thomas Jefferson's Poplar Forest." *Journal of Middle Atlantic Archaeology* 20: 89–97.

Turner, Charles W. 1952. "Virginia Agricultural Reform, 1815–1860." *Agricultural History* 26(3): 80–89.

Twyman, Robert W. 2003. "Fall Line." In *Dictionary of American History,* vol. 3, edited by Stanley I. Kutler, 310. Charles Scribner's Sons, New York.

Tyler, Lyon Gardiner (editor). 1915. *Encyclopedia of Virginia Biography.* Vol. 2. New York: Lewis Historical Publishing.

Upton, Dell. 1982. "Vernacular Domestic Architecture in Eighteenth-Century Virginia." Winterthur Portfolio 17(2–3): 95–119.

Van Dyke, Ruth M., and Susan E. Alcock (editors). 2003. *Archaeologies of Memory.* London: Blackwell.

Vaughan, Joseph Lee, and Omer Allan Gianniny Jr. 1981. *Thomas Jefferson's Rotunda Restored: A Pictorial Review with Commentary, 1973–76.* Charlottesville: University Press of Virginia.

Veech, Andrew Stoesser. 1998. *Signatures of Gentility: Assessing Status Archaeologically in Mid-Eighteenth-Century Fairfax County, Virginia.* PhD dissertation, Brown University. Ann Arbor, Mich.: University Microfilms International.

Veit, Richard. 2009. "Memorial—Norman F. Barka, 1938–2008." *Historical Archaeology* 43(2): 1–8.

Verner, Coolie. 1967. "The Fry and Jefferson Map." *Imago Mundi* 21: 70–94.

Vlach, John Michael. 1991. *By the Work of Their Hands: Studies in Afro-American Folklife.* Charlottesville: University Press of Virginia.

———. 1993. *Back of the Big House: The Architecture of Plantation Slavery.* Chapel Hill: University of North Carolina Press.

Walker, William H., and Michael Brian Schiffer. 2006. "The Materiality of Social Power:

The Artifact-Acquisition Perspective." *Journal of Archaeological Method and Theory* 13(2): 67–88.

Wall, Diane diZerega. 1994. "Family Dinners and Social Teas: Ceramics and Domestic Rituals." In *Everyday Life in the Early Republic,* edited by C. E. Hutchins, 249–283. Winterthur, Del.: Henry Francis du Pont Winterthur Museum.

Walsh, Lorena. 1993. "Slave Life, Slave Society, and Tobacco Production in the Tidewater Chesapeake, 1620–1820." In *Cultivation and Culture: Labor and the Shaping of Slave Life in the Americas,* edited by Ira Berlin and Philip D. Morgan, pp. 170–199. Charlottesville: University of Virginia Press.

———.1997. *From Calabar to Carter's Grove: The History of a Virginia Slave Community.* Charlottesville: University Press of Virginia.

———. 1999. "New Findings about the Virginia Slave Trade." *Colonial Williamsburg Interpreter* 20(2). research.history.org/Historical_Research/Research_Themes/ThemeEnslave/Slave-Trade.cfm, accessed April 27, 2011.

———. 2001. "The Chesapeake Slave Trade: Regional Patterns, African Origins and Some Implications." *William and Mary Quarterly,* 3rd ser., 58(1): 139–170.

Watelet, Claude-Henri. 1774. *Essai sur les jardins.* [*Essay on Gardens*]. Paris: Prault.

Watkins, Malcolm C. 1968. *The Cultural History of Marlborough, Virginia.* Washington D.C.: Smithsonian Institution Press.

Weaver, John W. 1979. "An Early Trash Pit at the Governor's Land." In *Pots, Pipes and Trash Pits,* edited by Edward Bottoms and Cynthia S. Hansen, 135–138. Vol. 1 of the Jamestown 2007 Trilogy. Richmond, Va.: Archeology Society of Virginia.

Weld, Isaac, Jr. 1800. *Travels through the States of North America and the Provinces of Upper and Lower Canada during the Years 1795, 1796, and 1797.* 4th ed. London: John Stockdale.

Wells, Camille. 1993. "The Planter's Prospect: Houses, Outbuildings and Rural Landscapes in Eighteenth-Century Virginia." *Winterthur Portfolio* 28(1): 1–31.

Wells, Tom. 1998. "Nail Chronology: The Use of Technologically Derived Features." In *Approaches to Material Culture Research for Historical Archaeologists,* compiled by David R. Brauner, 318–339. 2nd ed. California, Pa.: The Society for Historical Archaeology.

Wenger, Mark R. 1997. "Jefferson's Designs for Remodeling the Governor's Palace." *Winterthur Portfolio* 32(4): 223–242.

Whately, Thomas. [1770] 1982. *Observations on Modern Gardening.* New York: Garland Publishing.

White, Esther C. 2006. "Archaeology and Restoration along Mount Vernon's South Lane." *Quarterly Bulletin of the Archeological Society of Virginia* 61(4): 197–208.

———. 2008. "'As You See It So It Was?' Reconstructing Historic Built Environment in the USA: The Case of Sites Associated with George Washington." PhD dissertation, University of Leicester, Leicester, U.K.

White, Esther C., and Curt Breckenridge. 2010. "'Gardens abounding in much gay and Variagated Foliage': Understanding George Washington's Upper Garden." Paper presented at the 43rd Annual Conference on Historical and Underwater Archaeology, Amelia Island, Fla.

Wilk, Richard R., and William L. Rathje. 1982. "Household Archaeology." *American Behavioral Scientist* 25(6): 617–639.

Wilkie, Laurie. 1997. "Secret and Sacred: Contextualizing the Artifacts of African-American Magic and Religion." *Historical Archaeology* 31(4): 81–106.

———. 2010. *The Lost Boys of Zeta Psi: A Historical Archaeology of Masculinity at a University Fraternity.* Berkeley: University of California Press.

Wilkins, Andrew P. 2009. "Identifying 18th Century Hidden Landscapes at Stratford Hall Plantation Using Portable X-Ray Flourescence Phosphorus Readings on Plowzone Samples." MA thesis, University of Massachusetts, Boston.

———. 2010. "Elements of a Landscape: Soil Chemistry at Stratford Hall Plantation." *Journal of Middle Atlantic Archaeology* 26: 155–164.

Williams, Dorothy Hunt. 1975. *Historic Virginia Gardens: Preservations by the Garden Club of Virginia.* Charlottesville: University Press of Virginia.

Williams, Martha R. 1975. "Sully Volunteer Archaeological Project: Preliminary Field Report, Fall, 1974." Manuscript on file, Division of History, Fairfax County Park Authority, Fairfax, Va.

Williams, Morley. 1932. "The Evolution of Design at Mt. Vernon." *Landscape Architecture* 22(3): 165–177.

———. 1938. "Washington's Changes at Mt. Vernon Plantation." *Landscape Architecture* 28(2): 62–73.

Wilson, Gaye. 2005. "'A Declaration of Wants': Provisioning the Monticello Table." In *Dining at Monticello: In Good Taste and Abundance,* edited by Damon Lee Fowler, 47–53. Charlottesville: Thomas Jefferson Foundation.

Windingstad, Jason D. 2008. "Some Preliminary Results of the Geoarchaeological Investigation at Thomas Jefferson's Poplar Forest." Archaeological Research Laboratory, University of Tennessee Department of Anthropology, Knoxville, Tenn. Manuscript on file, Thomas Jefferson's Poplar Forest, Forest, Va.

Winner, Mildred D. 1992. "Mr. Jefferson's Delinquent Account at Lynchburg's First Dry Goods Store." *Lynch's Ferry* 5(2): 37–39.

Witthoff, John. 1949. "Stone Pipes of the Historic Cherokees." *Southern Indian Studies* 1: 43–62.

Yaeger, Jason, and Marcello A. Canuto. 2000. "Introducing an Archaeology of Communities." In *The Archaeology of Communities, A New World Perspective,* edited by Marcello A. Canuto and Jason Yaeger, 1–15. London: Routledge.

Yentsch, Anne. 1994. *A Chesapeake Family and Their Slaves.* Cambridge: Cambridge University Press.

———. 1996. "The Symbolic Divisions of Pottery: Sex-Related Attributes of English and Anglo-American Household Pots." In *Contemporary Archaeology in Theory: A Reader,* edited by Robert W. Preucel and Ian Hodder, 315–349. Oxford: Blackwell.

Young, Amy L. 1997. "Cellars and African-American Slave Sites: New Data from an Upland South Plantation." *Midcontinental Journal of Archaeology* 22(1): 95–115.

Zukin, Susan. 1991. *Landscape of Power: From Detroit to Disney World.* Berkeley: University of California Press.

# Contributors

Jessica Bowes is an anthropology graduate student at Syracuse University.

Jack Gary is director of archaeology and landscapes at Thomas Jefferson's Poplar Forest.

Barbara J. Heath is associate professor of anthropology at the University of Tennessee–Knoxville and author of *Hidden Lives: The Archaeology of Slave Life at Thomas Jefferson's Poplar Forest*.

Lori Lee is laboratory supervisor at Thomas Jefferson's Poplar Forest and a doctoral candidate at Syracuse University.

Stephen A. Mrozowski is director of the Andrew Fiske Memorial Center for Archaeological Research at the University of Massachusetts–Boston and is professor of anthropology at the University of Massachusetts–Boston.

Eric Proebsting is associate archaeologist at Thomas Jefferson's Poplar Forest.

Heather Trigg is a research scientist at the Andrew Fiske Memorial Center for Archaeological Research at the University of Massachusetts–Boston.

Timothy Trussell is associate professor of anthropology at Millersville University.

# Index

*Page numbers in italics refer to illustrations.*

CPSIA information can be obtained
at www.ICGtesting.com
Printed in the USA
LVHW052058180523
747395LV00005B/816